HINDU AST
L E S S O N S

36 TEACHERS SHARE THEIR WISDOM

gp
Groundswell
Press

A Division of ARC Associates, Inc.

Hindu Astrology Lessons

Copyright ©1997 by Groundswell Press

Groundswell Press
Division of ARC Associates, Inc.
Post Office Box 8925
Gaithersburg, MD 20898 USA
Phone/Fax: 301-353-0212

Cover by Paula Houck and layout by Angeline Marino.

ISBN 0-9641612-6-5

Library of Congress Catalog Card Number: 97-70272

Printed in the United States

First Edition

1 2 3 4 5 6 7 8 9 10 15 25

EDITOR'S INTRODUCTION AND ACKNOWLEDGMENTS

There is an old aphorism which says that if you want to get something important done, ask a busy person. As this unique anthology amply demonstrates, the reason that aphorism persists is because it is true. The biographical sketches that trail each article clearly show that this comprehensive, collaborative effort is blessed by a remarkable collection of individuals, almost all of whom are now caught in the grip of a life-long passion for propagating into the West the philosophy and tools of Jyotish.

For that matter, in many of these biosketches much goes unstated. As just two examples among many, one writer was a Presidential Scholar who was personally honored by President Lyndon Johnson. Others have spent large amounts of their own time and risk capital organizing Vedic astrology conferences. In the beginning their reward for this was understood ahead of time to lie on a continuum somewhere between financial ruin and meager profitability.

In terms of profit this book is no different. The likely target market for its contents is highly specialized (most probably interested Western astrologers who have already introduced themselves to the basics of Indian astrology), and even the most optimistic expectation for its success is quite subdued in material terms. But in our current culture legitimate astrologers are accustomed to swimming upstream. Consequently all these original articles were donated so that this industrious effort could come to fruition. The only consistently noteworthy complaint from the writers was that the format forced them to write so little. Such is the determination of the inspired Jyotishi.

Another factor that I suspect motivates many of these dedicated writers is that we are all pleased to be encountering more and more sophisticated consumers of astrological products and services. Through their own efforts, these consumers are developing the skill set to learn what a legitimate astrologer should be able to provide. Consequently these consumers are becoming more and more subtle and discriminating in their choices and expectations (in fact, they often become solid amateur students). These people then become leaders in overturning our popular culture's ignorance of legitimate astrology. This benefit is yet another reason to present a mid-level survey anthology which will aid them in their quest.

Jyotish is a lifetime (pre)occupation. Like any other sophisticated area of inquiry, it requires study. If you go to just one of the seminal sources such as the *Brihat Parasara Hora Sastra* (I recommend the Sharma translation), you will see that the topic is vast. So don't be discouraged if some of the material in this anthology is over your head. This condition is only temporary. If you have the life path of an astrologer then you will grow into it. The objective of each of these articles is not to be definitive; the objective is to stimulate the reader down different paths of inquiry.

We suggest you reinforce your grounding in the basics via one or more of the introductory survey books. Then consider attending Hindu astrology conferences and/or engaging a tutor from among these contributors. You will find that their fees compare very favorably with any other educator, consultant, or highly specialized professional. Also "astrology" is neither monolithic nor impersonal; each astrologer has his own style, areas of specialty interest, and personal approach to this work. So don't generalize about astrology from your personal encounter with this or that particular astrologer; learning is often just a matter of personal chemistry.

Maybe you prefer a very scholarly astrologer, or a funny one, or a kind one, or a psychic one, or a very technical one, or a sarcastic one. They are all out there, as is their combinations, so just persist and you will soon get to where you want to be. Also like everyone else, astrologers periodically relocate. Therefore, if you are trying to find one of these individuals and you can't, just call another writer for help because we tend to know how to locate each other.

Prepare your eyes for the fact that they will be seeing various spellings of the same word. For example, in this book you will see the nakshatra Jyeshtha also spelled as Jeshtha, Jyestha and Jyeshta. We've remained editorially flexible on this matter since this is what you will actually see when you read astrology books from India. I personally don't know how to establish authority in this conversion from Sanskrit to English. You may wish to defer to the preferred usages noted in the books of our more scholarly Western contributors. Note that we have also decided to generally defer to the formatting conventions of each writer rather than overly homogenize the final result.

I want to thank my friend Angeline Marino for her fine technical assistance in setting up the text and graphics. I can tell you for a fact that Saturn made her do it. Thanks also to Bill Bodri, Jim Butler, Alan Goodman, Mimi Mukherjee, Liz Stierman and others friends who offered detailed assistance, and very lively reaction, along the path to publication.

Let me also convey a special word of thanks to my wife, Paula, whose artistic efforts bring a bright and charming aura to the cover. Who could not at least pick up this book! This is Ganesh, the popular and beloved Hindu god of wisdom and illumination. Paula first created a most interesting image of how Ganesh was likely to be popularly assimilated by our modern Western culture. As we decided against this image in favor of the more traditional, this decision symbolized for me how difficult it is for this anthology to simplify and "Westernize" the astrological ideas of a complex, and very different, spiritual culture — especially when the vast bulk of related materials still remains either closely held or untranslated.

Parenthetically, Ganesh is also the pre-eminent god of merchants. To this day in India, when a merchant goes bankrupt, his customers often learn this from the fact that all the office Ganeshas are turned upside down! Be advised: in true American tradition Groundswell Press has bolted its office Ganeshas into the upright position. Our logic is that this action should help assure the success of this book.

The mathematically inclined may also notice that there are actually 38 articles here and not 36. On the one hand, we could just state the more mundane truth that we had a couple of post-deadline submissions that we thought were entertaining and worthy of your time. But in a more metaphorical vein, the other reason is that this anthology is really like a package loaded with little treats. If you go to a decent bakery and order three dozen of their confections you should be given a few extra ones. So we figured it was the *yeast* we could do!

We can't close without a minor apology to the reader. In the interest of brevity the writers were encouraged to limit charts and graphics, or else to exchange charts for equivalent text. But some articles ended up more technically intense than expected, and some of these could have benefited from additional graphics of one kind or another, including charts.

Within the constraints of our format, something had to give. So what we assumed is that the reader will be inspired to buy some good software and personally run charts in those few cases where only the data is supplied.

Let's also note here that, for technical reasons, the publisher holds the copyright to these articles. But, in fact, the publisher considers these articles to be the property of the individual authors. So please contact them for authorization or questions about any further use of their articles.

It is with honor and pleasure that we now present to the reader some of the more dedicated and lively practitioners of this ancient art. As we are all students, each at our own level, may you now grow with us all in our enthusiasm and awe for this "Science of Light."

For all dedicated astrologers
now bringing
Eastern concepts and techniques
to the West.

TABLE OF CONTENTS

HOW SHAD BALA REVEALS YOUR KARMA

Marcello Borges

Of what practical use are the numerical values provided by the Hindu planetary strength methodology called *shad bala* — the system of "six strengths" related to position, direction, time, declination, motion and brightness? This article will highlight the generally unrealized connection between the relative strength of planets, as revealed in this system, and the extensive, and very well documented, information (via "readings") unconsciously channeled by the world famous psychic Edgar Cayce.

Here I will just make the assertion (proofs are reserved for another article) that there is a nearly exact correspondence between the planets that Cayce listed in *sequence* as being the most dominant in a person's life and the *same* relative sequence of planetary strengths as calculated via shad bala. Having stated that, let's move immediately to how to *apply* this fact.

First, there is the concept of the *individual* planet. The strongest planet in a natal shad bala should be understood as the main significator of that individual. It is the *most visited* planet during the intermission of lives (the period between two incarnations), and shows also the nature of the individual, sometimes even better than the Moon, Ascendant or Sun.

To be clear: this is *not* a Vedic concept but a concept introduced by Cayce during his many trance states. Though he knew neither astronomy nor astrology in his waking state, many keywords I'll use to describe the planets were used by this world famous psychic as he repeatedly described them during his thousands of trance readings. For the purposes of this article, my key "lesson" concept is that the term "strongest planet" means what you have done and how you have behaved most of the time during your previous incarnations. And because of this habitual pattern, this further implies that you will *probably continue* to behave similarly this time around.

To understand this concept, take a look at the houses which are ruled by the strongest planet in your Vedic chart. These are the areas of life that will probably be the easiest for you to work out. Also, evaluate the Dasas and Bhuktis for your strong planet. Those will be periods where the activities indicated by that planet, as well as by the houses it rules and by the house in which it is posited, will be more easily done.

Now use the same logic to evaluate the weakest planet in your shad bala. This indicates areas of life and character traits which have been overlooked in previous existences, and that would probably be neglected in the present incarnation.

So viewing the planets in this way shows them as guides to understanding the *main pattern* in an individual's successive incarnations. I have seen this concept of planetary patterns work consistently with my clients, so I feel very confident about presenting these ideas which might otherwise be considered especially speculative.

As I make assertions about the relative strength and meaning of relevant chart data—and this will be expressed in rupas and virupas (with 60 virupas in each rupa)—it may initially be the most meaningful and fun if you have your own data in front of you. Many Vedic astrology software programs can easily provide this data for you. *[Editor's Note: Those readers especially new to this class of data may also want to first review the article written by Alan Goodman.]*

Let me mention that the ideas presented below were extracted from my book *Tecnicas de Equilibrio Holistico (Holistic Balance Techniques)* published in Portuguese in 1992. I have never before presented them in English.

The Sun

A strong Sun (in absolute terms, more than 415 virupas or 6.92 rupas) indicates one who is bringing into the present life a pattern of leadership and drawing the focusing of attention. In this case, the self-confidence is highly developed, thanks to the support received in past existences as a chief, raj, leader, patriarch, etc. of a familiar group, clan, community, nation, tribe or religion. Classically, the "bad" side of a strong Sun is arrogance. When not treated with the pomp and circumstance he/she expects, the reaction of the individual with a strong Sun may be similar to that of a spoiled child. Madonna and Marilyn Monroe are two examples of solar types as identified via this shad bala methodology.

A Sun which is weak in shad bala (less than 415 virupas) indicates one whose past-life patterns may not have included power or self-centering. They may be shy and even avoid any display of self. They are more followers than leaders, for they lack the habit or the practice of self-affirmation. Since the Sun indicates the soul, these people are not lively.

The Moon

We may say that people with a strong Moon in shad bala (in absolute terms, more than 435 virupas or 7.25 rupas) are quite at ease to deal with issues like homemaking, marriage, etc. Edgar Cayce suggested that each of us should make [homemaking] "a career, because it represents the highest career any soul can have on Earth... [the Moon] is the symbol of something that the entities aim at: a celestial home".

Those readings suggest that home life is very, very important from a spiritual point of view, and should be taken out of its purely feminine aspect; everyone, men and women, must cooperate on homemaking. Another familiar keyword we find for the Moon in the readings is emotions, which is very cogruent with the Western astrological tradition. However, Vedic astrologers say that the Moon is associated with memory, an indication which is quite congruent with Mercury. They also say that the Moon's position helps us understand the area of life where the individual will fulfill his/her karma.

There is a direct relationship between the attachment to matter, to the physical side of life on Earth, and to the density or "heaviness" of the emotional body. Thus, the more "physical" individuals will take longer to dissolve their emotional body during their temporary station on the Moon. On the other hand, those who took the material world more lightly will get rid of their emotional bodies quickly, and according to the information given by Cayce, will soon be leaving the Moon to continue forward with their planetary sojourn.

This is emphasized by the importance the readings gave to the relationship between the Moon and the physical body. The gratification of desires, especially sexual ones, is also ruled by the Moon. This is not a traditional concept in Western astrology, but Vedic astrologers do use the Moon in this sense. Even the main Sanskrit word for the Moon (soma) means "body" in Greek!

A weak Moon in shad bala is related to fear, especially during the full Moon. This also includes emotional highs and lows. La donna è mobile ("woman is volatile"), says the song. This means that people with a weak Moon are highly sensitive to their emotions, and do not exert much control over them.

Mercury

Edgar Cayce's readings frequently employed certain words to describe Mercury's traits including mental attributes, learning ability, teaching, ease with idioms, the search for knowledge, quick conclusions, and adaptability to circumstances.   Also referenced are talent with communications, good development of the five senses, strength in speech and listening, talent as a mimic, the ability to easily picture something in one's mind, and attention to details. The Mercurial type is a good judge who uses wisdom. All these key-words remind us of the astrological tradition, both Western and Eastern.

The readings suggest that those with a strong Mercury in shad bala (in absolute terms, over 440 virupas or 7.33 rupas) may have had past lives as writers, heralds, journalists or teachers. They may have worked intensely with the analytical mind in activities such as accounting, mathematics, statistics, engineering, research or business. Every task that depends on data, facts and numbers, as well as on curiosity may have been a part of the Mercurian individual's past profile.

The negative side of a strong Mercury may appear in many guises. The individual may be stubborn, or else insist on doing something only in his/her own way.   Excessive criticism (toward self and/or others), an inclination to argue too much or to be cynical, are not rare. A misused Mercury may give the individual a propensity to believe only in his/her own perceiving senses. They may despise their own emotions, handling them as if they were not their own. The worst aspect of a negative Mercury is the mental snobbism: to think that what others say is not worthy of the snob's precious attention.

Venus

Whenever we find someone with a strong Venus in shad bala (in absolute terms, more than 390 virupas or 6.5 rupas), this individual may have dedicated some of his/her past lives to positive practices and actions which may have accelerated his/her spiritual development. This is much more probable if Jupiter is also strong in the natal chart. In these cases, the present life may be the last (or one of the last) earthly sojourn of the individual, if he/she learns the lessons they have not mastered and persists in his/her virtuous practices, while remaining unattached to the results and effects of those good deeds.

A confirmation of this "law" is found in the *Brihat Jataka*. Writing about the planets, Varaha Mihira says that Venus (Sukra) and Jupiter (Guru) represent Vipras, that is, one who is pure and devoted to God. Commenting on this, the translator of the *Brihat Jataka*, S. Rao, said that "when these [Venus and Jupiter] are powerful the horoscope may be attributed as belonging to a Brahmin...". Well, a Brahmin is one who dedicates his/her life to the service of God and to related sublime activities, presumably over a series of past lives, and this agrees with what Cayce said!

What is the basic meaning of a strong Venus? Love, be it spiritual, physical or romantic. Other keywords found in the readings are joy, companionship, good conversation, ease in making and maintaining friends, deep emotions and feelings, empathy, tenderness, affection, optimism and kindness. Individuals with a strong Venus are kind toward those who suffer (remember, Venus is exalted in Pisces, the sign of sacrifice). The Venus-type individual also tries to create peace and maintain harmony in their zone of influence. Their motherly instinct is strong, as well as their connection with the home and family (evoking the Moon, the other main yin planet).

While it is not a pattern in itself, we may say that a strong Venus individual had previous incarnations where the yin aspects of life were well-handled. If the present gender is feminine, this life will present an easy experience; the yin attributes developed before will soften the present obstacles. This reminds me of an Eastern esoteric tradition: a life of "rest" and "ease" at each seventh incarnation! If the individual is now a male, his life will be graced with a much richer and fuller inner life than his fellow men because he will learn and experience things in a way that the others—devoid of a good contact with love and sensitivity—usually handle badly.

The strong Venus individual may be quite at ease with artistic activities—music, the use of color and harmony, decoration, architecture, drama, dance or writing. Their imagination is good, as well as their esthetic sense. Edgar Cayce told one Venus individual that her main task in this life would be to see God in each manifestation of beauty. Establishing and maintaining relationships are quite easy for the Venus type.

The bad side of Venus is related to too strong a set of likes/dislikes as well as an exaggerated attention to the appeal of the flesh ranging from sensuality to sexuality. This may also include people with past lives as prostitutes, gigolos, geishas, etc., where they became attached to the pleasures and vices of Venus. They may be possessive, passionate, and self-indulging excesses of food, drink, smoke, sex, etc.

On the other hand, a weak Venus may indicate an individual that did not have a chance to handle and understand the other in previous lives, especially in one-to-one relationships. Monks who have dedicated their lives to the highest ideals, and to helping others to get there, will not know how to relate to a lover in a future incarnation because they simply lack the practice, not because they lack the love! Also, a weak Venus may show up as hesitation—a word we often associate with Libra.

Mars

It is easy to understand why the Cayce readings make many more "difficult" or troublesome references to Mars than those which are easy or tranquil. After all, in Western astrology Mars is called "the lesser malefic." However, I have seen a strong Mars (in absolute terms, more than 380 virupas or 6.33 rupas) in the charts of people who have a strong capacity to battle against adversity, who "go for it." This is not negative or bad. Cayce also said that the red planet has a relationship to power, determination, drive, executive capacity and strong mindedness—the very traits of many successful professional people!

The readings also used the word "pacifier" to describe a strong Mars. This may sound paradoxical, but I have two thoughts. First, it may be that the Martian types—people with past lives as soldiers, warriors, involved in military activities—became spiritually exhausted with fighting, and they now prize peace, even if it's the pax romana. Alternatively, their well-developed fearlessness (if only developed through athletic competition) could preclude a psychological need to respond to challenges with foolish aggressiveness. This could also link into an ability to have a subtle psychological sympathy with the presentation of any aggressive circumstance, and via this synergy, dissolve it—such as in The Way of Aikido.

A strong Mars may also indicate such past-live profiles as adventurers, explorers, pioneers—people who had only themselves to rely upon. For this reason they may now feel quite comfortable as the "loner" type, having quite a hard time when dealing with others; yet this is one of their main karmic tasks. Their other task is to learn how to handle their extraordinary energy—often including "rage" and "fury." Physical activities such as sports (preferably non-competitive so as not to further stimulate this aspect) are highly recommended to Martian types. Thus they may burn off their excessive energy, getting it down to normal levels.

The Martian individual is stubborn and has a "short fuse," being quick to ignite and react. They have a propensity to dominate, to fight (in every sense), and to wage war. Self-control is very important here. As a result of their inner pressures, headaches, fevers, etc. may occur frequently. A weak Mars, on the other hand, is someone who has difficulty in handling his/her own problems, depending much on others. They may be anxious, be unable to "stand their ground," and may fear many things.

Jupiter

One of the two most important planets—as a "school" for perfecting the soul and for spiritual evolution—is Jupiter. Regarded as the "Greater Benefic," we may say that a strong Jupiter in shad bala (in absolute terms, more than 430 virupas or 7.17 rupas) indicates someone who is living under a "good star," so to speak.

If the Cayce readings were prolific in praise for Venus, they overflow with it concerning Jupiter. People with a strong Jupiter received comments such as broad vision and high ideals, benevolence and kindness, charity, tolerance, understanding, unattachment, and perception of the universal forces. They usually have a good sense of humor—a traditional concept in astrology—and a pleasant personality, qualities that make living with a Jupiter individual something quite easy. They protect and receive protection—including that from "above."

The readings show that Jupiter is connected with economy and businesses, especially those involving huge sums or big projects. As a kind of karmic payback for the noble purposes that motivated the Jupiter individual in previous lives, they almost certainly will be affluent. Scarcity seldom appears, and even in the hardest moments they will find the flexibility needed to cope with the occasion. Their contact with people in powerful   positions is easy, but they know equally well how to deal with the humble; the range of their relationships is enormous.

Jupiterians know how to lead and how to inspire responsibility.   Their main asset is their ability to advise; they are the best counselors.   For this reason, Cayce recommended that they follow professions such as law, politics, public life, diplomacy, religious activities and psychology, especially of groups. Also recommended was teaching, study (they are avid for knowledge), writing and oratory, and travel. Their mystical bent is strong.

Cayce readings were sparse when it came to the negative side of a strong Jupiter. They may eventually connect themselves to the material (or carnal) aspects of life.   Those with a weak Jupiter (in absolute terms, less than 430 virupas) probably didn't have a deep contact with the Jupiterean traits, or else they mishandled them.   They must develop a broader perspective of life.

Saturn

No other planet in the Cayce readings is so "different" from the traditional astrological descriptions than Saturn. While astrologers usually regard it as a limit or barrier, the lord of Karma, etc., the readings portray it in dark shades and rough lines all right, but in a different way.

Those with a strong Saturn (in absolute terms, more than 375 virupas or 6.25 rupas) are able to face changes in life: changing situations and renewals. In this sense its characteristics are more similar to the Western symbolism assigned to Uranus.   Their main previous lives were marked by historical periods of transformation, of upheaval from the established and the traditional. They faced these changes with ability, survived the traumas and learned how to rebuild the structures. After all these obstacles, they now aim at higher positions—the themes of Capricorn and of the 10th House, both connected to Saturn. This also highlights their traditional ease at organizing things around them.

"Trials," "tests," "evaluations" are words commonly used, among others, in the readings to describe Saturn. We could say that a sojourn in Saturn is similar to a school exam or summer course; the Saturnian individual has to show that his/her lessons were learned. It is the "environ into which all insufficient matter is cast." When someone made too many mistakes, he/she has to go to Saturn and "clean the slate" to start anew.

However, this is not easy. The readings employ words such as "separation," "changes," "disappointments," "sadness," etc. regarding Saturn. The Saturnian individual knows the tasks that are ahead for him/her, and they are not heavenly. It is—and here is the main difference from the traditional model for Saturn—the planet of "changes." For example, Reading #1089-3 says, "In Saturn we find that influence of an ever-changing nature, of a seeking, of a renewing, of making starts."

On the other hand, those with a strong Saturn have a tremendous sense of responsibility. They may think that the care and attention for their loved ones is never enough, and so they carry the world on their shoulders. As a result they don't taste much of life's pleasures. Their childhood may have been "mature," and their adult life is filled with duties and demands. The physical body reacts with "afflictions" or diseases, as the readings say. The main reaction is the hardening of the shoulder muscles. It's the "Atlas" effect....

The Outer Planets

As we know, the outer planets—Uranus, Neptune and Pluto—are not part of the Vedic tradition. If we don't have the shad bala for those planets, how do we know if they are strong in a given chart? We must use factors such as the planet's position in the natal chart—rising or culminating, a conjunction with a Light (Sun or Moon), a concentration in its sign (a stellium in Aquarius may imply a strong Uranus, for instance), velocity, etc.

Edgar Cayce's own chart (March 18, 1877 at 3:03 PM LMT in Hopkinsville, KY 87W29 36N52) shows Uranus exactly conjunct his Leo Ascendant. Accordingly, in a reading given for himself (#294-8), he said that "we find this entity almost entirely influenced by, and came from that in the last plane of Uranus, with Neptune, Venus and Jupiter... [from] the ultra forces, as of Uranus and Neptune, come much of the influence of the various planes...."

[Editor's Note: For those who are not used to reading the transcribed Edgar Cayce material, it takes some getting used to. Also, the references to reading numbers are a reference to the notation used at the library of the Association For Research & Enlightenment (ARE) in Virginia Beach, Virginia.] His chart also shows Neptune close to his MC, as well as Pluto. This reading is a confirmation of the importance of the rising and culminating planets, just as Ptolemy and Gauquelin have said.

Uranus is the source of exceptional abilities, especially psychic, and the best example is Cayce himself. He also related Uranus to Atlantis. The Uranian individual is subject to extremes. Neptune is also highly mystical and sensitive, and those with a strong Neptunian connection were advised to stay near lakes, rivers or the ocean in order to balance their powers. Pluto was called Vulcan and Septimus by Cayce before it was discovered, and the readings weren't very clear about it.

Although Marcello Borges has a B.Sc. in electronic engineering, he began working full-time as an astrologer in 1986. Self-taught in esoteric fields, he is a lecturer and researcher on karmic astrology, having taught this and synastry at the first Astrological College in Brazil. He is a member of the A.R.E., NCGR and was formerly ISAR's International VP in Brazil. His research and article on "The Astrological Profile of Astrologers" was published in volume XX, #2 (March, 1991) of KOSMOS. He is also a regular contributor to The Vedic Voice. *Research interests include Hindu/Vedic techniques, sexuality, spirituality (astrologers, psychics, and past life/death/reincarnation charts) and UFO contacts, having collected and researched 500 UFO cases. An English/Portuguese translator, he has just earned a B.Sc. in Law, and recently completed a study of the position of astrology within the body of Brazilian Legislation. Contact: Rua Iubotinga, 389, Apto. 162, 05716-110, Via Vila Andrade, São Paulo, SP, Brazil. Phone & fax: (5511) 846-8627.*

THE HIDDEN POWER OF MANTRAS AND YAGYAS

James Braha

I'm told that the original title of this anthology was going to make reference to "secret tips." In this regard the thought that immediately came to my mind was that of *yagyas* and *mantras*. A *yagya* (sometimes spelled *yajna)* is a religious or spiritual ceremony performed by one or more Hindu priests in order to alleviate karmic difficulties. It is a kind of offering or sacrifice in which a priest appeals to the planetary beings, or the gods, for grace and intervention on behalf of the person requesting the yagya. During a yagya, the priest lights a fire, burns incense, and throws rice and ghee (clarified butter) into the flames. This symbolizes the burning of negative karma from the past so the person may be relieved of the most intense influences of past destructive actions.

During the yagya, the priest continuously chants astrological mantras. Astrological mantras are Sanskrit prayers which entreat higher evolutionary beings to remove obstacles appearing in a particular birth chart. According to Indians, chanting a mantra is a way to invoke a planetary being into one's life. Mantras may be used by anyone, not only priests, and many of my clients have received excellent results from chanting them.

As for yagyas, they are very effective and should be performed during a *Dasa* period or *Bhukti* sub-period that is expected to be difficult or life-threatening. The most common yagya is the *nava-graha* (nine planet) yagya. This can also be performed during good periods to help fulfill heartfelt desires or to remove unrelenting impediments in life. Over the years, I have seen yagyas work miracles, so I am amazed that more astrologers do not prescribe them for their clients. They can make such a difference in peoples' lives; I would be lost without them.

During my early years as an astrologer, I was reticent to prescribe mantras or yagyas unless the particular client was spiritually or metaphysically inclined. I thought my advice would not be taken seriously. I quickly learned, however, that trying to determine who would or would not be willing to chant a mantra was a mistake. My lesson came via a Midwestern housewife who knew almost nothing about astrology and had called to have her very first birth chart interpretation. Her husband's life had been rapidly falling apart, thereby dramatically affecting her happiness.

Upon hearing her expression of desperation, I decided to prescribe a mantra relating to the planetary Dasa she was experiencing. Although I never expected this woman, a total novice to the world of metaphysics and mysticism, to actually chant a two-sentence, Sanskrit mantra for fifteen or twenty minutes a day, what else could I do but give her the proper astrological remedial measure? To my surprise, my client called a few months later to profusely thank me, saying that chanting the mantra had powerfully and blatantly changed her and her husband's lives! Since then, I have never censored myself from prescribing a mantra or a yagya for someone in need. Indeed, what is the point of predicting the future if we cannot significantly alter it?

Given below are some examples of the results that I, or my clients or friends, have gained through planetary yagyas. Aside from the wonderful practical effects, however, it must be made clear that yagyas are, in fact, the heart and soul of Hindu astrology. The whole point of a predominantly predictive astrology is to discern upcoming karma, and if it is negative or destructive, to alter it. That is exactly what yagyas are about. Further, in order to appreciate where predictive astrology fits into the scheme of Hindu culture and the human experience, one must experience at least two or three yagyas firsthand. Particularly as an astrologer, it is profoundly satisfying to observe a Hindu priest performing a religious ceremony that is entirely astrological in nature. During a yagya, one feels a sense of wonder and miracle, and a distinct connection to the cosmos as the priests pay full homage to all the astrological influences.

The astrological mantras (listed in my Hindu astrology books and certain standard texts) of all nine planets are chanted. The Moon *nakshatra* (lunar mansion) of the person requesting the yagya is spoken, as are the *rasi* (sign) of the Moon and of the *lagna* (ascendant). A day or two after a yagya, one typically feels a boost of positive energy and a relief of negative karma.

Since yagyas are important, powerful and effective, they should be prescribed for any and all clients who are in bad Dasas or Bhuktis or who need help in fulfilling heartfelt desires. Astrologers of the Hindu system who have not experienced at least two or three yagyas firsthand are doing a disservice to themselves and their clients.

Here is just a partial list are some of my experiences in prescribing yagyas:

1. A man to whom I prescribed a Jupiter mantra doubled his salary (from $50,000 to $100,000) in one year. He was so impressed, he made me recite the mantras for all the other planets so he could try all of them.

2. A friend was involved in a bitter divorce and was having unending troubles in court, including the problem of gaining access to equal visitation rights with his daughter. At the time, he was in a Jupiter Bhukti (within a Venus Dasa), and Jupiter in his horoscope occupies its "fallen" sign of Capricorn. Because Jupiter, the natural indicator of both law and children, was so afflicted, my friend was having trouble in both areas. Within one week after obtaining a yagya, the judge in the court case was called out of town and replaced by a thirty-five year old woman who quickly decided that my friend deserved to have equal custody access to his daughter. The judge also noted for court records that my friend's daughter was being manipulated against her father by a bitter ex-wife.

3. A client who had lost a court case was being sued by the opposing party for court costs. The judge told my client's lawyer that unless he could cite a precedent court case working in the client's favor that she would have to pay the costs—a whopping $25,000. The lawyer searched high and low and concluded that a favorable precedent court case did not exist. I advised the woman to obtain a yagya. Within a week or two, her stunned lawyer called to say he just found a magazine article about a recent similar court case that worked in her favor. Result: she was spared the $25,000 court costs.

4. A local priest in South Florida did a yagya in my apartment in 1992 for myself and all friends with relationship problems caused by kujadosha (Mars affliction) in their horoscopes. One friend at the yagya, who had been divorced seven or eight years earlier and had been enduring one bad relationship after another, met his second wife less than a week after the ceremony. My girlfriend, present with me during the yagya, and I married within a year. My brother, whom I invited to the yagya not for relationship purposes but because of a terrible Mars Dasa, was fired from his job two days after the yagya. For months, I had pleaded with my brother to quit his job because he was being blatantly sabotaged by jealous or resentful bosses. Within a week after the yagya, he found a far superior job with employers who did everything they could to ensure his success.

5.   In 1995, I interpreted a horoscope for a person who had just entered a Mars Dasa and was experiencing all kinds of Mars problems—rashes, accidents, and so on. I went to the yagya with this man because I wanted to visit the new Hindu temple that had recently opened in South Florida. Although the yagya was for my client, I assumed it might have a good effect on me just by being present. The reason I believed that was because years earlier a female friend (not a lover) had attended a yagya that was done for me and had called the next day to say that the yagya had worked for her. The day after the yagya, she received a completely unexpected phone call from the largest newspaper in the state wanting to do a full-page article about her. So I concluded that yagyas might affect whomever attends the ceremony.

After my client's Mars yagya, I waited to see if I would gain any benefits related to Mars in my birth chart. Mars rules the seventh House in my horoscope (relationships), and so it was that my marriage was altered in a positive way. Two nights after the yagya, just as I was falling asleep, I was awakened by my wife who suddenly asked, "Is something bothering you about our relationship?" I was startled by her question which seemed to come from nowhere. Within minutes, we were discussing our marriage with great intensity and concentration. The results were potent and I awoke the next morning with profoundly greater awareness and patience about the problematic issue we had discussed. The peace of mind, and the understanding I gained from the experience, have endured to this day.

6.   During a very rough Rahu-Venus Dasa-Bhukti, I decided to have a Venus yagya for some debilitating health problems I was experiencing (Venus rules my 1st and 6th Houses, i.e., health matters). During this afflicted period, my health was so sensitive, and my immune system so weak, that I was habitually catching colds and the flu whenever I was under the slightest stress. Medical doctors could find nothing wrong with my health. Meanwhile I was getting sick every other week.

I told Pandu, the Hindu priest, of my health problems and requested him to perform my yagya on a Friday, the day ruling Venus, the planet causing the problems. As it happened, the yagya was performed the day before a weekend booksellers convention where I would be selling my astrology books.

When I awoke on Saturday, I saw that it was raining heavily outside and realized I would definitely be getting sick. The previous book conventions I had attended were extremely demanding, and in this instance I would be carrying numerous heavy boxes of books from the outside rain into an artificially controlled and heavily air conditioned environment. Experience suggested little doubt that I would end the weekend with a cold.

As it turned out, I carried the heavy boxes of books I needed, walked endlessly around the convention center for two days meeting publishers, booksellers and book buyers, and walked in and out of the rain for two days. On Monday evening I was surprised on two counts. First, I had escaped getting sick. Second, a friend and his wife remarked that I looked healthier than ever and that, in their words, my face was glowing. Within weeks of the yagya my strength and vitality improved dramatically, and my health, though not perfect, was on the upswing. The yagya had proven more effective than months of vitamins, acupuncture, special diets and visits to traditional doctors.

Yagyas can be obtained by calling any Hindu temple in the U.S. or India that employs a Hindu priest. (Two temple addresses are given below.) There are many kinds of yagyas available. There are yagyas for wealth, childbirth, removal of obstacles, family happiness, acquisition of a spouse, and so on. For the purposes of ameliorating a difficult period or sub-period, the navagraha or nine-planet yagya is usually recommended because it is both effective and easily affordable. The usual donation for the two-hour ceremony is around $150 as of this writing.

It is preferable to be present with the priest during the yagya, but if this is impossible, the ceremony can be performed in absentia with fine results. Another way to heal afflicted planets and difficult Dasas and Bhuktis is to chant astrological mantras. These are the same mantras that the Hindu priest chants while performing a yagya, although yagyas include additional ceremonial material. Some Westerners will find chanting astrological mantras comfortable while others may not. Those with strong interest should consult any of my three texts on Hindu astrology.

To find a Hindu priest in your area, consult your local phone directory under the heading: Churches and Temples. If no Hindu temple exists, consult one of the temples listed below.

Hindu Temple
    of Greater Chicago
P.O. Box 99
12 S. 701 Lemont Road
Lemont, IL 60439
Phone: 708-972-0300

Sri Shirdi Sai Baba Temple
3744 Old William Penn Hwy.
Pittsburgh, PA 15235
Contact: Pandu Malyala
Phone: 412-374-9244 or
    412-823-1296

Those with extreme problems, or those who desire a more profound altering of karma, may contact me directly for information regarding large yagyas performed in India. For about $800 (as of 1996), 108 priests can be hired to perform a yagya where mantras are chanted for eight hours a day, for seven days. But also note that some specialized yagyas can cost quite a bit more. Or, for about $400, twenty-eight priests will chant for three consecutive days, eight hours per day. Yagyas as large as these are significantly more powerful and profound than two hour nava-graha yagyas.

For clients whose problems are so severe they render even yagyas ineffective, the person should perform charity work once or twice a week. This is a powerful way to burn off bad karma quicker than normal, as well as constructively redirecting the person's attention away from his or her own pain and suffering.

James Braha is recognized and respected internationally as the astrologer who first brought Hindu predictive astrology to the West in understandable form. All of his books are acclaimed for their clarity, directness and accessibility. These include 1. Ancient Hindu Astrology for the Modern Western Astrologer, *2.* How To Be a Great Astrologer, *3.* How To Predict Your Future, *and 4.* Astro-Logos, Language of Life. *Although he maintains a very busy private practice, James has traveled worldwide giving numerous well-received lectures and workshops. He can be reached at 700 Fox Street, Longboat Key, FL 34228-1020. Phone: (941) 387-9101.*

ALTERNATE DASA SYSTEMS

James C. Butler

Vimshottari Dasa is the most famous of the Dasa systems, and justifiably so. It is the greatest of the universal Dasas given by the Sage Parasara (this is as opposed to conditional Dasa, applicable only to certain horoscopes). For a Western astrologer learning Jyotish, it is sufficient for at least a lifetime of study. Yet in practice, some charts do perform better when their implied cycles are viewed in a different light.

This article will highlight three additional universal dasa systems: Yogini, Kalachakra, and Chara. Quite a few Vedic astrologers use these alongside Vimshottari and transits, usually to refine and confirm what is judged from these two primary tools. However, it is possible to use any of these as the sole Dasa system, and some astrologers do. Chara Dasa, in particular, is part of a complete sub-system of astrology in its own right.

A caveat here is to avoid straying too far from the "basics." After reading this article you might want to begin just by glancing at the mahadasas for your own chart, or that of someone close to you, to see if anything significant stands out. Nothing here is presented as gospel. Consider my statements as "generally accurate propositions" which you're welcome to refine.

Fortunately, at least three software packages currently support two of the three Dasas discussed here, as well as one method (used in North India) for Kalachakra Dasa. As of late 1996, none that I know of supports the South Indian method for that Dasa although I expect that able programmer-Jyotishis will soon add this option. In any case, I strongly recommend calculating all of these Dasas by hand, at least initially, and double-checking this wherever possible against the computer's results. Because of its brevity, this discussion will make a lot more sense if you have the output from all three systems in front of you.

Yogini Dasa

This is a popular Dasa in North India, often used in conjunction with Vimshottari. Though not necessarily as powerful as the latter, it can provide added color. It is very easy to calculate, and can be done mentally with minimal practice. The name refers to the eight Yoginis (astral beings not unlike Goddesses) each ruling over a Dasa, and with each having a fixed correspondence to a ruling planet (including Rahu but not Ketu, although Rahu's period is sometimes considered as the entire nodal axis).

Calculation: Like Vimshottari, this is a lunar Dasa, but with a total cycle of only 36 years. Once complete, the cycle repeats where it started. (Presumably, up to two cycles would be seen for medium spans of life, and up to three for long spans.) Unlike Vimshottari, there is a different system of nakshatra rulership, as shown in the table below. Take the nakshatra of the natal Moon numerically (starting with Ashwini = 1) and add three. Divide by eight and take the remainder (which, if zero, is taken as equal to eight). That remainder corresponds to the mahadasa running at birth (and conveniently, also to its duration in years):

YOGINI	PLANET	# of YEARS	NAKSHATRAS
Mangala	Moon	1	6,14,22
Pingala	Sun	2	7,15,23
Dhanya	Jupiter	3	8,16,24
Bhramari	Mars	4	1,9,17,25
Bhadrika	Mercury	5	2,10,18,26
Ulka	Saturn	6	3,11,19,27
Siddha	Venus	7	4,12,20
Sankata	Rahu	8	5,13,21

The Dasa balance remaining at birth is calculated in a manner similar to Vimshottari. Simply multiply the percentage of the nakshatra yet to be transited by the Moon times the number of years allotted to the ruling planet (or Yogini). As in Vimshottari, subperiods begin with the mahadasa-ruling planet, and are proportional in length to the mahadasas.

Judgment: As with Vimshottari, judge the periods based on the inherent nature of the ruling planet, its strength natally, and the house in which it is posited. My impressions, confirmed by other astrologers, are that results do seem to reflect house placement much more than ownership. Basically, a Saturn period in the Yogini Dasa system adds a Saturnian flavor to the concurrent Vimshottari period. A Jupiter period, with a strong Jupiter in the 11th, will be good for income and group work, other factors permitting. In my opinion, Yogini is around one-third as important as Vimshottari; it is particularly interesting when its cycles synergize with Vimshottari.

In Yogini, periods of the natural malefics (including the Sun) are classically considered as generally malefic, and the converse is true for periods of the natural benefics (including Mercury). Thus one sees that, according to the Dasa cycle above, ups and downs will alternate because malefics and benefics occur in turn. This principle is basically in tune with the observation, made above, that house ownership doesn't contribute much to the determination of benefic/malefic status.

Yogini Dasa is discussed further, with a number of case studies, in two useful books, both published recently in India: *Yogini and Kalachakra Dasa*, by Sumeet Chugh (1995, Sagar Publications, New Delhi, India), and *Applications of Yogini Dasa,* by Rajiv Jhanji and N.K. Sharma (1994, Vision Wordtronic, New Delhi, India).

Chara Dasa

Whereas Yogini Dasa has much in common with Vimshottari, Chara Dasa is quite distinct. It is not a lunar Dasa, but rather depends on the Lagna's sign (and is otherwise independent of the time of birth, making Chara Dasa applicable if such time is known only approximately). Also, its periods are not indicated by planets but by signs, so that one might be running an Aries–Gemini period, for example.

Though this Dasa is mentioned by Parasara, it is applied and interpreted within a sub-system of Jyotish known as Jaimini astrology (after the sage who wrote the sutras revealing its rules). Although popular in the large South Indian state of Andhra Pradesh, Jaimini astrology has, until recently, remained obscure to most Westerners and many Indians. Astrologer K.N. Rao has researched and tested Jaimini astrology and made it accessible to modern astrologers. This brief discussion is based upon the delineations he has given and that I have tested.

Jaimini astrology differs from Parasari astrology in several important ways.

For our purposes, three are worth noting:

Aspecting: In essence, signs inherently aspect certain other signs, and these aspects become "activated" if a planet is present in a sign, in which case it casts that sign's aspects. Thus, planets cast aspects according to the sign in which they are posited, independent of the planets' Parasari aspecting powers. For example, according to Jaimini rules, any planet in Aries aspects the signs Leo, Scorpio, and Aquarius.

Karakas: Here, a planet takes on a certain fixed symbolism depending on how far it has advanced in degrees within its sign. Thus, the planet in the highest degree, regardless of which sign it is in, is called the "Atmakaraka," and it symbolizes the soul or self. Karakas are tabulated accordingly for the rest of the planets (excluding the nodes), down to the "Darakaraka," which is the least advanced in degrees (and signifies the spouse). In tabulating the karakas, Lahiri or Krishnamurti ayanamsha is strongly recommended; others will change the karakas completely.

Yogas: Jaimini astrology also has its own system of yogas wherein planets form good and bad combinations based on house rulership and karaka status. Keep in mind, though, that planets must conjoin or combine by Jaimini aspect (which, it turns out, are always "mutual" aspects). For example, either Atmakaraka or Darakaraka combining with the 5th lord forms a good yoga.

Rather than go into further detail, I refer the reader to Mr. Robert Koch's article in this anthology, and to Mr. K.N. Rao's books and articles on Jaimini techniques.

Calculation: Depending on the lagna, the order of Dasas is invariably sequential, either forward or backward through the zodiac. As this Dasa is now widely software-supported, and space does not allow calculation to be shown, the reader is referred to the references by Mr. Rao, cited below.

Judgment: A general rule with all Dasas is to take the Dasa ruler as the lagna and judge the chart accordingly. This is certainly applicable in Chara Dasa, where the currently running Rasi becomes the temporary lagna. For example, if the natal chart promises children, look to a Dasa from which the 5th House is strong by accepted methods. Look also to the Dasa period or subperiod of the sign that is the 5th House from the natal lagna.

Another example: let's say that the Sun is in the 10th House in Aries natally, with Jupiter in Leo in the 2nd. Jupiter aspects the Sun by the rules of both Parasara and Jaimini. Look for recognition, perhaps from the government, during not only Aries and Cancer periods, but also Scorpio periods. Why? Because the Sun is strong in the 6th from Scorpio, and Jupiter is now in the 10th aspecting him. Subperiods of the signs aspected by the Sun or Jupiter could also be relevant.

The above example is intended to illustrate the principle of turning the horoscope. In practice, one should also take into account a planet's karaka status. This, along with other issues, is explained further in the references cited herein.

If you plan on exploring this Dasa, the book to get is K.N. Rao's *Predicting Through Jaimini's Chara Dasa*. Consider the symbolism behind the following principle discovered by Mr. Rao: marriage may occur during the Chara Dasa of the sign which is the 7th (spouse) sign from the sign in the navamsha (marriage subchart) containing the Darakaraka (indicator of spouse). Fascinating material. Also useful is *Predicting Through Karakamsa and Jaimini's Mandook Dasa*, by the same author (as well as articles in *The Astrological Magazine*). *Jaimini Sutram*, translated by Prof. P.S. Sastri, is available but difficult to follow, and not useful for issues related to timing.

Kalachakra Dasa

Literally, Kalachakra means "wheel of time." This Dasa is given a great deal of emphasis by Sage Parasara. Like Vimshottari, it is a lunar Dasa; like Chara, its periods are indicated by signs rather than planets. The order of Dasa or Bhukti periods is usually sequential through the zodiac, either in a forward or reverse direction, with certain important exceptions. Kalachakra Dasa ("KCD") is unique in a number of ways, and it is classically known as the most highly-praised Dasa as well as the most difficult. Thus, this brief treatment is only intended to raise the reader's interest and to provide an introductory basis for further study.

As I was completing this article, I became aware that there are multiple systems used in calculating KCD, each giving totally different results. The North Indian *vakyakrama* system seems to be the best known in the United States, at least judging from the fact that it is widely software-supported. But in South India, a quite distinct system called *rashikrama* is favored. Apparently, there is disagreement over the interpretation of certain relevant passages in Sage Parasara's work.

I was more or less convinced that the North Indian system I'd been using was correct, but having experimented with rashikrama, I'm not so sure! Therefore, both systems will be presented, and no prejudice should be inferred, i.e., the reader should experiment with both. Two talented astrologers are to be credited with illustrating KCD as described here: Sumeet Chugh for the system used in North India, and Martin Gansten for that used in the South.

In the Northern system, KCD is almost unbelievably sensitive to small differences in birth time; just one minute of birth time can throw the periods off by three months (!), and switching ayanamshas creates even worse havoc. Consequently Northern Jyotishis recommend sticking close to Lahiri. The Southern system is not nearly so sensitive.

Calculation: This is quite detailed and therefore won't be shown here. The Moon's passage through individual navamsas (a.k.a. nakshatra padas) defines the specific Dasa balance and, in the North, also the Dasa order. Note also that KCD also uses a unique order of navamsa divisions which differ from those used in the regular varga chart.

Judgment: To start, apply the same principles as described above under Chara Dasa, wherein the ruling Dasa is taken as the lagna. If an event is promised natally, look to the KCD periods wherein the corresponding houses (counting from that rasi period as lagna) are emphasized. Also, of course, look to the KCD periods of the relevant rasi natally.

Although it's obvious that Dasa and Bhukti shifts ought to correlate with significant changes in a person's life, it is considered especially important (especially in the North) to look at "out-of-order" shifts, given Sanskrit names meaning "Frog's Jump" (skipping over one sign), "Monkey Jump" (skipping back or forward one sign, out of the overall forward or reverse order), and "Lion's Leap." The latter occurs when one sign jumps to the next in trinal fashion. In the Northern system, out-of-order shifts can transpire at the level of the Dasas. In the Southern system, they occur only at the level of the Bhuktis.

There is far more to this Dasa system than I have described, or even understand to this point, since much of its application is still "hidden" in the oral traditions, and perhaps in the vast body of still-untranslated works. The sensitivity and difficulty in calculation of this particular "wheel of time" has probably discouraged research and general use. Fortunately, new hope is offered by modern birth data and computer-aided calculation. Certainly most important will be further research into which system gives the best results.

Brihat Parasara Hora Sastra has entire chapters devoted to KCD, although the English translations are not very clear. (Nor are the translators necessarily to blame, given the importance of oral teaching in explaining the classical texts.) For practical information on the Northern system of KCD, consult Sumeet Chugh's *Yogini and Kalachakra Dasa*, cited above. K.N. Rao has published some articles about Kalachakra Dasa in *The Astrological Magazine* (Bangalore). For more on the Southern system, see Martin Gansten's forthcoming article (most likely to be published in *The Traditional Astrologer*; otherwise, contact the author via his address in this anthology). Mr. Gansten's exposition is much clearer than that given by V.S. Sastri in his commentary to *Jataka Parijata* (Ranjan Publications, New Delhi, India, pp.1000-1002).

To conclude, deep thanks are due the astrologers, both ancient and modern, mentioned in this article on whose researches these principles are based. Any oversimplifications will, I hope, be offset by inciting the reader to further refine techniques. As long as we keep one eye on the more traditional methods (Vimshottari, transits), studying life's cycles from additional perspectives should prove quite rewarding.

James C. Butler (born 4/26/63 at 4:46 AM EST in Detroit, MI, USA) is an astrologer and scientist who currently lives in metropolitan Washington, DC. He studied organic chemistry at Harvard University, obtaining his Master's degree there, and helped found a privately-held pharmaceutical company engaged in cancer research. Having just returned from an extended sojurn in India, Jim is now back in academia, teaching, consulting, and pursuing his doctorate. He sees astrology as a natural arena for research, self-discovery, and consequent expansion beyond the materialistic paradigm. You can contact him at P.O. Box 7067, Arlington, VA 22207. Ph: 703-526-0136.

EVERYDAY PRASHNA

Stephen & Edith Headstrom Chuhta

At the First East Coast Hindu Astrology Conference that occurred in the Washington, DC metro area in September, 1994, Hart deFouw presented a very interesting lecture titled "Everyday Prashna" which greatly aroused our curiosity. Subsequently we and two other conference attendees (Barbara Rosholdt and Kathy Campbell) got together to test the concepts and theories presented during this lecture.

In fairness to Mr. deFouw we need to point out that this is *our* understanding of what he presented, and second, that it is, as he noted, just one simplified technique extracted from the vast field of Vedic astrology. For Western astrologers who may be new to the term *prashna,* it is the same as the word *horary* in Western astrology. It has to do with setting up a chart for the moment of a question and then extracting the answer from the chart of the question.

TABLE 1

CLASS	HOUSE	PRIMARY QUESTIONS
CHYUTI	1	Change of Social Status, Promotion/ Demotion, Victory/Loss, Fame/ Infamy, Honor
VRDDHI	4	Gains/Losses Especially of People, Material, Things, Money, Property, Vehicles, etc.
NIVRTTI	7	Matters that are Restored to their Original State, Returning of Lost Objects, Regaining of Health, Regaining of Lost Position in Life
PRAVAS	10	Journeys, Foreign Residents, Being Away from one's Home, Immigration, Relocation, Travel, Move of Residence, etc.

TABLE 2

	SIGNS				ANSWERS
CARDINAL	AR	CA	LI	CP	Change
FIXED	TA	LE	SC	AQ	No Change
MUTABLE	GE	VI	SA	PI	00-15° (No Change) 15-30° (Change)

Rules:

1. In order to analyze a question, it is very important that you have a *strong desire to know the answer.* One way of determining that the question is not frivolous is by reviewing the horoscope to ensure that it reflects the question. Table 1 defines the relation of the *question* to the *House,* while Table 2 shows the relationship of the *answer* to the *sign* of the *House of Question.*

2. To answer a question, it is required to determine which House listed in Table 1 applies to the question. If it is difficult to determine the proper House then you should use the *Lagna* as the House of Question.

3. The question should be reduced to its *primary purpose.* For example: Shall I sell my House? The question should be re-stated as follows: Is the sale based on making money (4th House question "gain")? or change in job (10th House question "relocation")? or inheritance (1st House question "status")?

4. If the applicable House (1, 4, 7, 10) is occupied, receives an aspect, or is besieged from adjacent houses by malefic planets, i.e., Saturn, Mars, Rahu, etc. then the person's feelings, values and expectations will be disturbed or disappointed. A malefic planet in its own sign, or aspecting its own or exaltation sign, will not yield detrimental results.

5. If a House is occupied by, or receives an aspect from a benefic, i.e., Jupiter, Venus, etc. then the answer will enhance the person's feelings, values and expectations.

6. If a House is occupied by, or receives an aspect from both a malefic and a benefic planet, then the person's feelings, values and expectations will experience both good and detrimental effects. The resulting effect will lean toward the stronger planet (whether malefic or benefic).

7. Timing takes place by noticing when the Ruler of the House in Question, or the Moon, transits the original Prashna Chart and aspects its House of Question. Common sense should be used when dealing with time. In some cases, you can use the changes in the Nakshatras or Navamsas of the slower moving planets to time events.

Guidelines:

1. First determine the sign in the House of Question, i.e., Cardinal, Fixed or Mutable (per Tables 1 & 2).

2. Next determine the occupation, aspects, or if the House of Question is besieged.

3. Finally determine the time required for the event to take place by using the Ruler of the House of Question, the Moon, or noting when the Nakshatras or Navamsa changes.

Examples:

Using the above Rules & Guidelines the following examples were analyzed during our weekly meetings:

	Ketu 18:36 Lagna 20:18	Moon 12:26	
Saturn 15:15	**CHART A**		
Mercury 15:12			Mars 07:28 Rx
Sun 28:16	Venus 11:24 Jupiter 13:13	Rahu 18:36	

A. Question: Will my sister move out of state? (See Chart A)

Analysis: Since this is a relocation question, the 10th House from the Lagna was used. It contains the sign of Capricorn which indicates that a change in her present status would occur. Because the 10th House is besieged by Saturn and the Sun (since they are in adjacent houses) this would tend to indicate that she would not be happy in the new location.

Result: She moved out of state when Mars, ruler of the Lagna, was just about to return to the 5th House from the 4th House in which it aspected the 10th House of relocation. She was not happy with the move. We were not successful in using Saturn to time the event, and as a result, Mars, ruler of the Lagna, was used.

Background: We received a call from a sister indicating that the company her daughter was working for was bought out, and the people working there feared they would all be laid off. Their fears were realized. Her daughter, who was living with the sister, received a job offer in a different state. As a result they moved four months later. The sister was not happy with the move since she lost money on the home sale, and her daughter was required to accept a position with a smaller salary and reduced benefits.

	Ketu 17:48		Lagna 20:24
Saturn 15:50			Moon 15:32
Sun 03:35 Mercury 22:31	**CHART B**		Mars 07:28 Rx
	Jupiter 14:14 Venus 16:47	Rahu 17:48	

B. Question: Will Bob's health return? (See Chart B)

Analysis: Since this is a Health Restoration question, the 7th House from the Lagna was used for analysis. It contains the sign of Sagittarius. Because the Lagna degree is greater then 15, we assumed that a change would take place. In other words, his health would return.

Result: Bob had a speedy recovery. He was released from the hospital when the Moon transited the 7th House.

Background: We received a phone call indicating that our friend had suffered a seizure and was rushed to the hospital emergency ward. He recovered and upon his release he was outfitted with a heart pacemaker.

C. Question: Will I resign as President of my Condo Association? (See Chart C)

Moon 11:34	Ketu 18:35		
Saturn 15:01		**CHART C**	
Mercury 11:15			Mars 08:31 Rx Lagna 23:02
Sun 25:36	Venus 08:47 Jupiter 12:44	Rahu 18:35	

Analysis: Since this is a question of Honor, the Lagna was taken as the House of Question. The Lagna contains the sign of Leo which indicated that no change would take place. The 1st House was aspected by both Saturn and Mars indicating that remaining in this position would cause a tremendous amount of frustration.

Result: I did not resign immediately. However two months later, when the Sun and Moon aspected the 1st House, I resigned to enjoy my retirement.

Background: The politics within the Association were becoming increasingly disruptive, to the point that the meetings were useless. Realizing that the situation was not going to change after conducting two additional meetings, I was no longer interested in wasting my energy and time.

Conclusion: Our untutored experiments with this system suggested it to be fairly useful in providing a yes/no answer, and it seemed to reflect the conditions surrounding the question. Timing, however, appeared to be very tricky and worked best with hindsight. But this is a complex area. To learn more about the intricacies of timing within Prashna we have heard reputable people recommend several books including *Essentials of Horary Astrology or Prasnapadavi* by M. Ramakrishana Bhat.

Stephen has been a student of Astrology for over 25 years. He has a Master of Science degree in Physics, studies Astrology as a hobby and uses it in his trading of commodity futures. Edith was born in Switzerland and relocated to the USA several years ago. She has a Commercial School Diploma from Switzerland with degrees in Commercial Arts and Foreign Languages. Before coming to the US, she was a practicing astrologer for 23 years in Europe. Edith has conducted seminars and taught advanced astrology courses at the University of La Laguna in Spain. She speaks fluent English, Spanish, German and provides tape consultations in those languages to clients in the USA and in foreign countries. Write: 7913 South Woods Drive, Fredericksburg, VA 22408. Phone/Fax: 540-891-2962. E-mail: SESTAR@erols.com

COMPATIBILITY IN VEDIC ASTROLOGY

Christina Collins

Chart comparison studies are primarily utilized for marriage suitability. In modern times they are also recommended for evauating business partnerships or employee compatibility, for gaining insight into family relationships, and even for comparing a nation's chart with its leaders. In addition to the more commonly known techniques for comparing charts—the connection between the Ascendants, the Suns, the Moons, the rulers of the Ascendants, the aspects between planets, the rulers of the 7th Houses, and so forth—Vedic Astrology gives us a greater scope within which to compare and interpret two charts.

For example, let's take the conjunction of the malefic planets Saturn and Mars. A person with this conjunction in their natal chart may exhibit or experience a lot of anger or frustration in his/her life, due to the warring qualities of these two enemies when posited together. However, if they sit in the 9th House and receive the aspect of a benefic Jupiter, then their nature can change to one of intense focus on the spiritual quest or the search for Dharma (life purpose). Be careful not to be too "black and white" in assuming the good or bad nature of a planetary connection. Separately study each chart thoroughly before comparing the two together. This will give you the "essence" of each person entering into any relationship.

Following are some additional considerations and techniques unique to Vedic astrology.

The Nakshatras

#	NAME	ANIMAL (Yoni)	GANAM (Class)
1	Aswini	Horse	Deva
2	Bharani	Elephant	Manusha
3	Krittika	Sheep	Rakshasha
4	Rohini	Serpent	Manusha
5	Mrigisiri	Serpent	Deva
6	Ardra	Dog	Manusha
7	Purnarvasu	Cat	Deva
8	Pushya	Sheep	Deva
9	Ashlesha	Cat	Rakshasa
10	Magha	Rat	Rakshasha
11	PurvaPhalguni	Rat	Manusha
12	UttaraPhalguni	Cow	Manusha

13	Hasta	Buffalo	Deva
14	Chitra	Tiger	Rakshasha
15	Swati	Buffalo	Deva
16	Vishaka	Tiger	Rakshasha
17	Anurada	Deer	Deva
18	Jyeshta	Deer	Rakshasha
19	Mula	Dog	Rakshasha
20	PurvaAshada	Monkey	Manusha
21	UttaraAshada	Cow	Manusha
22	Sravana	Monkey	Deva
23	Dhanishta	Lion	Rakshasha
24	Satabisha	Horse	Rakshasha
25	PurvaBhadrapada	Lion	Manusha
26	UttaraBhadrapada	Cow	Manusha
27	Revati	Elephant	Deva

What this table illustrates is that the Nakshatra (also known as constellation, lunar mansion, or star lord) provides information about the individual's caste (personality nature and disposition of consciousness) and their life-quality connection with the natal Moon. What star the Moon is in will indicate the mind, feelings, cravings, desires and emotions. Just as certain zodiac signs are compatible or inimical, the 27 constellations of the zodiac equally carry qualities of harmony or dissonance when associating with each other.

Kuta Agreement

Kuta ("points") highlight 10 factors for marriage agreement. There should be agreement in at least 5 of the 10 kutas. And, to be explicit, these kuta agreement factors are based upon comparisons of the Moon's sign or nakshatra of the prospective bride and groom.

DHINAM	(Karma) Luck.
RAJJU	Marital happiness and freedom from widowhood.
GANAM	Wealth/prosperity, nature of consciousness or life outlook, class. (Deva = Angelic, Manushya = Human, and Rakshasha = Demonic or Worldly.)
RASI	Growth of Family (sign comparison)
YONI	Physical rapport based on the animal types (for increasing the number of children).
MAHENDHRAM	Comfort and the relationship's longevity.
STHREE-DHEERGHAM	General welfare.
RASYADHIPATHI	Prosperity through foods grown in the soil.
VASYAM	Development of posterity/harmony.
VEDHAI	Gives many children.

In considering agreement, there are also methods for comparing the caste types (such as spiritual, commercial, military, and serving). Certain castes are more sympathetic with one caste type versus another. Also, consider the age of the couple. If they are young, this is their first marriage, and they are desirous of children, Kuta is more important. Strong Kuta agreement brings emotional harmony in marriage and many children.

Constellational Astrology by Robert Deluce, and B.V. Raman's *Muhurta* are good initial references for more detailed information if you want to know the step-by-step details on how to determine Kuta agreement. Additionally, certain computer programs (such as *Visual Jyotish* and *Parashara's Light*) have Kuta compatibility modules. Even though a computer will aid you in speed and preparation time, it is also important to learn how to determine Kuta yourself, among other reasons in order to understand to what level of strength (full or partial) each agreement is compatible.

Karakas (Significators)

Jupiter is the karaka for the Vedic marriage itself. Jupiter is also the karaka for the husband in a woman's chart. Venus is the karaka for the wife in a man's chart. A woman's Mars should aspect the man's Venus, and his Venus should connect with her Sun.

Western astrology is more likely to view Venus, the planet of love, as the significator for marriage. In the Sanskrit language Jupiter, "Guru" or teacher, governs all sacraments, rules, knowledge, divinity and wisdom. Jupiter is the teacher or guide of the Deva or angelic realm. Venus *(Sukra)* translates as "luminosity" and refers to the reproductive fluid in both males and females. Venus teaches and guides the Asuras or "demonic" realm towards love, beauty, harmony and balance.

Jupiter denotes the spiritual, sacramental and educational qualities of life, while Venus represents the material, love, pleasure-seeking and worldly qualities of life. This rulership of quite different realms also helps explain why Jupiter and Venus are considered planetary enemies in Vedic Astrology.

Cultural Considerations

Cultural differences between India and the West suggest another reason why the significators differ. An Indian marriage is traditionally based on a sacramental, religious or spiritual relationship while the Western marriage, though frequently having spiritual qualities of its own, is more often based on pleasure and personal fulfillment, with self choice of partner, and so forth.

Another way to view this is that Jupiter is the natural significator of the 9th House of wisdom, the 12th House of enlightenment, and is ruler of all spiritual sacraments. Venus is significator for the 2nd house of family life, the 7th house of marriage and partnership, and generally governs all pleasures. In the West, we observe Venus as equal significator, for in the Western culture, where divorce is much more prevalent, a strong love factor may be the very thing to hold a marriage together in a lifelong bond.

The Navamsa Chart (9th Harmonic)

"Nav" means nine, and "amsa" means division. One of the uses of the 9th divisional chart is to view the spouse. That the marriage karaka, Jupiter, is the natural 9th House ruler may be a potential reason for the use of this chart for spiritual or karmic marriage compatibility. One technique compares the Navamsa to the natal chart of the other person, and vice versa. Some astrologers also compare the two Navamsas to each other.

Another technique observes the marriage karakas, Jupiter and Venus, in the Navamsa and determines if they are well situated and well aspected. Also, we view the Navamsa 7th house along with its rulers and their condition. Next locate the natal chart's 7th House ruler's position by sign and house in the native's Navamsa chart. Then add this viewpoint to the study of both charts, to see if their 7th House ruling planets connect in the Natal or Navamsa of one or both people.

Sometimes, when a strong, long-term married couple seem to have many incompatibilities in their natal charts and you wonder how they have stayed happy and together, you will find the connection in the Navamsa. Or, if you have always wondered why you get along so well with the sign of Leo when that is not a good connection for your natal chart, you might observe that you have a full moon in Leo in your own Navamsa chart. Then you may begin to understand why you have so many Leo people in your life.

The Saptamsa Chart (7th Harmonic)

"Sapta" means seven. This chart is reviewed to determine the potential for having children, and the qualities of the children. Again, the karaka Venus ("Sukra") governs reproductive fluid for fertility and is the ruler of the 7th house (Libra) in the "natural" zodiac. As Saptamsa is the 7th or marriage house harmonic chart, it can be viewed in respect to what kind of qualities or results marriage will hold for an individual. I do not give this harmonic as much weight in comparing it with the natal chart of the other person, but do consider it when evaluating physical desire and the ability to produce children.

Kuja Dosa

Kuja Dosa ("Mars poison") occurs when major malefic Mars, the planet of conflict, is posited in house 1, 2, 4, 7, 8 or 12. If both individuals have Mars in one of these houses, it neutralizes the dosa. However if Mars is posited in the 1st House, it can still bring a fiery temperament and a "pitta" constitution to that individual. The thinking is that if both individuals have Kuja Dosa, then each will have a quality of this malefic content in their own nature, thereby creating a balance between them.

However, if one person has Kuja Dosa and the other does not, it can create difficulties. Naturally, a well-placed Mars in each chart (for example, a functional benefic or situated well by house placement) will manifest less conflict between the parties. In other words, don't be too quick to apply the seemingly simple concept of Kuja Dosa in a cursory way. I do give more focus to Kuja Dosa in the charts of potential business partners.

Dasas & Bhuktis (Time Periods)

The time periods in operation for each individual should be in harmony. Ideally, each should be friendly to the other. If one person is running Saturn and the other Mars, there may be trouble. When the Mars Dasa changes to Rahu (who acts somewhat like Saturn) there can be improved harmony. Also, it is not advisable to marry during the interval when one person's major Dasa will be changing within three months of the other person changing their Dasa.

Another consideration is Ketu Dasa. It is not considered wise to marry during this time period. It is a short period (7 years); therefore, the sub-periods (Bhuktis) and sub-sub-periods (Antaradasas) change very quickly. When one person is going through constant change it can be hard on a marriage. If the decision is to marry anyway, then it is wise to wait at least until the first Bhukti is complete (Ketu/Ketu).

Yogas & Aspects

Look to the Yogas present in each chart. Dr. B.V. Raman's *300 Important Combinations* and Dr. K. S. Charak's *Yogas,* are good references for more information. Some of the things I watch for are Kala Sarpa yoga in either chart. [*Editor's Note: See Linda Johnsen's related article on this.*] Also note if Rahu and Ketu (the lunar nodes) are running through Houses 1 and 7 (opposition) for either person. Just as in Kuja Dosa, if both charts contain it then the negative effect is neutralized. Remember to also check the Navamsa for this cancellation.

I also pay particular attention to what I have termed "nodal reverse," when one person's Rahu is conjunct the other's Ketu (typically about nine years younger or older). On the premise that Rahu is what you've come to learn in this life, and Ketu is what you bring in with you as karma (which can be good, bad or both), reversed nodes are opposing lessons. Often it produces a situation where one person is accomplished where the other is lacking, and where the working out of one's past issues is constantly triggered by the other's node.

For example, a person with Rahu in Aries needs to learn to be more adventurous and more of a risk taker. A person with Ketu in Libra may be somewhat accomplished with harmony and balance (good or bad aspects to these planets and their lords give this determination). Conversely, Ketu in Aries shows affinity for adventure and risk while Rahu in Libra suggests a need to learn balance. You can see where conflict could enter. I commonly see this combination between people who consult me when their relationship and/or marriage is already very troubled. It *can* work (because what one person needs to learn, the other has experience in) if both are committed to constantly be working on their issues (which I have observed to be rare).

Vedic Astrology within its many branches offers even more techniques. Sarva Ashtakavarga can be observed for high or low bindus (points) in the 7th house. The nadi system can also be applied. For more information, or to be on the list for the forthcoming book on Compatibility that I am honored to be co-authoring with Dr. Dennis Harness, please write or fax to the address below.

Christina Collins (Rani Bhuvana Tara Chandi Saraswati) is Director of the Academy for Vedic Studies in Boulder, Colorado. She is a 1994 recipient of the Jyotish Kovid title, awarded by Dr. B.V. Raman, President of the ICAS (International Council of Astrological Sciences) in New Delhi, India. She is also one of the first five Americans, and the sole female recipient, of the 1996 title Jyotish Vachaspati, awarded in Bangalore, India in November, 1996 by Dr. Raman and the ICAS. She is a Vice President and a steering committee member of ACVA (American Council of Vedic Astrology), also serving on its Education Board, and she is on the Executive Editorial Board of the ACVA Journal. Practicing since 1968, she relocated her international Beverly Hills practice and school to Boulder, Colorado in 1992. Christina has done thousands of consultations, serving students to celebrities, and has been teaching Vedic Astrology locally and at International Symposiums since 1989. Write: 3165 Arnett Street, #2, Boulder, CO 80304. Phone: 303-786-7868. Fax: 303-786-7336.

ASHTAMANGALA DEVA PRASNA

Shyamasundara Dasa

On the morning of July 23, 1982, I found myself outside a Durga temple on the outskirts of Trivandrum, South India. I was gathered with six learned astrologers of the area, including my teacher Krishnan Potti, the author (in Malayalam) of over a dozen books on astrology, to do Ashtamangala Deva Prasna ("ADP").

The setting was lush and exotic with many flower and fruit-bearing trees, and incense wafted in the breeze. Ashtamangala is a method of numerology and Deva Prasna is a special kind of Prasna dealing with temple matters. Both are explained in *Prasna Marga*. However, as I was soon to discover, successful ADP required more than knowledge of these two subjects. Success depended on a thorough knowledge of *Prasna Marga*, high intelligence, strong powers of observation, and keen intuition stemming from spiritual practices and pure lifestyle. Because of its nature, only the very best astrologers were called upon to conduct the Prasna.

This was not my first ADP. On my previous stay in India (1977-78), I had begun my general study of astrology. On this sojourn (1980-83) I wanted to focus on Prashna. I had been studying Jataka in Calcutta, but unfortunately I had not found astrologers in North India who knew Prasna. I knew that Prasna and other branches of astrology were well preserved in South India. So after I finished my studies in Calcutta, I headed south to Bangalore armed with a letter of introduction from the late Y. Keshava Menon (then president of the Calcutta Astrological Association) to Dr. B.V. Raman.

I had just read Dr. Raman's translation of *Prasna Marga* and hoped that he would guide me to a expert teacher. Dr. Raman kindly consented to see me but threw a wet blanket on my dreams saying that it would be practically impossible for me to find a good teacher of Prasna. "Good scholars of astrology are rare," he said, "of these, those that could teach were rarer still; and of these, those who had time to teach a neophyte were even more rare. And out of all of these astrologers one who could speak English was the rarest of all."

I was undaunted and determined to prove him wrong, but I soon found that he had not spoken lightly. Eventually, after many months of searching,

I finally found two sources for in-depth knowledge of Prasna. The first was a family of astrologers in Bangalore headed by the late B.G. Sasikantha Jain (M.K. Gandhi had also been his student) who practiced Bhrgu Prasna. And the second was Krishnan Potti the scholar of Prasna Marga. Convincing Sasikantha Jain to teach me took me over 10 months, but that's another story. And while Krishnan Potti readily agreed to teach me, there were two problems. He lived in a scenic but remote, hilly area outside of Trivandrum with no access by bus or taxi. Second, he didn't speak English.

The first I solved by learning to drive a motorcycle. Considering that there are practically no enforceable traffic laws in India, this meant risking my life. When the light was low, there was also the very real danger of running into greasy, soccer ball-sized lumps of elephant dung (not even counting the many kinds of animals always in the roads). Consequently, I would regularly pray to Lord Nrsimhadeva to spare my life. The second problem was more difficult. I didn't know Malayalam and was no Sanskrit scholar. However, I did have a fairly large Sanskrit vocabulary from studying *Bhagavad-gita* and *Srimad-Bhagavatam,* ayurveda, and of course astrology. I found that as long as we conversed in Sanskrit about astrology I could follow what was being said, and thus I passed more than a year studying with Krishnan Potti.

Despite his remote location he had a steady stream of people who would show up for consultations. He handled all kinds of Prasnas, but ADPs were special. These required that several scholarly astrologers gather at a venue away from their normal place of practice. In addition, ADPs required the use of nimitta (omens) and other special procedures. Because the ADPs involved many people, and were all in Malayalam, I arranged for a translator to accompany me on this day-long affair.

Despite my notes from that day, it would be impossible for me to include everything that was said and done in the 6-7 hour period necessary to conduct the ADP. However I hope the reader will be able to appreciate the mystical nature of the experience which, even for many students of Vedic astrology, will seem to border on magical. Countless experiences like this destroyed in my mind the mechanistic world view of modern science and permanently established the Vedic, God-centered world view of Krsna Consciousness.

Even as astrologers we are sometimes bound up in thinking that everything revolves around symbols drawn on a piece of paper. This limiting paradigm is shattered when we realize that everything in existence is a message from

Sri Krsna if we only knew how to read them. An astrologer must always keep his eyes and ears open and be prepared to read everything that is happening during a crucial moment such as a Prasna.

The Ashtamangala Deva Prasna Begins

To begin the ADP the astrologers first prepared a small, clean area of land and then covered it with a layer of raw rice. The questioners were asked to adorn it with a ghee lamp, white flowers and make offerings such as Tambula (Pan leaves). They then performed worship with devotion on all the articles that would be used in the process of divination and meditated on Lord Krsna as the Supersoul within their hearts (Bhagavad-gita 15.15) for the ability to predict correctly.

The astrologers then asked an official of the temple with no knowledge of astrology to come forward. They showed him a South Indian diagram of the zodiac and ask him to duplicate it on the prepared ground. Using a stick he carefully prepared the diagram by first drawing the Western line, then the Southern line, then Eastern and finally the Northern line. (In Prasna the directions of the diagram are such: the side that has Aries and Taurus is East, Cancer and Leo is South, Libra and Scorpio is West, and Capricorn and Aquarius is North).

The pandits noted very carefully the order that he drew them. One stated that because the priest drew the Western line first it was a highly inauspicious omen indicating that diseases (or general harm) would increase. And this was made worse because he had drawn the other lines in a counter-clockwise order which indicated many serious obstacles ahead. In general these two things were looked upon as unfavorable omens. They then looked for any irregularities in the way the lines were drawn, that is, if they were thick or thin, broken, etc. But none were observed.

The astrologers then called on any young child not conversant with astrology to come forward. The adults pushed a child forward. The astrologers directed the child to worship the ghee lamp and other divinatory paraphernalia with flowers. They then placed in the child's right hand a piece of gold, along with flowers, water, sandal wood paste and aksata—rice mixed with turmeric. The child was then instructed to go around the Cakra of the zodiac and stand near it facing east. Meanwhile, the questioner who had called this convocation of astrologers was instructed to be meditating on God to reveal His will. All the astrologers then reflected on the problems of the querent and meditated on the Lord, while the chief astrologer who would do the Ashtamangala was touching his cowry shells. At the end they asked the child to deposit the gold in any one of the signs that had previously been drawn by the priest. The child placed the handful in the square for Virgo.

This Swarna Lagna (gold ascendant), as it is also known, became the Arudha Lagna for the ADP. The exact time the Swarna Lagna was chosen was 8:45 AM, thus the Udaya Lagna, the time-based Lagna, was Leo. The planetary positions at the time were fixed, and the chart was filled in with all the planets including Mandi, who is very significant in Kerala astrology, and South India in general, but not much used in the North. (Most computer programs calculate Mandi according to their own methods. However, when I wrote the *Jyotish Vedic Program* for Matrix Software, I duplicated the methods of Prasna Marga and the Kerala tradition as I personally saw it practiced.)

The position of the Swarna Lagna was then examined. The piece of gold was located in the middle of the square designating Virgo; however, it was face down, on top of the aksata and flowers. It was also tilted and slanted toward the South. The astrologers declared this to be indicative of death and other evils.

While the Swarna Lagna was being chosen, Krishnan Potti did the first part of the Ashtamangala, and this requires a little explanation. A major instrument for divination in Kerala are cowry shells which have been specially selected, cleaned, sanctified, and used only for divination. In less complex Prasnas the Arudha Lagna is often found by manipulation of the cowries alone. For divination 108 cowries are used. To do the first part of the Ashtamangala, the astrologer first touches the cowries while meditating on Krsna and asking for spiritual guidance. Then the astrologer arbitrarily divides the shells into three piles, one to his left, one in front of him and one to his right. After examining the Swarna Lagna Krishnan Potti did the second part of the Ashtamangala by going to each pile of cowries and counting off multiples of eight and keeping the remainder, if the remainder is zero then let it be eight. You now have a three digit number in which no digit is greater than eight.

The digits represent past, present and future respectfully from left to right. 1=Sun, 2=Mars, 3=Jupiter, 4=Mercury, 5=Venus, 6=Saturn, 7=Moon, and 8=Rahu. Odd numbers are considered good, even numbers bad.

The Ashtamangala number that was obtained for the Prasna was 8 3 1 ruled by Rahu, Jupiter and the Sun respectfully. It seemed clear to me that 831 indicated that the past was bad, the present and future looked good. But the assembled scholars claimed that for special reasons this was not true. They said that because the numbers were in a descending order from left to right this indicated that the past was good, the present was bad and the future would be worse. Other parts of the reading seemed to confirm this.

The ghee lamp was now lit, and the flame was observed to lean toward the South. This was again declared to be an evil omen. Then one of the astrologers stated that the deity must have been moved at least twice before being established in the present temple. The temple managers replied that this was true and wanted to know how he knew. The astrologer said this was so because he had observed that the ghee lamp had been picked up and moved twice before the Prasna started.

The astrologers then examined the Tambula that was offered for worship. These Tambula represent the 12 houses of the Deva Prasna chart, and the condition of these houses can be determined by the condition of the leaves. In this case since there were only three "Pan leaves" only the first three houses of the Deva Prasna chart could be examined by this method. The first, representing the Lagna, had marks and cuts, thus things had not been good up until now. The second was smaller than the others and had cuts, thus there were financial problems. The third was in much better shape, so they declared those who served the temple were capable of doing good.

The number of leaves were now used to determine the Tambula Lagna (TL). TL = the remainder of $(T \times 10 + 1)/7$ where T is the number of Tambulas. Since T=3 we get a remainder of 3 which represents Mars in the normal order of planets. Since Mars is in Libra, this becomes the Tambula Lagna. Mars alone indicates that there had been strife and conflicts, and because Mars is in Libra they deduced that the deity afflicting the temple was goddess Bhadrakali.

Since Rahu ruled over the first Ashtamangala number, and he was in the 10th with Venus, one astrologer declared that the temple must have been east of its present place, in a location occupied by a naga (serpents endowed with mystical powers). This was admitted by the temple mangers. Since Mars had only just transited into Libra one astrologer stated that there must have been a fire in the temple recently. Affirmative was the response.

Another astrologer pointed out that Rahu and Venus in the 10th also indicated that someone must have died from poison nearby, and the ghost was still lingering in the vicinity. We were told that in the past a child had taken poison and died in the compound.

Up to this time we were not informed why the ADP was taking place. But as the ADP proceeded the details started to come out. At this point the original question was finally ascertained by the astrologers. One astrologer said that because Saturn is in the Arudha Lagna they want to know: why has Durga devi (goddess of the material world) left the temple? The people agreed that, indeed, this was their question. The reason she left, the astrologers said, is because the rules of conduct were not properly observed. This included entry into the temple of impure people, such as persons who had a recent death in their family, or women who were menstruating, etc.

Since the Arudha Lagna is Virgo the astrologers deduced that the land was owned by the women of the family by special arrangement. This was also confirmed to be true.

The astrologers agreed that since Mars and Jupiter are badakas for Virgo (Raman, 1980 pp. 545–547) and are in the 2nd House, and since Ketu is in Virgo navamsa, the same sign as the Arudha Lagna, then some other person must also have died. This dead person, and the poisoned child, having no shelter came to this temple and have contaminated the place. The querents admitted that indeed another person did die nearby, a family member, because of a fall from a tree.

The astrologers continued that since Jupiter is a bhadaka conjoined with Mars, significator of land, and this same Jupiter is aspecting Venus then the land the temple is on was previously owned and that now a ghost of a fallen brahmana is haunting the place. They also concluded from the symptoms that Bhadrakali, the ferocious form of Durga, has also manifested and is covering over Durga. The temple managers have to remove Bhadrakali and leave only Durga.

After examining all the houses of the Deva Prasna the astrologers concluded that because of Ketu in the 4th, and 4th lord Jupiter afflicted, the temple should be reconstructed. They also concluded that some theft had taken place, and that they needed decorations in the temple. Further, the affliction to the 10th and 12th Houses indicated much improvement was necessary in regards to the priestly functioning in the temple. They also recommend, on the basis of the condition of the 8th House, that they should make special offering and worship to pacify the deity.

Several questions were asked regarding what exactly should be done to pacify the deity and remove Bhadrakali. Suggestions for remedies were proposed. To determine if a proposed suggestion would work the astrologers would consult the cowries for a yes or no answer. After posing the question and proposed solution Krishnan Potti would meditate and then take a handful of cowries. Then counting off multiples of twelve he would arrive at a number, if the remainder was zero then it was 12. This number represented a new Arudha Lagna. Iupiter was found to be in a trine or quadrant from this new Arudha Lagna the answer was "yes," otherwise it was "no." In this way for several hours various strategies were tried to find a solution to the temple's problems.

As we have seen from this one example, the system of Vedic Prasna, as preserved in Kerala, is a very powerful method. To master it requires a lot of hard work, training and above all faith in Sri Krsna. Great faith is necessary because we are conditioned to think in a mechanistic way. We must go beyond that and understand that from a spiritual perspective everything is conscious and is controlled by and connected to God. The process of divination allows us to carry on a dialog with God through apparently inanimate objects or chance occurrences. This dialog can only be accomplished if we train and purify our intelligence, mind and senses, through study of appropriate texts, as well as a pure brahminical lifestyle based on the teachings of the Vedas.

PLANETARY POSITIONS (LAHIRI)
July 23, 1982, at 8:45 AM, IST, Trivandrum, India, 76E55, 08N29

RASI		NAVAMSA
Arudha Lagna	12-VI-13	AR
Udaya Lagna	12-LE-13	CA
Sun	06-CA-21	LE
Moon	08-LE-44	GE
Mars	00-LI-08	LI
Mercury	03-CA-46	LE
Jupiter	07-LI-46	SA
Venus	09-GE-21	SA
Saturn	22-VI-52	CA
Rahu	19-GE-39	PI
Ketu	19-SA-39	VI
Mandi	12-LE-17	CA

References:

Bhat, Ramakrishna, M., 1992, *Essentials of Horary Astrology or Prasnapadavi*, Delhi, India: Motilal Banarsidass Publishers.

Raman, Bangalore, Venkata, 1980, 1st Edition, translation, *Prasna Marga*, part 1, Bangalore, India: IBH Prakashana.

Raman, Bangalore, Venkata, 1985, 1st Edition, translation, *Prasna Marga*, vol. 2, Bangalore, India: IBH Prakashana.

Shyamasundara Dasa has been a disciple of A.C. Bhaktivedanta Swami Prabhupada since 1976. He began his study of Vedic astrology in 1977 and spent 5 years in India studying several branches of astrology with masters of the subject. Shyamasundara Dasa is a pioneer of Vedic astrology in the West. In 1979 he completed the first Vedic astrology software. In 1983 he wrote the first Vaisnava (Vedic) lunar calendar computer program which has become the official calendar for many ashramas worldwide. His 3rd generation astrology software was published by Matrix Software in 1988 under the title Jyotish Vedic Astrology *program. In 1987 he organized the 3rd Annual Vedic Astrology Conference sponsored by Matrix software. In 1996 he completed writing a series of courses for the Vedic astrology syllabus of the Florida Vedic College (FVC). The FVC is recognized by the state of Florida (and thus the whole USA and the world) as a degree-granting institution. The FVC is the only institution of higher learning in the West offering degree courses in Vedic astrology. Contact: 6793 West Newberry Road, suite 105, Gainesville FL, 32605. (352) 332-3931. shyamasundara.acbsp@com.bbt.se.*

THE BHAVA CHART: BIRTH & REBIRTH
(TEN POINTS OF DELINEATION)

Eve de Alberich

It is within the Bhava chart that the "history" of an individual may be studied, much in the same manner as one might look to a history book to discern the past patterns of a country. It has been said that unless we study the past we are doomed to repeat it. It is the Bhava chart which addresses this very axiom.

To begin with, the Bhava chart has an unusual structure. Its house cusps are actually the midpoints of its true houses. Its Ascendant, though, is always regarded as its Ascendant "proper" as distinct from its 1st House cusp. The Bhava chart may be compared to a sidereal chart that uses the Porphyry house system to derive its midpoint cusps. Its true house cusps can be marked in various ways: by using dashed lines, highlighted lines, solid lines, or whatever works best visually for each person. In eastern astrology it is simply "understood" that the cusps are there.

According to the Sanskrit source on calculation known as the Sripati Paddhati: the Bhava Midheaven and Ascendant are first established, whereupon the intermediate house cusps used for the Bhava midpoint house cusps are derived by a tri-section of the distance between the Midheaven and the Ascendant to form initially the 11th House cusp and then the 12th House cusp. Next, the same procedure is followed by tri-secting the distance between the Ascendant and the Nadir to establish the 2nd House cusp and then the 3rd House cusp. This is the same method used to derive the house cusps in the Porphyry house system. The Porphyry house system marks or divides space across the ecliptic, as distinct from other house systems which mark space across the prime vertical or that of the celestial equator.

Fundamental to the interpretation of the Bhava chart is an understanding of some of the underlying symbolism associated with the Bhava chakra (chart). The symbolism I refer to is to be found pictured in a fresco in the Tashi'ding monastery at Sikkim, a small Indian state near Tibet. This fresco depicts the Bhava chakra or "Wheel of Law." This wheel is divided into two halves, upper and lower, which are said to describe the various possible states of the human condition during any physical incarnation.

These two hemispheres are further divided into six sections or "states of being" called *lokas* from which can be determined the attitude or orientation most familiar to an individual prior to their present life. These lokas are derived from the Drekanas and suggest what an individual innately tends to focus upon before adopting different attitudes from the present life experiences. It is also said that an individual has one of these lokas that he is working *toward* in the future, and that this too can be determined from the Bhava chart using the Drekanas.

To Buddhist philosophy, all six of these lokas are considered to be illusions as a result of mankind being bound to physical existence through the three major illusional emotions, namely: Ignorance (symbolized by a pig), Anger (symbolized by a snake), and Lust (symbolized by either a dove or a rooster). These three major illusions comprise the Realm of Desire within which mankind is said to reside while experiencing physical life. The Buddhists believe that until a man frees himself from Desire, he is doomed to be born in one of Twelve Compartments of Life called the "Twelve Nidanas" which encircle the six lokas on the Wheel of Law.

These 12 Nidanas can be said to correspond to the 12 constellations. But, while they are associated with the six lokas, they do not correspond to them in any "even" manner. The whole of the Bhava chart is supported by the figure of one "Dag-Zin," a demon-like figure said to be symbolic of the unenlightened ego or unenlightened personality of mankind which believes in selfishness. This selfishness, in turn, supports the Wheel of Illusion itself which signifies the belief that matter and the world of illusion (i.e., the world of physical matter) are the truest reality.

The Eastern astrologer who searches the Bhava chart is very interested in his client's position on this wheel. Walt Whitman is quoted as once having said, "That which is mine own shall know my face." It is within the Bhava chart that the astrologer seeks the characteristics of his client's "face"—a face which certain others, according to Walt Whitman, will always unwittingly recognize.

The progression through the lokas is *not* linear, nor is the most materially comfortable loka the most desirable, nor is there any permanence in any of the six states. Its names refer not to actual beings, or embodiments or places, but instead to "states of consciousness" which the Buddhists believe are but states of illusion.

The upper half of the Wheel of Law contains the Illusions of Happiness, called Su-gati; while the lower half of the Wheel alludes to the Illusions of Unhappiness, or Dur-gati. Both have three further divisions:

SU-GATI

Sura-loka: Ruled by Jupiter, its symbol is a Lute, signifying the transitory nature of whatever the person has. They must learn always to keep uppermost in their minds the transitory nature of all things. This loka often indicates people who have come to help others, and the riches that they may possess are often the product of effort that has been performed by others. They are said to be fortunate, but still unenlightened. Their pitfalls can be pride or complacency that occurs as a result of their failure to understand that their condition is but temporary.

Asura-loka: Ruled by the Sun or Mars, its symbol is that of the Sword representing Knowledge, which these people are here to seek. These are persons who can be achievement-ridden, envious and obsessed with a desire for success, yet tortured always by the knowledge that other people exist who are better off than themselves. Theirs is usually an existence of continual striving and their chief characteristic is envy.

Theirs is a "fortunate" realm of power and money; but they are possessed by the fact that they are not quite at the "top" as they see it. They are often driven to seize what they want by force. They are urged in the present life to seek wisdom and peace of mind instead of power and wealth. These are people who are closely aligned with the material world and are therefore learning about issues having to do with hunger, self-preservation, and the use of their libido.

Nara-loka: Ruled by Mercury and symbolized by a Begging Bowl and Staff which signifies a need for these people to turn to a spiritual life. These individuals are said to have great freedom of choice regarding such things as work, recreation, and giving birth. They can, in fact, become bewildered from having so many choices. As a result, many may feel they lack a central purpose to their life and may wander from one activity to another.

These people may be fairly well off, but they are *not* achievement-driven. They may have better lives than most, but can be confused by all the choices in the world and sometimes may become intimidated by the degree of responsibility to which human beings can be heir. These are people who are said to be working toward acquiring higher principles in general and seeking to develop themselves further in the areas of love and virtue. Although intelligent, they may yet be lacking in wisdom.

DUR-GATI

Preta-yoni: Ruled by the Moon and symbolized by Amrit (the elixir of the gods), it is a symbol of the Vitalizing Properties of Life and the quality of Generosity to Others. These individuals have come to address the problem of greed and its attendant problems. These are people who never seem able to acquire quite as much as they want. They tend to the attitude that "nothing ever seems to work out for me," and "everything I do to extract satisfaction from life only seems to make things worse."

Such people are said to need to learn to identify more with the vital aspects of life, and to learn to cultivate generosity toward others as a way of rising above their own self-centered desires, expectations and cravings that only serve to keep them tied to their sense of misery. It may also be that these people will need to experience the generosity of others in their life to serve as an example. They may also find themselves needing or striving for beauty, their own concept of harmony, as well as pursuing design and form in all they do.

Tiryyak-yoni: Ruled by Venus and symbolized by a book signifying the liberating quality of clarity of thought which these individuals need to develop. Those souls found here exhibit an initial tendency to go passively through the motions of life, following their instincts and urges without ever really exerting the will and reason to take control of their own existence.

These individuals generally do not seem to experience great aspirations, nor the greater "peaks and valleys" of life. Instead they seem to be possessed of a sort of general malaise or lethargy exacerbated by an apparent lack of awareness concerning what they might be missing. Such people have come into this life to acquire the faculty of clear thinking in order to rise above their tendency to live their life by unwittingly reacting primarily to their instinctual drives. They do, however, seem to need, and strive for, their own concept of harmony, design, form and beauty in whatever they do.

Naraka-Loka: Ruled by Saturn, and symbolized by a Flame as representative of purification through suffering and the transmutation of the emotions into a more positive form of expression, persons referred to here may have many painful experiences or may even experience pain in many different ways, but all for a specific purpose. For these people, life in general seems to most strongly resemble a mirror in which they must constantly be shown their own true nature, especially their own mistakes and inadequacies, for the purpose of self-growth.

Often these people can experience much despair through self-examination in which they may feel grief or regrets over past wrong deeds and the knowledge of their own inadequacies. The issue of hatred is explored here—both hatred that can be directed outwardly through temper and anger, and hatred that can be directed inwardly through self-loathing and despair. Purification through suffering and the transmutation of negative emotions or drives into positive ones is the goal here. The experience of alienation occurs here as well until one learns to have sufficient compassion for other people and to recognize the tendencies toward alienation within their own nature.

There can be internalized anger related to the issue of Belonging. Lack of self-esteem can occur here as one comes to terms with one's past mistakes and inadequacies. Then, as one learns to forgive one's self, one can learn to translate this lack of self-esteem into compassion for others. The transmutation of limitations and errors into positive attitudes is the goal. Along the way, lessons concerning the issues of self-preservation, hunger and the proper use of the libido may also be encountered here.

The 12 Nidanas

1. Avidya: Spiritual misunderstandings, spiritual blindness, and new
                spiritual beginnings for good or ill.

2. Saniskara: How a man decides to shape his own nature. A person's
                foundations. What a person conforms his energies to.

3. Vijnana: Restless activity, what one is attracted to through curiosity,
                restlessness or consciousness.

4. Namarupa: How one sees oneself as distinct from others. The Mind and
                Body.

5. Chadayatana: What sort of understanding a person fills himself with. The
                filling of the self with understanding of one sort or another.
                The Senses.

6. Sparsa: The desire not to be alone. The desire for physical contact
                with others.

7. Vedana: The factors of pleasure and/or pain in the world and the
                ability of pleasure and/or pain to distort man's perception.
                Sensation.

8. Trishna: Becoming intoxicated with desire.

9. Upadana: Attachment. What an individual gathers unto himself.
                Becoming obsessive and/or acquisitive. Being committed to
                something.

10. Bhava: Existence. A valued outcome. Creativity used to achieve a
                productive and much desired end result.

11. Jati: The fulfillment of responsibility. Birth. Making creativity
                manifest in a practical way.

12. Jaramaran: The ending of one particular cycle. The completing of a life
                or a matter. Breakdown or decay.

The study of the Bhava chart can become very involved but there are 10 steps of delineation that can quickly outline the nature of the soul's journey upon the wheel. These ten steps are as follows:

Ten Steps of Delineation

1. *Where the Natural Inclination of the Individual resides* is indicated by the placement of the ruler of the 1st Bhava cusp.

2. *What an Individual Comprehends* is indicated by the placement of the Moon.

3. *The Personal Will & Spirit; One's Capacity for Honour & Glory* is indicated by the placement of the Sun

4. *Where the Soul Has Been; the Loka of the Past* is indicated by the Drekana Ruler of either the Sun or the Moon, whichever of the luminaries is the stronger.

5. *What the Soul Is Moving Toward; the Loka of the Future* is indicated by the 16th or 22nd Drekana ruler, whichever is strongest (as counted from the Ascendant with the Ascendant's Drekana counted as "one").

6. *What the Soul Has Done or is Most Familiar With Doing* is indicated by the ruler of the 12th House Drekana and any planets in the 12th house.

7. *What the Soul Is, or Is Not, Prepared For* is indicated by the condition of the 9th House and what it contains.

8. *What Will dominate or Stand Out in the Life* is indicated by using a 06° 00' orb and determining what is conjunct the Bhava (midpoint) cusps.

9. *The Crossroads of Life, Pivotal Decision Areas of the chart that Can Greatly Affect the Life, Its Direction and Its Goals* is indicated by a comparison of Rahu and Ketu.

10. *Obstacles & Challenges* are indicated by Retrogrades while *Past Lost Opportunities that are now Present Life Areas which must be Re-Faced* are indicated by Interceptions.

Instructions

Combine the factors called for in each of the 10 categories and transpose their meanings into a sentence using the following order in applying whatever components are called for in a particular step and excluding those which are not: **PLANET, NIDANA, DREKANA, NAKSHATRA, BHAVA HOUSE CUSPS, FIXED STARS**

Notes

- It is important to realize that the Nakshatras are areas of the sky whose boundaries are defined and marked by specific fixed stars and whose areas consist of fixed stars and whose meanings are derived by combining meanings of the fixed stars contained in each section of the sky as well as those fixed stars which mark each section's boundaries. Thus the individual stars are examined as to meaning as well as looking at the Nakshatras as a whole. Whenever a specific fixed star is conjunct a planet which in turn is conjunct a Bhava mid-point cusp, special emphasis is given to their combined meanings. For orbs of aspect, I use the orbs based upon a star's magnitude as given in Joseph Rigor's *Fixed Stars.*

- For determining Past and Future Lokas, which depend upon relative strength of planets, an appropriate computer software program may be of help if needed when determining Virupa Strength.

- The definitions used in this article for the Nakshatras, Planets, and Houses are related to the specific use of the Bhava chart and so may or may not conform to that with which the reader is more customarily familiar.

Sample Chart

The following chart will be used to illustrate the ten delineation steps. The chart's subject is the nativity of Adolf Hitler. Chart data was researched through the material collected by Lois Rodden and Bill Land. The source for Hitler's documented time of birth is the German magazine *Zenit* (November, 1933) which quoted the actual birth records.

April 20, 1889
6:30 PM C.E.T. (17:37:52)
BRAUNAU-am-INN, AUSTRIA
48°N 15' - 13° E 02' (-00;52;08)
Fagan-Bradley ayanamsha
Ascendant is 03° Libra 29'

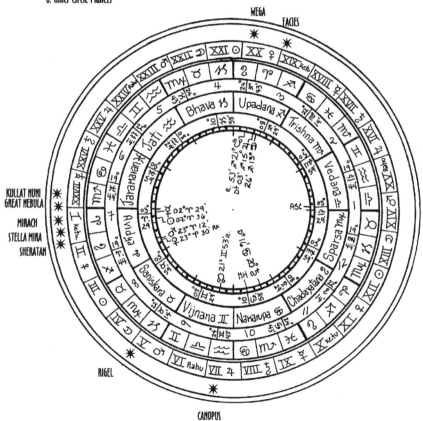

10 Points of Delineation Applied to Adolf Hitler's Bhava chart

1. **Natural Inclinations:**   1st Bhava cusp (19-VI-44)
                                      Ruler of 1st Cusp: Mercury
                                      Nidana of 1st Cusp: Sparsa
                                      Nidana of Mercury: Avidya

By combining the meanings of the elements listed above we find: The inclination not to be alone. To have contact with others. The inclination to interpret sense impressions. To establish mental connections with others through
language, gestures, and symbols through spiritual blindness or ignorance.
Perhaps wanting to establish what is believed to be new spiritual beginnings.

2. **Comprehension:**   Moon: 13-SA-26
                                      Nidana of Moon: Upadana
                                      Nakshatra of Moon: -20-

Combining the meanings of the elements listed above we find: One who
comprehends the concept of being committed to the hunting down of one's
enemies as an objective to pursue, or who also comprehends the pursuing of
one's objectives.

3. **Personal Will:**   Sun: 07-AR-36
                                      Nidana of Sun: Avidya
                                      Nakshatra of Sun: -20-

One whose Personal Will is applied to establishing new spiritual beginnings,
but also one who may be possessed by spiritual blindness, and who will seek
the ruin of his enemies.

4. **Past Loka:**   Sun & Moon in Mars Drekana
                                      Mars Drekana: Su-gati - Asura Loka

The past state of consciousness is achievement ridden, envious and obsessed
with a desire for success, yet tortured by the thought that other people (or
groups) are better off than himself. One who embodied a continual state of
striving and though possessed of, or having acquired power and money, was
driven to seize what was wanted by force. One who was familiar with the
issues of hunger, self-preservation, and never felt that he had attained the
"real" "top-of-the-mountain."

5. **Future Loka:**   22nd Drekana Ruler: Venus
                                      Drekana of Venus: Dur-gati -Tiryyak-yoni

Leaning towards the tendency, or gradually going more towards the attitude,
of going passively through the motions of life, and following his instincts and
urges without ever exerting his will, and without reason or motivation to take

control of his own existence. One who reacts primarily to his instinctual drives, but may still strive, or be driven, to seek beauty, design and form through artistic expression of some kind.

6. What is Familiar: 12th Bhava cusp: 22-LE-14
                             Nakshatra of 12th Cusp: -11-
                             Ruler of 12th Bhava: Sun
                             Nakshatra of Sun: -1-
                             Drekana of Sun: Mars
                             Drekana of Mars: Jupiter
                             Drekana of Jupiter: Mars

A person fascinated with or fearing death, who is used to or familiar with experiencing the esteem, respect and ambition of others. An organizer and a leading personality. A revolutionary who seeks the ruin of his enemies. One who is familiar with the concept and/or experience of career advancement.

7. What the Soul Is, or Is Not, Prepared For:

9th Bhava cusp: 22-TA-44
Nidana of 9th cusp: Saniskara
Placements in 9th Bhava: Rahu
Fixed Stars: Rahu w/Canopus,
            9th cusp w/Rigel

A person who is prepared for great persistence and perseverance in conforming to the image of a leader—possibly a military man, politician, government official or the leader of a political party—but who is given to enmity, vengeance and deceit.

8. What Will Dominate or Stand Out in the Life:

Mercury conj. midpoint cusp (01° 00')
Nidana of Mercury: Avidya
Nakshatra of Mercury: -1-
Mercury in 7th Bhava House
Fixed Stars: Mercury conjunct - Mirach,
             Stella Mira & Sheratan
Sun conjunct midpoint cusp (04° 07')
Nidana of Sun: Avidya
Nakshatra of Sun: -1-
Sun in 7th Bhava House
Fixed Stars: Sun conjunct - Kullat Nuni,
             Great Nebula
Moon conjunct midpoint cusp (04° 57')
Nidana of Moon: Upadana
Nakshatra of Moon: -20-
Moon in 3rd Bhava House
Fixed Stars: Moon conjunct Facies

One whose personal will is directed toward forming a mental connection with others through language, gestures, and symbols, but applied through spiritual blindness or with the idea of starting a new spiritual beginning. He will work to bring about the ruin of his enemies abroad as well as those he has openly named. He is driven to succeed and may commit suicide in critical situations. He has the ability to conquer and is possessed of demonic power and possibly even fiendishness. He will tend to be merciless, mean and given to war. He will achieve notoriety and will persist or endure to the bitter end. He is given to secret, bad habits and can tend to be a private person and unstable.

There will be peculiar events in the life. He is one who comprehends commitment to objectives and the pursuing of his prey or victims in order to master his immediate environment. He may be ingenious in the promotion of ideas either ahead of their time, or that are unpopular. He may rise to high position, but can be subjected to severe losses, violence and self-destruction.

9. Pivotal Decisions: Ketu: 21-SA53 R.
                                      Nidana of Ketu: Upadana
                                      Nakshatra of Ketu: -20-
                                      Ketu in 3rd Bhava House
                                      Rahu: 21-GE-53 R.
                                      Nidana of Rahu: Vijnana
                                      Nakshatra of Rahu: -7-
                                      Rahu in 9th Bhava House

Pivotal decisions will revolve around whether to persist in or commit to becoming a military-political leader through distorted perceptions; and whether to follow his instinctual drives that attach him to mastering his immediate environment through the pursuit of his victims.

10. Obstacles and Challenges:
                                      Venus is Retrograde
                                      Nidana of Venus: Avidya
                                      Nakshatra of Venus: -2-
                                      Venus in 8th Bhava House

He attempts the pursuit of personal happiness through spiritual blindness, and/or he attempts to initiate a new spiritual beginning in matters relating to death or endings. His ability to relate to others with affection and feeling is blocked or impaired and may express itself instead through endings or death.

Eve de Alberich has been a professional astrologer, teacher, lecturer, and consultant to psychologists since 1977. Her background is in the fine arts, advertising, technical writing and research. She has published articles in the NCGR Journal, Urania Magazine, *and was in collaboration with Charles Emerson, founder of the NCGR, before his death to rewrite and co-author lessons in his Uranian Astrology course which focused upon the medical and psychological indicators in a natal chart. Eve can be reached at: POB 86879, Baton Rouge, LA 70879-6879. Phone: (504) 791-5871. Fax: (504) 755-1411 or alberich @ ix.netcom.com.*

MATERIAL PROSPERITY USING THE YOGI AND AVAYOGI

Hart deFouw

Many people ask me about the use of the Yogi and the Avayogi, two planets that are calculated by several Jyotish computer programs. The Yogi and the Avayogi were popularized by the late brilliant astrologer, Mr. S. Iyer, of Bangalore, India. My own Jyotish mentor taught me Iyer's system over a period of two years and eventually put me in touch with him. Iyer indicated that the concept of the Yogi and Avayogi were inspired by Nadi manuscripts that were available to him. Whatever their origin, the addition of the Yogi and the Avayogi to chart interpretation enriches the understanding of many horoscopes.

The Yogi is calculated by the formula: (Longitude of the Sun + Longitude of the Moon) + a constant of 93° 20'. All longitudes are expressed as an arc from 0° of Aries. The derived longitude is known as the Yoga Point. The planet ruling the nakshatra of the derived longitude is the Yogi of the horoscope. In the chart of Bill Gates (born 28 Oct 1955 @ 9:05 PM in Seattle, WA - see chart below), the respective longitudes for the Sun and the Moon are (191°46' + 344°28') + 93°20' = 629°34' - 360° = 269°34' or 29°34' of Sagittarius. This is the Yoga Point. Because the Yoga Point falls in the nakshatra of Uttarashadha, which is ruled by the Sun, the Yogi of this horoscope is the Sun.

The Avayogi is calculated by the formula: Longitude of the Yoga Point + 186° 40'. The derived longitude is known as the Avayoga Point. The planet ruling the nakshatra of the derived longitude is the Avayogi of the horoscope. In the referenced chart, the longitude of the Yoga Point is 269°34' + 186°40' = 456°14' - 360° = 96°14' or 6°14' of Cancer, which becomes the Avayoga Point. Because the Avayoga Point falls in the nakshatra of Pushya, which is ruled by Saturn, the Avayogi of this horoscope is Saturn.

Moon 14:28		Ketu 26:13R	Lagna 22:59
		BILL GATES	Jupiter 04:34
	Rahu 26:13 R	Sun 11:46 Venus 26:57 Saturn 28:20	Mars 16:51 Mercury 23:19

Although its very name would suggest a spiritual theme, in everyday chart analysis the astrological Yogi has little to do with spirituality. It is, in fact, a key indicator of material prosperity in the horoscope. The Avayogi implies the opposite. It is the obstructer of material prosperity.

A Yogi or Avayogi is well placed in a horoscope if it is in an angular (1, 4, 7, 10) or trinal (1, 5, 9) house. Both are poorly placed if in houses 3, 6, 8 or 12. The remaining astrological houses are neutral. According to Iyer, the Indian unequal house system known as the "Shripati" method should ideally be used to evaluate the house placements of the Yogi, the Avayogi, and the other planets.

My mentor was more flexible. He sometimes applied the usual one sign/one house chart of Vedic astrology to evaluate the Yogi and the Avayogi. A Yogi or an Avayogi is strong if it is exalted, in its own sign, in its own nakshatra, or when it is retrograde. Both are weak when debilitated (without the cancellation known as neecha bhanga) or combust, especially within 3° of the Sun. In theory, the Yogi should be well placed and strong while the Avayogi should be poorly placed and weak for ideal results, a rule which is still subject to the general principles of horoscope interpretation. For example, a planet who participates in a combination for wealth will have that meaning emphasized if it is connected with a well placed and strong Yogi; it will have its results diminished if it is connected with a well placed and strong Avayogi. In either case, the basic combination for wealth prevails but is colored by the Yogi or the Avayogi.

The Yogi and Avayogi have many applications in horoscope interpretation. They are used in the analysis of houses, planetary periods, divisional charts, transits, and yogas. In Iyer's method of horoscope interpretation, the Yogi and the Avayogi ultimately form part of an elaborate but elegant and principled system of horoscope analysis. Here are some simple and useful fundamental principles which enhance—but usually do not override—the general rules of horoscope interpretation.

1. A person born with the degree of the Ascendant in the nakshatra that contains the Yoga Point is inclined to considerable prosperity if the Yogi is well placed and strong.

2. A person born with the degree of the Ascendant in the nakshatra that contains the Avayoga Point is inclined to considerable obstruction in material prosperity if the Avayogi is well placed and strong.

3. The major or minor planetary periods of planets who are in the nakshatraof the Yoga Point and its trines enhance financial prosperity during their periods. The same is true for planets associated with, or aspected by, the Yogi. The impact will be maximized if the Yogi is well placed and strong.

4. The major or minor planetary periods of planets who are in the nakshatra of the Avayoga Point and its trines obstruct financial prosperity during their periods. The same is true for planets conjoined with, or aspected by, the Avayogi. The impact will be maximized if the Avayogi is well placed and strong.

5. When the ruler of a major or minor planetary period transits during its period the nakshatra of the Yoga Point or its trines, prosperity is enhanced noticeably if the Yogi is well placed and strong.

6. When the ruler of a major or minor planetary period transits during its period the nakshatra of the Avayoga Point or its trines, prosperity is diminished or obstructed noticeably if the Avayogi is well placed and strong.

7. The participation of the Yogi or the Avayogi in major yogas (especially raja yogas, dhana yogas, etc.) highlights the effect of the yogas.

8. The Yogi will enhance prosperity during its major or minor planetary period if it is well placed and strong.

9. The Avayogi will obstruct prosperity during its major or minor planetary period if it is well placed and strong.

In the example horoscope, several of the above conditions apply. Note that they are interpreted in the overall context of the horoscope, which contains a formidable array of promising and brilliant combinations such as Sasaka Yoga, Malavya Yoga, Bhadra Yoga, Lakshmi Yoga, Chandra Mangala Yoga, Raja Yogas and Dhana Yogas. The structure of the horoscope strongly suggests power and affluence, which the involvement of the Yogi and of the Avayogi further dramatize.

The following comments reflect on four of the nine principles noted above:

Principle 3: Bill Gates is in the major period of Venus from December 16, 1982 to December 16, 2002. Venus is associated with the Sun who is the Yogi. The Sun is well placed because it is in the 5th House both in the one sign/one house chart and in the unequal Shripati house chart. The Sun, although debilitated, is strong because of the clear cancellation of its debilitation in this chart. The period of Venus, who is associated with a well placed and strong Sun, has seen him rise to the position of the wealthiest man in America.

Principle 4: Venus, the main period lord, is associated with the Avayogi Saturn. Saturn is in the 5th House in the one sign/one house chart, but it is in the 6th House of the Shripati house chart. It is therefore poorly placed but Saturn's exaltation makes it strong. This association of the poorly placed but strong Avayogi with the current major period of Venus correlates to the many financial setbacks that have also occurred during the Venus cycle.

Several lawsuits that have required substantial settlement payments have been reported.

Principle 7: Venus, the major period lord, is a participant in the classical wealth-indicating combination known as Lakshmi Yoga. Lakshmi Yoga is present when the lord of the 9th House and Venus are in their own or exaltation constellations in an angular or trinal house. The influence of both the Yogi and the Avayogi by their association with Venus, a key participant of Lakshmi Yoga, dramatically highlights this and the several other yogas in which Venus participates.

Principle 8: The main period of the Yogi (the Sun) will follow the main period of Venus. Because the Sun is well placed and strong due to the cancellation of its debilitation, whatever else it may imply, its indications for material prosperity are favorable.

Although several other principles too detailed for this article come to bear on the placement of the Yogi and the Avayogi in Bill Gates' horoscope, it is my hope that sufficient particularity has been given to illustrate the important effect of the Yogi and Avayogi on material prosperity.

It is my contention that if the Yogi and the Avayogi are not actively and prominently involved in important horoscope features such as the Ascendant, the Yogas, or the main planetary periods, then the effects of such features will be diminished if they imply something about prosperity. The involvement of the Yogi and the Avayogi with the main features of a horoscope greatly emphasizes those very features, often increasing their importance spectacularly for better or for worse.

Hart deFouw has been studying and practicing astrology for the past 25 years. He studied Jyotish for 15 years with his guru, who also introduced him to meditation, Sanskrit, philosophy and ayurveda. Hart travels worldwide 6-8 months of the year giving individual Jyotish consultations, and he appears as a featured lecturer at many conferences. He is the co-author of Light on Life: An Introduction To The Astrology of India, _published by Penguin Books. Hart can be reached at: 115 Maplewood Avenue, Toronto, Ontario M6C 1J4 Canada Phone: (416) 653-4005._

TIPS ON INTERPRETING VIMSHOTTARI MAHA DASA

Narendra Desai

Dasas are periods in which the native undergoes good or bad experiences as a result of his past karmas as indicated by planetary conditions in his horoscope.

The ancient sages in India have declared the span of human life to be 120 years. This period is distributed among nine "planets," each division being referred to as the Dasa of that particular graha (planet). As to the allocation of a certain number of years to each graha, I refer you to the book by Dr. V. G. Rele titled Directional Astrology of the Hindus.

Vimshottari Mahadasa uses the angular distance of each Nakshatra which is 13° 20', and this is the approximate daily movement of the Moon. If we multiply this by the 9 planets we get 120 degrees. Therefore, the Moon defines a life cycle of 120 years. And as the Moon passes through three individual, but related, sets of 120 degrees each then we complete the zodiac of 360 degrees. The Moon represents the mind which plays a very great part in man's evolution. We typically find that the Moon is at the root of almost all problems.

The Tara System and Vimsottari Dasa

With this as some brief background, let me illustrate something about the Tara (star) system. Observe the following table. It will list nine nakshatras (stars) for the Moon starting with the one in which the Moon is located at birth, and then each subsequent one. The last column makes a judgment statement about the property (or Tara) of any nakshatra in that position:

TABLE 1

STAR	TARA	MEANING
1st	Janma	(The birth nakshatra) (+)
2nd	Sampat	Wealth or prosperity (+)
3rd	Vipat	Difficulties, loss or obstacles (-)
4th	Kshema	Happiness and prosperity (+)
5th	Pratwara	Loss in business and obstacles (-)
6th	Sadhaka	Success/accomplishment in work (+)
7th	Nidhana	Death (-)
8th	Maitree	Friendship (+)
9th	Param-Maitree	Great or thick friendship (+)

With reference to Table 1 (above), keep in mind that there are, in fact, three sets of nine nakshatras, so the second and third groups follow the same pattern. Watch now how this is applied to, for example, the chart of O.J. Simpson in the following Table 2 (nakshatra names have been abbreviated to fit into the table). O.J. Simpson's birth data is as follows: July 9, 1947 at 8:08 AM PST in San Francisco, CA (37N47 & 122W25). His natal Moon is in Poorvabhandra:

TARA	THE 27 NAKSHATRAS		
Janma	P. Bhandra	Poornarvasu	Vishakha
Sampat	U. Bhandra	Pushyami	Anuradha
Vipat	Revati	Ashlesha	Jeshtha
Kshema	Ashwini	Magha	Moola
Pratwara	Bharani	P.Falguni	P.Shada
Sadhaka	Krittika	U.Falguni	U.Shada
Nidhana	Rohini	Hasta	Shravana
Maitree	Mrigasira	Chitra	Dhanishtha
Param-Mai	Aridra	Swati	Satabhisha

TABLE 2

We will now apply the Tara sequence of Table 2 above to each of the nine planets in his chart (plus his Lagna), and conclude on his net condition. See the following Table 3:

TABLE 3

GRAHA	NAKSHATRAS	TARA	CONDITION
Asc/Lagna	Magha	Kshema	Good
Sun	Purnavasu	Janma	Okay
Moon	P.Bhadra	Janma	Okay
Mars	Rohini	Nidhana	Bad
Mercury	Purnavasu	Janma	Okay
Jupiter	Vishakha	Janma	Okay
Venus	Ardra	P.Maitree	Best
Saturn	Pushya	Sampat	Best
Rahu	Krittika	Sadhaka	Best
Ketu	Anuradha	Sampat	Best

So we can conclude that most of his planets are in nakshatras which are favorable for him—except for Mars which has caused a great deal of trouble for him. But because of the other favorable placements, he emerged unscathed from his personal crisis (he was arrested on June 12, 1994 and acquitted on October 3, 1995; neither period involved a Mars Dasa or Bhukti). This generally good distribution also accounts for his ability to overcome many childhood difficulties and achieve worldwide fame.

Ashtaka Varga and Vimsottari Dasa

The next portion of this article assumes that the reader knows the basics of ashtakavarga. It describes a less commonly known method for estimating the result of any particular Dasa period.

First, complete the ashtakavarga chart for the graha whose Dasa result is to be known. Then divide the Dasa years of that graha into 12 equal parts. For example, if the period being studied is that of the Sun (a 6-year period) then the 12 parts will each be six months long. These 12 periods are to be equally distributed among the 12 signs beginning with the rasi (sign) where the Dasa graha is situated.

The result of the 1st 1/12th portion will be according to the number of bindus contained in that rasi where the graha is situated. The result of the 2nd portion will be according to the next (2nd) rasi, and so forth. If there are more than four bindus in any particular rasi, that will promote good results. To the extent that there are less than four bindus, the period will be more difficult. The Bhukti periods can also be divided by 12 and the same principle applied. For the ashtakavarga of the nodes, treat Rahu like Saturn and Ketu like Mars.

Also review the nature of the rasi sub-period so far as the graha is concerned. If it is in a friendly or unfriendly rasi, if it is exalted or debilitated, and so forth, then adjust your interpretation accordingly. For example, if there are four bindus but the graha is debilitated by rasi, the results may be unfavorable. But even if the bindus are a little low, if the rasi happens to be the planet's exaltation rasi then the results will not be so bad.

Other General Rules

During the Dasa or Bhukti period of a graha (particularly a benefic), if Jupiter or the Sun happens to transit the exaltation rasi of that graha then it will give favorable results. Planets transiting their exaltation rasis during the sub-period of that rasi will give especially good results. This logic can be applied to related patterns.

Generally, for good results there should be harmony between the Dasa lord and Bhukti lord. Conversely, if these two lords are situated in a 2/12 or 6/8 relationship to each other, then unfavorable results typically occur.

During the Dasa of a malefic, when the sub-period of planets governing the 3rd, 5th and 7th nakshatras from the natal star (Janma nakshatra) are in progress, the native will be put to many trials and hardships (as per the Tara system discussed earlier).

The Dasa of a graha posited in the 8th Bhava (House) from the lord of the Lagna will be harmful to the native, and depending upon the overall circumstances, may even cause his death towards the end of the Dasa.

Important events in a person's life such as marriage, birth of a child, promotion, transfer, etc. can only happen in the Dasas and Bhuktis of particular planets. To determine the probable period of a marriage in a horoscope, the 7th, its lord, planets posited in the 7th, the navamsha lord of the 7th and Venus—all of these have to be considered, their strength carefully analyzed, and the graha which is most beneficial to impart marital happiness must be found out. Then the Dasa or Bhukti of that graha may be predicted as the probable marriage indicator.

During the Dasa of a graha the native will experience those effects which are attributed to that graha, and also the effects of the Bhava and rasi occupied and aspected by it, and also the yogas produced by the graha. The qualities and function stamped upon the Dasa lord will be modified, to a considerable extent, by the nature of the Bhava it occupies, the nature of grahas aspecting it, the nature of the lord of the constellation in which the Dasa lord is placed, and the position of the graha in rasi as well as navamsha.

While making predictions the general effects due to that graha should be carefully weighed, and particular care should be taken to avoid incongruent results wherever they occur. Also the result predicted should be consistent with the person concerned under the circumstances in which he is born and brought up, and also his physical condition at the time of the consultation. Some additional general rules which help in the prediction of Dasa effects are these:

- If a Dasa graha is weak or debilitated we cannot expect anything helpful from him, even if the lord of the sub-period is strong.

- During the Dasa of a graha who is inimical to the lord of the lagna and the Moon-sign lagna (Chandralagna) the native will have troubles from enemies, quarrels, medical and financial problems, etc.

- This can also be true during the Dasa of a debilitated graha, or a retrograde graha, or a graha posited in the Bhava of an enemy. The person concerned will be banished, hated by relatives, and will be addicted to forbidden acts.

- The Bhukti of a malefic in the Dasa of a malefic will be dangerous, and possibly even calamitous, especially if they happen to be in mutually hostile positions.

- If the Lagna is powerful, favorable results can be expected during the Dasa of the lord of the Lagna.

- The period of the Dasa lord of one trine (5th or 9th) and the sub-period of the lord of another trine (5th or 9th) is good.

- In the Dasa of a yogakaraka graha the effects of rajayoga will be experienced during the Bhukti of the associated karaka.

- Even though a graha may be debilitated, combust, or in the Bhava of an enemy, his Dasa will yield mixed results in general, and will be favorable toward the end of the Dasa period, if he occupies a good Bhava in both the rasi and navamsha.

- The Dasa periods of Venus and Jupiter are not auspicious if they own kendras (in general, benefics should not own kendras).

- If any graha occupies the maraka places, i.e., the 2nd and 7th Houses, their Dasas can prove fatal to the native if the balance of the chart supports this conclusion.

The results of the major period or sub-period are modified by the influence of transits (gochara) at that time. Saturn is typically associated with obstacles, the retardation of progress, etc. If he is afflicted in the horoscope, the hardships and afflictions will be even greater. Jupiter on the other hand will shield the native from obstacles if he is favourably disposed in the horoscope.

The influence of these two planets is greatly felt in transit. If Saturn is adversely placed relative to the Dasa lord, even if the latter is himself well placed in the horoscope, Saturn will retard the good effects of the Dasa and release them only when his transit is over. But, on the other hand, Jupiter in conjunction with the Dasa lord will promote his better results to the extent possible.

Finally, an important thing to remember while making predictions is that the mere presence of rajayogas or other fine planetary combinations in the horoscope is not enough. These rajayogas will not give their effect if they are devoid of strength; in this case any good results would be reduced to a minimum. It is even said that the yogas produced by planets which are devoid of any strength will be experienced only in thoughts or in dreams.

Narendra Desai is a world-renowned astrologer who has read more than 50,000 horoscopes. His clients have included many well-known artists, entertainers, industrialists, financiers, and spiritual seekers. He was born in 1924 in the same village as the hermitage of Sage Bhrigu. He is a life member of the Bombay Astrological Society and past President of the C. J. Krishnaswami Foundation and Astrological Academy. He has received several honorary degrees and gold medal awards from various astrological institutions in India. For the past 13 years he has written a column on astrology for the Mirror Magazine in India. He is also the author of Essentials of Numerology and numerous articles on astrology and palmistry. He can be reached at: Bldg. D, Apt. 7, Troy Gardens, 220 Littleton Road, Parisippany, NJ 07054. Phone: (201) 334-6086

ON STUDYING JYOTISH IN INDIA

Ronnie Gale Dreyer

Studying Jyotish in India is something that I feel every Western practioner of Vedic Astrology should seriously consider doing if only for a limited amount of time. Having initially learned Jyotish in the milieu where this subject developed and thrived, I cannot imagine what it would have been like had I never spent any time there at all. Not only was I able to experience Indian culture firsthand and learn through observation, but I had the rare opportunity to study with practitioners whose craft was, in part, relayed to them through an oral tradition not found in the Scriptures.

Had I not spent time in India, I never would have known that when someone inquires "What is Your Sign?" they are asking about your Lagna, or ascendant, and not the Sun sign at all as here in the West. This is quite logical since the Moon, not the Sun, is the most influential heavenly body, and the placement of the Sun itself is oftentimes no more or less significant than the position of Venus or Mars.

Since Jyotish employs a whole sign house system, knowing the sign of one's Lagna also allows for an immediate understanding of some basic chart dynamics. With a Leo lagna, for example, you are not only instantly aware that the first house of personality and health is ruled by the Sun, but that the second house is ruled by Mercury, the third house by Venus, the fourth house by Mars, etc. Furthermore, it is easy to ascertain at once which houses of the horoscope are affected by current Jupiter and Saturn transits. Had I not spent time in India constantly identifying myself by my ascending sign, I would never have realized how significant the Lagna is actually considered.

In addition to recognizing the Lagna's importance, I was able to fully grasp the enormous weight carried by the 27 Nakshatras, or fixed star clusters, commonly referred to as Moon Mansions. It is the Moon's Nakshatra position which determines the sequence of Dasas and Bhukties throughout one's life thus allowing the astrologer to choose the appropriate timing for important events such as education, job, marriage and children. Although the planets placed in their signs and houses have always been primary when learning Western horoscopic Astrology, the earliest Hindu astronomers placed the planets in the Nakshatras long before they were acquainted with the zodiacal signs.

While we in the West know how vital a role the Moon and its mansions play in Vedic Astrology, I never would have realized the full extent had my first teacher, Dr. Muralil Sharma, professor of Jyotish at Sanskrit University in Benares, not insisted that my first assignment was to memorize and recite the 27 Nakshatras. This was not an easy task considering that I had to learn to pronounce the Sanskrit sounds by placing my tongue in different parts of my mouth which I normally do not use. Since I was there for a limited stay, I gladly adhered to Dr. Sharma's preferred teaching methods and sure enough pronounced the 27 nakshatras perfectly by heart.

In fact, my initial meeting with Dr. Sharma was in itself a wake-up call to precisely how sacred knowledge is regarded in India. As if the heavens had actually heard my call, I met Dr. Muralil Sharma at the precise moment I was inquiring in the Mathematics Department office of Sanskrit University if there was a professor who would be willing to teach me Jyotish. After hearing my plight, Dr. Sharma promptly offered to tutor me for one hour every day in exchange for merely being an attentive student. In response to my question about payment, Dr. Sharma assured me that because I had travelled so far in search of knowledge, a gift from the Gods, it was his professional obligation to teach me whatever he could for the duration of my stay. In fact, this is the perfect meaning of the word "Guru" which literally means both "one who imparts knowledge" as well as "Jupiter," the planet which represents the quest for knowledge.

Seeking out a Guru, a teacher who guides you creatively, intellectually and/or spiritually, is a concept which is difficult to understand here in the West where the mode of education usually involves attending a university. While there may be individual mentors and professors who guide one's course of study, the notion of Guru implies a master/apprentice relationship of which there is no equivalent here in the United States. More than the actual astrological knowledge which I received, the most important aspect of my stay in India was not only witnessing various Guru/student relationships but being able to experience it myself in a culture where Jyotish is not only highly respected but taught in the Universities.

But the true beauty of learning Jyotish lies in its rich oral tradition much of which is simply not found in written texts. For the most part, Indian astrologers who hang their singles have learned their craft from members of their family whose teachings have been passed down through many generations. K.N. Rao, noted astrologer and teacher, learned astrology initially from his mother, while my second astrology teacher, Deoki Nandan Shastri, a commercial astrologer who still practices in Varanasi, was taught by his father who was also a professional astrologer. Without the good fortune to have studied with teachers whose own education was passed on orally, I would have thought that the entire basis of Jyotish was found in the written Scriptures.

Another subtlety which is greatly misunderstood in the West is the question of Marakas, the so-called "death inflicting" planets which occupy and rule the 2nd and 7th Houses. Studying in India sheds great light on this very sensitive issue which, when not fully understood, could result in misuse of knowledge and abuse of power. I have heard many Western jyotishis predict death and misfortune by simply looking at the Dasa and Bhukti periods which correspond to these planets. One of the things I learned in India was before even attempting to predict death, the first order of business is to calculate whether the individual will have a short, middle or long life span. But even if the Dasa periods ruled by marakas do correspond with the approximate life span, astrologers cannot always, nor should they (due to ethical reasons), portend the end of life.

While Indians are certainly more philosophical about death than we are here in the West, most practitioners of Jyotish are still as close-mouthed about predicting death as are Western astrologers. According to B.V. Raman whom I interviewed at the First International Vedic Astrology Symposium in San Rafael, California several years ago, astrologers should never forecast death. Instead, the astrologer's obligation is to subtly discourage planning future events and suggest getting one's affairs in order.

It is my opinion that only by studying astrology in India or, to a lesser extent, with a reputable Indian astrologer here in the West, can certain practical applications of Jyotish come to light. This is not to say that one cannot learn Vedic astrological techniques here in the West. There are obviously many Westerners well-educated and experienced in Jyotish (some of whom have studied under Indian teachers either here or abroad) who can provide the basis of a comprehensive study. It is just that there is always that little something missing which can only be found by observing the cultural and spiritual environment in which Hindu Astrology developed and flourished. Of course, many of us will never have the opportunity to go to India for an extended period of time. There are, however, many Hindu communities in the United States and Canada where customs can be observed and even astrologers can be found.

For information about where to study Jyotish in India, please contact: Indian Council of Astrological Sciences, 64 Gowdiamutt Road, Royapeeta, Madras-600 014 INDIA.

Ronnie Gale Dreyer, recipient of the Jyotish Kovid award from the ICAS, is an internationally known astrological consultant, lecturer and teacher based in New York City. She is the author of Indian Astrology: A Western Approach to the Ancient Hindu Art (1990), Venus: The Evolution of the Goddess *and* Her Planet (1994), *and* Vedic Astrology (1997). *Ronnie is also a contributor to the anthology* Astrology for Women: Roles and Relationships *(1997) and* Llewellyn's 1998 Sun and Moon Sign Guides. *In addition to writing gift books, columns, articles and book reviews, she has served as editorial consultant for new age and self-help books for several major publishing companies. Ronnie lectures extensively for astrology groups and national conferences, and conducts ongoing courses and workshops in Vedic Astrology.*

Ronnie holds a Bachelor of Arts in English/Theater Arts from the University of New Mexico, and studied Jyotish, both privately and at Sanskrit University in Benares, India. She co-founded the first astrological computer service in the Netherlands where she lived for ten years and was the official Dutch representative for Astro*Carto*Graphy. She is currently the recording/corresponding secretary of the Association for Astrological Networking (AFAN) and is on the staff of the New York Astrology Center. Contact: P.O. Box 8034, FDR Station New York, NY 10150-8034. Tel: (212) 799-9187. Fax: (212) 799-2748. E-mail: RGDreyer@Prodigy.com. Web page: http://members.aol.com/rgdreyer.

VARGA KUNDALI:
THEIR ROLE IN PREDICTIVE ANALYSIS

Brendan Feeley

My interest in varga charts began when Hart DeFouw first presented the topic at a weekend seminar to a small group of students about seven years ago. The subject excited me as it introduced another level of refinement in predictive analysis, and particularly because it provided tools for rectification and fine tuning the birth time in cases where the precise moment of birth was uncertain.

I spent the following six months dedicated to the analysis of varga charts, and I was finally able to arrive at an accurate birth time for my own horoscope by adjusting specific vargas so that the result of the Dasha/Bhuktis corresponded to life events. Since that time, varga chart analysis has become an integral part of my repertoire of skills in predictive analysis.

An accurate birth time must be known to rely on the divisional charts. Many astrologers avoid using them for this reason. Time and patience is well spent in careful research of these charts, for the experience can lead to quick determination of the accuracy of the birth moment as well as an increased level of predictive accuracy. In cases where the birth time is close but uncertain, the varga charts can be used to rectify the correct time.

One of the benefits of varga chart analysis is that the indications of a Bhava in the rasi chakra can often be understood in a manner that resolves possible conflict or confusion in the mind of the astrologer. For example, let's assume that the 9th House in the rasi chakra is favorably disposed. The lord is well placed and aspected, and benefic planets influence the house itself. Now the 9th Bhava has to do with bhagya, father, Guru, God, as well as travel and higher education. An astrologer has to be able to advise his client in each of those areas, but we know it is unlikely that the benefic influences are going to manifest equally for all of the significations of the 9th House in a particular Dasha/Bhukti.

Any astrologer would immediately examine the Sun, and the 9th from the Sun and Moon, to gain additional insight into the life of the father. He or she would examine Jupiter for luck, fortune, spiritual inclinations, and education. But another way to differentiate between these different 9th Bhava significations is to examine planetary placements in specific varga charts relating to these matters.

For example, the Navamsa is said to tell us about the luck of the native as well as marriage. The Dwadasamsa tells us about his father, his accomplishments and his health; the Vimsamsa about spiritual life as well as periods of initiation, spiritual realization, and devotion to God; the Chaturvimsamsa about education.

The same treatment could be applied to the 4th House which represents mother (Dwadasamsa), property (Chaturtamsa), and vehicles (Shodasamsa). This is the benefit of varga chart analysis. We can determine the outcome of a particular signification of a Bhava with a greater degree of accuracy during particular periods of time. The vargas provide additional insight into the results that will manifest for the native.

Before I discuss the methods that are generally used to determine planetary strengths in the varga charts, I want to present the 16 vargas or divisions of a sign that were defined by Maharishi Parasara.

[Note that the following references numbers located within parentheses indicate, respectively, the divisions' degree span, and the average length of time it takes for such a division to rise, or put another way, the length of time that each rasi rises in that particular varga. Also note that for certain of the divisions there are special rules for assigning rulership. This is unlike the navamsha where rulership is sequential through the zodiac. For further discussion see *Elements of Vedic Astrology*, Volume 1, Dr. K.S. Charak (Vision Wordtronic, New Delhi, 1995).]

Rasi = Natal Chart (30° 00', 120 Mins.)

The rasi tells us everything about the native. It is the foundation of the individual life, and it shows the karmic strength and weaknesses that the individual has to experience in the different areas of life.

Hora = 1/2 Division (15° 00', 60 Mins.)

Horas of the Sun are masculine and cruel; those of the Moon are feminine and mild. When most of the planets are placed in the Sun's Hora then we find that the person is inclined to worship God for protection and guidance in periods of difficulty, whereas if more planets are placed in the Moon's Hora then the person will be more inclined to seek consolation from parents and family.

When most of the planets are in the Sun's Hora, the individual will have strong masculine qualities, but may be overbearing and egotistical, and this brings with it the corresponding challenges in close personal ties such as marriage and family. If more planets are in the Moon's Hora, the individual will have feminine qualities, and will derive pleasure from interpersonal relationships and family life.

The Hora has to do mainly with wealth. In general, malefics in the Sun's Hora and benefics in the Moon's Hora are preferred. Malefics in the Sun's Hora give determination and courage.

Drekkana = 1/3 Division (10° 00', 40 Mins.)

This chart is principally concerned with brothers and sisters, and the happiness or benefits we experience through them. Difficulties or benefits for brothers and sisters can be seen in this chart. It can also be used to evaluate one's courage, one's ability to be successful in the business world, or indeed any adventure in life that requires fortitude and enterprise. The Drekkana is also important in predicting the nature of death.

The 22nd Drekkana and the Sarpa Drekkanas are particularly evil when it comes to matters of health, and they must always be examined when we are analyzing a chart for periods of challenge and difficulty such as diseases, accidents or injury. The 22nd Drekkana is counted inclusively from the Drekkana of the lagna, and its lord is considered to be an adverse factor. The Sarpa Drekkanas are certain Drekkanas of the watery signs: for Cancer, the 2nd and 3rd; for Scorpio, the 1st and 2nd; for Pisces, the 3rd.

Chaturtamsa = 1/4 Division (7° 30', 30 Mins.)

This varga chart is said to bear upon one's fortunes and financial stability. It can be used to determine the luck of the native in this area of life. It indicates one's ability to own and prosper through property. For instance, if the planets that form Dhana Yogas in the rasi chakra have a similar disposition in this varga then the power of the yogas to produce wealth will be greatly enhanced.

Sapthamsa = 1/7 Division (4°17' 8.57", 17 Mins., 8.57 Secs.)

This varga indicates favorable and unfavorable periods for the children of the native. It indicates the birth of children, as well as the periods of benefit or difficulty to be experienced through them. It shows the health and prosperity of the children in the different periods and sub-periods.

Navamsa = 1/9 Division (3°20', 13 Mins., 20 Secs.)

This is said to be the most important divisional chart. It is the one-ninth division and is therefore a harmonic of the 9th House. In this sense, it tells us a great deal about the bhagya, or luck, that the soul will manifest over the span of the life. For example, the Navamsa can be used to determine whether the promise in the natal chart is going to manifest with difficulty or ease throughout a particular Dasa or Bhukti. If the Navamsa is well fortified, with strong planetary placements and good yogas, and if it shows a significant improvement over the Rasi for a particular period, then the promise of the period will improve over that span of time. It is a favorable indication.

The Navamsa is specifically used to tell about the condition of married life as well as the number of marriages. It tells the character, temperament, and mental or moral disposition of the spouse. The 7th House in the Navamsa gives a general description of the mental and emotional characteristics of the husband or wife, as well as the capacity for harmonious relationships and partnerships. This chart is also used to determine the auspicious periods for relationships and marriage, as well as the timing of marriage, separation, and divorce.

But the Navamsa can be used to examine all portfolios of life and not just marriage. If a house is strong in the Rasi chakra, but in the Navamsa it becomes weak and afflicted, then caution must be used in predicting the outcome for that area of life. In South India, the Navamsa is used much like the Rasi chart, and it is considered to be of equal importance.

The 64th Navamsa is said to carry with it evil influences, and my experience has shown me that this is particularly so when it conjoins with other malefic combinations in the chart. [*Editor's Note: For further discussion of the 64th Navamasha, please see the article by R. G. Krishnan. In the present article, the 64th Navamsha from the Moon is being referenced. This may be easily found by taking the sign that is the 4th from the Moon in the Navamsha chart.*]

Dasamsa = 1/10 Division (3°00', 12 Mins.)

This chart is very important in examining one's profession—status, position, fame and power. Along with the Rasi, it can be used to predict the type of profession that the native is likely to choose. It will also indicate the successes and failures in the profession or the chosen path in life.

Dvadasamsa = 1/12 Division (2°30', 10 Mins.)

This chart tells us about the life of the parents, their health, happiness and longevity. This chart can also be used to determine periods of spiritual development, and some astrologers maintain that the Dwadasamsa can be used to reveal past and future lives.

Shodasamsa = 1/16 Division (1° 52' 30", 7 Mins., 30 Secs.)

Conveyances, vehicles and their comforts. Benefits and adversities from vehicles, such as the purchase of vehicles and the timing of accidents or injuries to be experienced through them.

Vimsamsa = 1/20 Division (1°30', 6 Mins.)

One's spiritual practice, devotion to Gods and Goddesses, and meditation. The formation of good planetary yogas in this chart can do a great deal to elevate one's spiritual achievements. It will show the Dasas in which the spiritual tendencies in the native will blossom or recede into the background.

Chaturvimsamsa = 1/24 Division (1°15', 5 Mins.)

Academic achievements, vidya, education. To consider periods of academic achievement for an individual, we have to examine the potential promised in this chart. If the Dasa lord occupies favorable positions in this varga, there will be achievements in education and learning.

Bhamsa = 1/27 Division (1°6'40", 4 Mins., 26.4 Secs.)

It's about one's strengths and weaknesses.

Trimsamsa = 1/30 Division (1°00', 4 Mins.)

This chart is used in female astrology. It is said to show the character and chastity of one's wife. But the chart can be used to determine the good and evil outcomes in any period, and it is particularly important to examine this chart for health issues.

Chatvarimsamsa/Khavedamsa = 1/40 Division (0°45', 3 Mins.)

For auspicious or inauspicious effects.

Akshavedamsa = 1/45 Division (0°40', 2 Mins., 39.6 Secs.)

For all general indications.

Shastiamsa = 1/60 Division (0°30', 2 Mins.)

Used for all general indications, the classical texts say that if the lord of the rasi Bhava occupies a malefic Shastiamsa it will be weakened. If it occupies a benefic Shastiamsa it will flourish. I have used this chart, as well as other varga charts, to successfully determine the differences in the destiny of the lives of twins. [*Editor's Note: See the closely-related article by Teresa Hamilton.*]

Varga Classification

According to Sage Maharishi Parasara, Vargas can be considered as in four groups:

• Shad Vargas (6): Rasi, Hora, Drekkana, Navamsa, Dvadasamsa, Trimsamsa

• Saptha Vargas (7): Add Sapthamsa to Shad varga

• Dasa Vargas (10): Add Shodasamsa, Dasamsa, and Shastiamsa to Saptha varga

• Shodasa Varga (16): All sixteen vargas outlined by Parasara

In fact, most astrologers do not go beyond the Dasa varga scheme.

In determining positional strengths of planets the Sapta Varga scheme, or seven divisions, are used by Maharishi. But for analyzing the important aspects of life, the Dasa Varga system or Shodasa Varga divisions are used. A special distinction is given to a planet if it occupies his own or exalted sign in the varga charts. If Jupiter occupies his own sign in all 15 vargas he is given a status referred to as *Vallabhamsa*. The person will be spiritually developed, intellectual keen, and will be recognized in his field. Results, of course, will be particularly fortunate in the Jupiter Dasa, assuming that the natal chart promises such results. If Mars occupies his own sign in 11 of the vargas, he gets the distinction of *dhanwantariamsa*. It is said to confer talents in the field of medicine.

Varga Chart Analysis

I have learned that there are two different approaches used by astrologers in the analysis of the varga kundali. These are as follows:

1. The varga chart is analyzed in the same manner as the rasi chart, and all the rules of Parasari astrology are applied to planetary placements, strengths, weaknesses, yogas, aspects, lordships, and house interpretation.

2. Some astrologers ignore lordships and simply base their judgment on the positional strength or weakness of the planets from the lagna. Planets in kendras and trikonas are strongly placed to give positive results in that varga, provided the planet is strongly placed and aspected by benefics. Planets in 3, 6, 8 or 12 are unfavorably placed and bring delay, obstruction and disappointment.

Further, some astrologers maintain that the Parasari aspects cannot be applied to the varga charts, as the planetary positions in those charts are not as tronomically correct. They do not consider those aspects. I have been using the Jaimini aspects, as well as the Jaimini karakas, in the analysis of varga charts, and I have found this to be an extremely valuable practice in my predictive work.

Principles of Interpretation

In conclusion, here are some important principles that must be used in examining the outcome promised by a particular varga. Note that when a planet occupies the same sign in the varga chart as its natal placement, it is said to be Vargottama, and it receives a special strength. Many astrologers claim that if the planet is debilitated, this Vargottama classification cannot help much, although it may be of some benefit.

- Examine the varga for its strengths and weaknesses just as you would examine the rasi chakra. Apply all of the Parasari rules for planetary strengths and weaknesses (exaltation, debilitation, friend or enemy sign, digbala position, etc.). Examine the placement of the benefics and malefic planets, and base your judgement on sound astrological principles. Examine the chart for yogas such as Pancha Mahapurusha yogas, Gaja Kesari, Chandra Mangala, Kartari, Lagnadhi, Vipreeta, as well as Parivartana and the Raj Yogas based on lordships.

- Examine the strength of the lagna in particular, as well as the house that relates to the portfolio of life. For example, the 10th house would apply in the case of the Dasamsa. A vargottama lagna increases the capacity of the native to manifest success in that area of life. If the lagnesh (lagna ruler) is poorly placed, say in the 8th House, and conjoined with malefics, it is not a good signification for that chart. Expect the results to be poor, even in a favorable dasa.

- Once you have determined the promise of the chart, examine the operative Dasa, Antaradasa, and Pratyantaradasa. A strongly placed Dasa lord, in a varga chart that promises good results, will bring success and favor to the native. Conversely, a poorly placed Dasa lord will bring disappointment and struggles. Narrow the periods further by examining the Antaradasa and Pratyantaradasa.

- In general, if planets are placed in dusthanas (3, 6, 8 or 12), they will not bring forth good results in their respective periods, particularly if the planet is weak and conjoined with malefic influences. However, if Mars is placed in the 6th House he can give good results since he aspects the lagna.

Brendan Feeley, M.A., has practiced astrology since 1975. He began his study of Western astrology with Howard Sasportas and Ronald Davidson while living in London. In 1986 he took to the study of Vedic astrology, and he has devoted himself exclusively to this system since that time. He studied initially with Hart deFouw, and later with K. N. Rao and Dr. Charak. He uses both Parasari and Jaimini astrology in his practice. He is also a professional Homeopath, and is the founder of the Center For Classical Homeopathy in Washington, DC where he teaches and practices this art of cure for both acute and chronic conditions. He may be reached at: 9211 Perfect Hour Columbia, MD 21045. Phone: (410) 290-9088. Fax: (410) 788-0190.

VEDIC ASTROLOGY, KARMA AND RIGHT UNDERSTANDING

Dennis Flaherty

The word *karma* has found usage in nearly all the languages of the world. It is found in English, French and German dictionaries, but the word's mother tongue is Sanskrit, the language of ancient India.

The etymological roots of *karma* are traced back to the ancient systems of Indian philosophy that were developed to understand the existence of the world we see before us. The great sages, or *rishis*, of ancient India had direct experiences of the truth of existence. They then codified those experiences into a series of *sutras*, which later were discussed orally and eventually systematized into particular schools of philosophical thought. Etymologically, the word *sutra* means a "thread" (see, for example, our English word *suture)*, implying a weaving process. Even though the threads of Indian philosophy are of differing colors, the weaving process is similar, resulting in a metaphorical garment of truth as to the nature and meaning of existence.

Many interpretations of the various sutras are possible, for words in Sanskrit can have several meanings. The fertile interpretations of various scriptures gave rise to a group of *acaryas*, or teachers, who created an ongoing process of vast philosophical debate which has resulted in the oldest and possibly largest philosophical and spiritual library the world has known. All these systems of philosophical thought, whether the systems are Buddhism, Nyaya, Sankhya, Mimamsa, or Vedanta, have one thing in common: the *immutable law of karma.*

How many times have we heard the phrase: "well, that's their karma." Much of the time the word karma is used in a pejorative sense as an indicator of negative events. This is unfortunate, for if there is bad karma, then surely there must be good karma. Perhaps a statement from one of India's greatest saints, Sri Ramakrishna, will clarify the question of karma.

In **The Gospel of Sri Ramakrishna** a devotee asks; "But the law of *karma* exists, doesn't it?" Sri Ramakrishna replies; "That also is true. Good produces good, and bad produces bad. Don't you get the hot taste if you eat chilies? But these are all God's lila, His play?" *Karma* is simply the law of cause and effect, good being causative of good, and bad being causative of bad. What you sow is what you reap. But our human nature much of the time is to concentrate upon and remember the negative. It is through this natural tendency that we become thoughtful of our actions, for it is usually some perceived loss, some suffering that starts the process of introspection, or self analysis, that precedes most changes in our life direction.

It is the consequence of suffering that concerns us all. The philosophy of Buddhism expounds upon suffering. The Buddha's **Four Noble Truths** are concerned directly with suffering. They are: 1. Suffering exists. 2. There is a cause of suffering. 3. There is a cessation of suffering. 4. There is a means to cease suffering. The philosophy of Buddhism proclaims that suffering is not accidental, but conditional, and can be brought under one's control.

The Buddha gave a systematic guide called The **Noble Eightfold Path** that leads to liberation from suffering. The eight stages are: right views, right resolve, right speech, right conduct, right livelihood, right effort, right mindfulness and right meditation. The word "right" is used here in the context of direct and correct knowledge of the **Four Noble Truths**, for the Buddha's view was that *avidya,* or ignorance, is the starting point in consciousness. This ignorance, or faulty viewpoint of the outer world, leads to false identification with the world—that is, false expectations from what the world has to offer us. This is the cause of all pain and suffering.

This article is not meant to be a discourse on Buddhism nor any Indian philosophical system in particular. The literature of India is already brimming over with discussion and debate regarding the very principles that are being discussed here. The intent here is to show that suffering, and joy for that can be traced to the law of karma and, according to Buddha's Noble Truths, that there is a way to cease suffering. This way involves direct knowledge of the nature of existence.

It is perchance no coincidence that the name of astrology in Sanskrit is *Jyotish*. Jyotish means the "knowledge of light." It is a system of direct knowledge of the light, which is the first causative emanation in the creation of the universe.

Astrology never exists in a cultural or philosophical vacuum. The fertile philosophical environment of ancient India profoundly influenced the development of Jyotish, or what is commonly called today Vedic astrology. The astrologer-seers of ancient India observed the coming and going of suffering, or negative karmas, and utilized the direct knowledge of Jyotish to ease these sufferings by revealing the causal roots, development and timing of the fruition of karmas within the life of the individual. Jyotish was also utilized to forecast the coming and going of positive karmas that would uplift the individual and bring them closer to *moksha,* or liberation.

The systematic framework of Vedic Astrology has the immutable law of *karma* at its very foundation. That is why it is often called predictive astrology. There are specific houses of the astrological chart that deal with *karma.* For example, the 5th House of the Vedic chart deals with *poorva-punya,* or the positive *karmas* of previous births. The 12th House deals with *vyayas,* or expenditure and loss, the negative *karmas* of previous births. The release of these expenditures, or karmas, liberates the soul. In this sense, the 12th House of the Vedic chart also specifically indicates *moksha:* the liberation and the ***cessation of all suffering.***

The systematic framework of Vedic astrology also incorporates the use of *yogas,* or planetary combinations. These various *yogas* have *karmic* attributes associated with them. This depends on the nature of the planets in the yoga, the houses they rule, and where the yogas are located in the chart. These yogas fall into several categories. To name a few: *Raja yogas* give rise to knowledge, spirituality and often fame and power. *Dhana yogas* give rise to wealth and prosperity, and *Arishta yogas* give rise to pain and suffering. Within these categories are many more types of *yogas,* such as *Pancha Maha Purusha yogas,* which give rise to great personages, and *Dharma Karma Adhipati yogas,* which give rise to souls of great purpose and commitment.

There are numerous more *yogas* of Vedic astrology, but specific to each is the fruition of the *karma* the yoga involves, and the timing of its revelation in the life of the individual. For this Vedic astrology uses varying *Dasa* systems, or planetary periods. These periods are used to determine when the *karma* of these yogas will fructify and manifest in the life of the individual. The Moon's Nodes, *Rahu* and *Ketu,* also play an important part in the fruition of *karma.* The great Vedic sage Parasara called the Moon's Nodes "the soldiers of the planetary army." They have their marching orders and are also utilized as *karmic* indicators.

As you can see, Vedic astrology developed in a culture whose philosophers deeply pondered the question of *karma.* It becomes important to understand this rightly, to coin a phrase from the **Eight Noble Truths** of Buddhism. A wrongful understanding of *karma* can leave one with a disastrous, fatalistic vantage point towards life. A little bit of knowledge is said to be a dangerous thing. The ancient philosophers of India spent lifetimes understanding the subtle principles of *karma* and how these *karmas* are continuously played out in the life.

Rightful understanding of *karma* begins with a study of the types of *karma,* such as past, current and future *karmas.* One must also know the difference between which *karmas* are fixed and which are non-fixed. For example, one cannot water a tree with tainted water for a decade and expect the fruit of the tree to be pure and free from defects when it matures, even if in the last year the tree had been watered with pure water just before harvest. We may have forgotten in the last year that there was a decade of toxicity preceding our current watering habits. Having forgotten, we will have wrongful expectations toward the harvest and be deeply disappointed with the harvest of fruit.

This wrongful attitude will lead to suffering, and this suffering can lead to resignation or it can lead to introspection. This can, according to the principles of the Noble Truths of Buddha, potentially direct us towards rightful understanding, and the cessation of our suffering on the road to liberation.

So as you see, each fruition of *karma* is, in fact, an opportunity for liberation. Unfortunately, it rarely comes in the good times, for we are caught up in our enjoyment. It mostly comes during the tough times when we are most motivated to ask ourselves why things are the way they are. It is said in ancient India that "the children of sorrow are the bringers of joy," for inherent within our suffering is always the hope of liberation. Thus, every significant event in our lives presents this opportunity.

It is therefore not what life presents you with that is of importance, but rather what you do about what is presented to you. Life will present us all with differing opportunities conditional upon our *karma.* No two opportunities are the same. An exemplary Vedic astrologer can forecast and discuss the coming and going of karmas. But only you can employ the principles of right understanding with the fruition of each karma as an opportunity for growth and liberation. No Vedic astrologer, however well intentioned, can perform this service for you.

In conclusion, I am of the opinion that it is imperative to employ the principles of *karma* from the Eastern culture, and the principles of free will from the Western culture to gain an in-depth vantage point in the understanding of our existence. Astrology in India is known as the "eye of the Veda," for its ability to penetratingly gaze into the very nature of existence. Jyotish can facilitate an understanding of what in life is unlikely to change, and what in life is likely to change, and when that change is liable to occur.

Here Vedic astrology does a great service for humanity. It is however your right to respond to the events that life presents to you in a manner according to your nature, or according to your conscious choice. This is the element of free will. Coupled with Vedic astrology, the philosophies of ancient India can cultivate an attitude of right understanding, which in time can help you develop the wisdom to discern between what you can change and what you must accept.

Dennis Flaherty is a certified practicing Vedic and Western astrologer, author and popular lecturer. He directs the East-West curriculum at Greenlake Metaphysics in Seattle, Washington. Dennis holds degrees in English and Sociology from the University of Massachusetts. He is past president of The Washington State Astrological Association and currently serves on the Steering Committees of ACVA (American Council of Vedic Astrology), and AFAN (Association for Astrological Networking). Dennis was nominated for a Regulus award at the 1992 United Astrology Conference, and is a recent recipient of the Jyotish Kovid from the Indian Council of Astrological Sciences, headed by Dr. B.V. Raman, in Madras, India. Dennis co-sponsored the Sacred Astrology Symposium in Seattle in 1995. He can be reached at Greenlake Metaphysics, 7212 Woodlawn Ave. NE, Seattle, WA 98115. Phone: (206) 525-2229.

VEDIC MEDICAL ASTROLOGY AND AYURVEDA

David Frawley

Vedic astrology, like other systems of astrology, has a special branch of medical astrology. This deals with a variety of health matters including longevity, individual constitution and disease potential. It considers both physical and mental health and disease.

Medical astrology, whether East or West, originally reflects the medical systems of ancient times which were energetic and naturalistic in their approach. Astrology employs a similar energetic language of qualities and elements as its related medical system. Traditional medical systems interface easily with astrology and have a common origin. However, while the older Western medicine of the Greeks has long disappeared, Vedic medicine, Ayurveda, has maintained a living tradition and practice to the present day.

Common Basis of Systems of Medical Astrology

Much of Vedic medical astrology resembles Western medical astrology. The attribution of the parts of the body to the different signs and houses, from Aries and the 1st House and the head, to Pisces and the 12th House and the feet, remains the same in both systems.

In the Vedic system, if the same numbered House and sign is afflicted, a health problem in that portion of the body is indicated. For example if, in a woman's chart, Saturn simultaneously aspects the 5th House and the 5th sign, the likelihood increases that she will be infertile or have a hysterectomy. This becomes even more probable if the 5th House from the Moon is also afflicted.

The Vedic system, like the Western, ascribes the same qualities and elements to the different signs, such as Aries being "cardinal and fiery." In addition it relates elements to the houses like that of the signs: the 1st House as fire, the second as earth, and so on. Planets will cause diseases relative to the signs they occupy. For example, planets in movable houses will cause diseases through too much change, travel or movement. Planets in watery houses will cause problems through exposure to damp environment or through the internal accumulation of phlegm.

The diseases attributed to the different planets are similar in both systems as well. For example, in both systems Saturn causes chronic, wasting and debilitating diseases. Jupiter causes diseases of excess, indulgence and obesity.

Both systems link the planets to the elements. They are the same in regard to fire and water, but differ on the other elements, partially because the Vedic system has five elements:

Ether - Jupiter
Air   - Saturn
Fire   - Mars, Sun
Water - Venus, Moon
Earth - Mercury

Ayurveda

Vedic Astrology interfaces tightly with Ayurveda. Ayurveda is the traditional natural healing system of Vedic knowledge, with its roots going back to the earliest Vedic texts some five thousand years ago. Ayurveda is the foremost of the Upavedas, or secondary Vedas. Astrology is the foremost of the Vedangas or branches of the Veda, being the very eye of the Veda. Ayurveda and Vedic astrology employ a similar language of elements, humors (doshas), and qualities (gunas).

The planets correlate with the different biological humors (Sanskrit doshas). These humors in their normal condition sustain health. In excess they become toxins and cause disease. Vata, or wind, is the biological air-humor responsible for all movements and discharges of impulses. Pitta, or bile, is the biological fire humor governing digestion and metabolism. Kapha, or phlegm, is the biological water-humor that makes up the bulk of the bodily tissues.

Each humor has its psychological counterpart. Vata on the positive side gives creativity and adaptability; negatively it causes fear and anxiety. Positive pitta creates intelligence and insight, while negatively it causes anger and hostility. Positive kapha promotes love and contentment, while negatively it breeds greed and attachment.

Planets and Doshas

Vata	-	Saturn
Pitta	-	Mars, Sun
Kapha	-	Jupiter, Venus, Moon
Mixed	-	Mercury

For the sake of symmetry one could argue that Mercury is a Vata planet. It is said to be mixed in nature owing to its mutability by which it takes on the influence of the planets and signs with which it is involved. Relative to the lunar nodes, Rahu, linked to the nature of Saturn in Vedic thought, usually comes under Vata. Ketu, linked to the nature of Mars, comes under Pitta. The nodes are prominent in psychic and psychological disorders. They play a crucial role in Vedic medical astrology.

Generally Saturn governs over all the Vata systems in the body, the Sun rules all the Pitta systems, and the Moon governs all the Kapha systems. Mars more specifically causes Pitta disorders. Jupiter sustains good health.

Most diseases in Ayurveda come under Vata, which governs the deeper and more enduring level of imbalances. It causes the debility, degeneration and decay that we can easily relate to Saturn. Pitta causes the second highest number of diseases, with febrile and inflammatory conditions such as are commonly associated with Mars and the Sun. Kapha causes the least number of diseases, mainly those of excess weight or self-indulgence, which benefics like Jupiter, Venus and the Moon tend to cause.

The Application of Medical Astrology

Vedic astrology first helps us determine the basic strength of a person and his or her longevity. This is determined by the strength of the Ascendant and its lord in both the rashi and navamsha (9th) charts. For more depth one can examine the drekkana (3rd), dvadashamsha (12th), and trimsamsha (30th) charts as well (keeping in mind that these sub-charts require an extremely accurate time of birth). The condition of the Moon in both the rashi and navamsha is also seriously considered because it is an Ascendant in itself. The Sun is important because it rules digestion and particularly when it is conjunct other planets.

The strength of the 6th House, and its lord, shows our power of immunity. The 8th House, and its lord, indicate life-threatening or congenital disorders. Rarely mentioned is that the planetary period at birth tells much about our congenital vitality.

The Vedic chart indicates the Ayurvedic constitution of the person according to the predominance of doshas and elements of planets, signs and houses. Generally the Ascendant determines the appearance of the person, but the strongest planet influencing the Ascendant and its lord determines the predominant constitutional humor. The nature of the Ascendant, and the location of the Ascendant lord, naturally are very important.

Significant groupings of planets, particularly influencing the 6th House, have their effect as well. Also, the influence on the Moon is very important, particularly its navamsha sign. The Moon gives more Kapha when full, more Vata when waning, and more Pitta when new. The Sun tends to take on the dosha of the planets with which it is joined (Sun-Mars being Pitta, Sun-Saturn being Vata, Sun-Jupiter being Kapha). Like any matter in astrology, constitutional analysis requires a synthesis of many factors.

Vedic astrology also helps us determine the periods in which disease is likely to occur. These are the periods of the 6th and 8th lords in Vimshottari Dasha. The periods of Maraka planets (planets ruling or located in the 2nd and 7th houses) gain the power to cause disease once their term is reached, depending on whether the overall chart indicates short, medium or long life.

Even a beginner in Vedic astrology can employ medical astrology for some benefit—not to predict disease, but to project its possible outcome once it has occurred. First one needs to examine the period in which the onset of the disease occurred. Then one should see if the coming planetary periods get better or worse.

If subsequent periods are ruled by natural or temporal malefics, this tends to exacerbate the disease. Those ruled by natural or temporal benefics will make it better. However the Bhukti of the Ascendant lord during the Dasha of a malefic can often be very challenging because it links the malefic influence to the very vitality of the person. A very afflicted chart will have much disease during the Dasha of the Ascendant lord.

Treatment of Disease

Vedic medical astrology employs a variety of treatment methods from Ayurveda and Yoga. These involve more the spiritual and occult side of treatment, the prescription of gems, rituals and mantras. [*Editor's Note: Please see the related article by James Braha on mantras and yagyas.*] These are particularly important for psychological disorders and for diseases that arise from karma, i.e., from our own past actions. By contrast, diseases arising from external pathogens or other purely physical factors can be treated on a physical level alone.

Ayurvedic doctors often use astrology or consult astrologers, particularly for patients who have many health problems or whose condition does not respond favorably to normal treatment methods. All of us can benefit from medical astrology at least to help us know likely times of good or bad health, and the basic vulnerabilities of our constitution.

Constitutional Studies

Following are three constitutional studies, or Ayurvedic readings, of charts. For purposes of brevity I have kept the examination simple and have not added the divisional charts.

			Jupiter
			Ketu
	CHART 1 **Vata Constitution** **(Male)**		
Rahu Moon			Mars Venus Lagna
		Saturn	Mercury Sun

At first sight, one might look at Chart 1 as Pitta, with Mars rising in Leo, a fiery planet in a fiery sign. Yet the Sun, ruler of the Ascendant, is in Virgo, a Vata sign, with Mercury, a Vata planet, which disposes it. The 6th House, however, is the decisive factor. The Moon is here, not only in the sign of Saturn, a Vata planet, but in close conjunction with Rahu, a Vata planet.

Though the Moon is waxing, it is isolated and devoid of any benefic influence. Vata-predominant Saturn is also strongly located, exalted in the 10th from the Moon (giving Mahapurusha Yoga for Saturn or Shasha Yoga). The positions from the Moon are thus primarily Vata, which makes Capricorn predominate over Leo in the constitution.

The Mars/Leo traits make the individual rather dramatic in self-expression, but the constitution is Vata, with Pitta second. The individual has a weak back, one lung unable to inflate, and a general Vata nature. The Moon-Rahu conjunction brought about a period of mental disorders and a nervous breakdown, but not severe. It gives the native nightmares and weak nerves. Yet the individual is active physically and does construction work, though not without periodic episodes of weak health. He is interested in spiritual matters but often lacks the energy or motivation to pursue them seriously. Here we see the importance of the 6th House, and the Moon, in determining health as well as how crucial conjunctions, particularly of the luminaries, with the lunar nodes can be.

	Rahu Mars	Mercury Sun	Jupiter Venus
			Moon
	CHART 2 **Pitta Constitution** **(Male)**		
Saturn		Ketu Lagna	

In this case a gemstone for the Moon is to be recommended—but perhaps on a pendant since the individual will be sensitive toward wearing gems in public, having Mars on the Ascendant.

Once again, Mars is clearly the strongest planet in Chart 2. It is in its own sign, Aries, in an angle from the Ascendant (the 7th) and from the Moon (the 10th). It aspects both the Ascendant (by its 7th aspect) and the Moon (by its 4th). This creates the Mahapurusha Yoga (Ruchaka Yoga) for Mars, which gives strong powers of action and self-expression, and a Mars-type personality. Rahu helps magnify the power of Mars, giving turbulence in the field of relationship and several unhappy marriages, along with charges of abuse against him.

Chart 2 is Clint Eastwood a successful actor (Rahu again) of the more violent type (Mars), who built his reputation primarily via violent westerns and police type shows. He also has been active in politics, as a mayor (note Libra Ascendant). The Moon in Cancer in the 10th gives popularity and prominence. Our focus here is the Ayurvedic constitutional type, but we can see how its psychological characteristics are evident in the character.

		Rahu Moon	Lagna
			Saturn Mars
	CHART 3 **Kapha Constitution** **(Male)**		
	Ketu Venus Jupiter	Mercury Sun	

At first sight Chart 3 appears rather airy with a Gemini Ascendant, Libra Sun, and the Moon with Rahu. However, note that the Moon is only one House after full, is in its sign of exaltation, and is aspected by both Jupiter and Venus (7th aspect), watery planets, and from Scorpio, a watery sign.

If we turn the Moon into the Ascendant, the Kapha nature of the constitution becomes evident. These planets dominate the 6th House which determines health. Jupiter and Venus in a watery sign give the tendency to weight gain and also sluggish liver function. Though the individual has been generally healthy past the age of 40, the tendency to heart disease and hypertension, which we note in the chart, is beginning to arise. The planets in the 6th also give a strong capacity for work, service and devotion.

The airy traits do come out in the character, however, as he is very communicative, fond of books, and pursues a variety of spiritual subjects. The Moon-Rahu conjunction did result in a mild mental breakdown in youth, but also shows a strong spiritual or devotional sensitivity. It has provided the individual with a government pension. In addition Kalasarpa Yoga prevails with all the planets between Rahu and Ketu, adding to the strong psychic nature of the person.

Note that there are no planets in fiery signs and both main fire planets, the Sun and Mars, are debilitated and not located in strong positions (they prefer angular or upachaya houses). There is not much Pitta in the constitution, Vata being second to Kapha in strength. This chart would benefit primarily by a gemstone for Mercury. This would also help the debilitated Sun.

David Frawley is the author of many highly regarded books on Vedic subjects including The Astrology of Seers: A Guide to Vedic (Hindu) Astrology, *and* Ayurvedic Healing: A Comprehensive Guide. *He is President of The American Council of Vedic Astrology (ACVA) and offers a correspondence course on Vedic astrology as well. David can be reached through: The American Institute of Vedic Studies, PO Box 8357, Santa Fe, NM 87504-8357.*

SECRETS OF BHRIGU NADI

Martin Gansten

Hindu astrological prognostication today is almost invariably based on the application of one or more of the numerous *dasha* systems mentioned in classical texts, coupled with transits. Other methods mentioned in later texts, such as the solar returns *(varshaphala)* of the medieval Tajaka school, or the more unique converse secondary progressions referred to in passing in the 19th century work *Sanketanidhi,* are ignored by most, as they do not form part of the traditional corpus of astrological lore believed to have originated with the *rishis,* or ancient sages.

But there is another predictive technique, embedded in texts ascribed to these same rishis. It is simpler than transits and as accurate as any Dasha system; and yet, despite the present popularization of Jyotisha, unknown to all but a handful of astrologers. This is the progressive system of Bhrigu Nadi.

The Mysterious Nadis

The word *Nadi* is perhaps familiar to most students of Hindu astrology, although not everyone may have had a first-hand experience of the phenomenon. In short, a Nadi or Nadigrantha is considered to be an ancient collection of ready-made horoscopes accompanied by readings of various length and precision, written on palm leaves or similar materials. These readings are ascribed to Hindu sages (such as Bhrigu, Agastya, Vasishtha, etc.) or divinities, and the texts are kept by special Nadi readers who decipher the often illegible or encoded script for a fee.

Thousands of people, including an increasing number of Westerners, visit Nadi readers every year in the hope of finding a reading for themselves, with varying results. It is not possible here to go into the differences between astrological Nadis proper and the so-called Mantra Nadis, etc. Suffice it to say that there are a large number of these texts, written in many different languages (mainly Tamil and Sanskrit), and apparently based on a variety of astrological and other predictive techniques.

In recent years, many books and articles claiming to unveil 'the' Nadi system of prediction have been published, as well as several English translations of (fragmentary) Nadi texts. Most of these leave the reader quite disappointed, as the *key* linking charts to predictions is never revealed – generally because it is unknown even to the translator of the text. I will describe such a key technique which apparently forms the basis of the Bhrigu Nadi found in South India[1]. (My investigations have brought me into contact with a Delhi astrologer who claims to have seen a Nepalese manuscript of the Bhrigu Nadi based on the same or similar principles.)

I would also like to mention that although I have met a few astrologers experimenting with similar techniques, the credit for the discovery of the exact principles presented in this article goes to Mr. Tommy Larsen of Copenhagen, a very able astrologer with a wide personal experience of Nadigranthas.

The Basis

In the Bhrigu Nadi, only Rashi charts are shown, and generally without mention of the ascendant. This may come as a surprise to many, since Hindu astrological work in general depends very much on the twelve houses reckoned from the ascendant. Indeed, another Nadi work *(Candrakala Nadi* or *Devakeralam)* states: "If the ascendant is not known, [the astrologer's] words will be false and will not bear fruit." But prediction in the Bhrigu Nadi is based entirely on the juxtapositions of the nine planets, and will still often be very precise, as we shall see.

In this connection, it may help to think of individual destiny as a combination of patterns; the patterns are universal, but their combination unique – or at least quite rare. B.V. Raman mentions the following idea in a lecture on Nadi astrology, speaking of other Nadis and their techniques:

> The various charts given should be taken as representative or symbolic, and they can be fitted into [a] person's horoscope which has almost a similar pattern. Thus, for a given horoscope, many judgments are given which agree with one another to a period and then differ.... The Dwadasamsa or the 1/12th division indicates a certain general pattern of future, the Thrimsamsa or the 1/30th division, a more specific pattern and the Nadi amsa, the exact pattern[2].

---

[1]See R.G. Rao: *Bhrigu Nandi Nadi,* Ranjan Publications, Delhi, 1986. This is really a fragmentary synthesis of two different Nadi works.
[2]*Hindu Astrology and the West,* Ranjan Publications, Bangalore, 1991, pp. 272-281.

From this point of view, the delineation of planetary positions as carried out in the Bhrigu Nadi constitutes the most fundamental pattern of a person's destiny, on which all individual variation rests. This predictive technique is powerful, but is not meant to replace considerations of house placements, Dasha periods, etc., which will still be needed for fine-tuning.

The Bhrigu Nadi system is built exclusively on planetary symbolism or *karakatwa,* and the essence of delineation, natal as well as prognostical, is the combination of planets in the same, opposing, trinal, and adjacent signs. Such symbolism may sometimes differ from that mentioned in the general Parashari canon. For instance, the significator of land *(bhumikaraka)* in this system is not Mars, but Mercury. As a South Indian astrologer once told me, "In Hindu mythology, Mars is the son of the Earth. How can the son have power over the mother? But Mercury is Lord Vishnu, the husband of Bhudevi (the Earth goddess)."

As I cannot include whole lists of planetary significations in this article, readers are referred to the books of R.G. Rao, especially *Transits of Planets*[3] , for such information. The same goes for the important issue of planetary friendships, which again differ somewhat from Parashari rules.

The Technique

The fundamental idea of prognostication in the Bhrigu Nadi is to move all planets forward, at uniform speed, from their radical positions in order to arrive at the likely time of an event. There are different levels of speed, just as there are *antar-* and *pratyantardashas* within a Dasha. On the first level, every 30° represent twelve years. Next, every 30° represent one year; and finally, every 30° may also represent one month. Here I will limit discussion to the first and most important level of progressions, where each planet thus moves forward by 2°30' a year.

The time of an event is determined by the distance one karaka planet has to move in order to exactly conjoin, trine or oppose another karaka planet. Squares may also produce some effect, but less marked and of a more transitory nature, unless two or more of them occur simultaneously. Squares can further be important in backing up events shown by simultaneous conjunctions, trines, or oppositions.

---

[3]Published by the author himself: R.G. Rao, Srinivasanagar II Cross, Kattriguppa Main Road (near Vidyapeeth), Bangalore-560 085, India.

In these progressions, the permitted orb of aspect is 6° (corresponding to 2.4 years) either way, making the possible time frame of any event as wide as 4.8 years. However, much more exact timing can usually be achieved by examining a number of progressions occurring more or less simultaneously. The time when two, three or more progressions of a similar nature overlap, thus exerting their influence on the native simultaneously, is the most likely time for an event to take place. I will illustrate this principle with an example chart taken from the Ranjan edition of *Bhrigu Nandi Nadi*.

An Example From The Nadi Text

Most of the planetary configurations of the 504 charts included in this volume have appeared in the present century (although, due to the use of faulty vakyas, or calculation formulae, there may be occasional discrepancies for planets near the verges of signs). Chart 184 of *Bhrigu Nandi Nadi* thus corresponds to the planetary positions on August 25, 1937 as follows (noontime positions are used):

```
Ketu     – 18-TA-07
Venus    – 00-CN-40
Sun      – 08-LE-57
Mercury  – 04-VI-53
Mars     – 15-SC-15
Rahu     – 18-SC-07
Jupiter  – 25-SA-11 Rx
Saturn   – 11-PI-00 Rx
Moon     – 23-PI-07
```

I will touch upon only two predictions given in the Nadi reading: first, a financial turning point with plentiful earnings at age 42-43, and second, an accident in the native's 43rd year.

1. The primary significator of wealth in the *Bhrigu Nadi* is Venus, who will cause prosperity when contacting or contacted by its friends Saturn, Mercury, and in particular, Rahu. Progressing Rahu from 18-SC-07 to 00-PI-40, where it will trine Venus, at the rate of 2°30' per year, we get 102°33' / 2°30' = 41.02 years. Progressing Saturn in the same way from 11-PI-00 to 00-CN-40, conjoining Venus, we get 109°40' / 2°30' = 43.87 years. Giving both these exact progressions an orb of 6° or 2.4 years, we find that the period of overlapping runs from 41.47 years to 43.42 years of age – in the Indian idiom, from the native's 42nd year of life until his 44th.

2. For accidents in a male chart, Jupiter (life) should be afflicted by malefics, Mars and Ketu being especially violent. Now, Jupiter in this chart is retrograde and will therefore give results from the preceding sign as well.[4] Progressing Jupiter as from 25-SC-11, we find that he will conjoin Saturn at 11-PI-00 after 105°49' / 2°30' = 42.33 years, trine Mars from 15-PI-15 after 110°04' / 2°30' = 44.03 years, and Rahu from 18-PI-07 after 112°56' / 2°30' = 45.17 years. These three progressions are simultaneously active from the age of 42.77, i.e., the native's 43rd year.

The several other events mentioned in the reading cannot be discussed here for want of space, and the same goes for important issues like retrogrades turning direct, mutual reception, etc. A book describing these techniques in detail may be published in the future. It should be noted that the transits of the slow planets (Saturn, Jupiter, and the nodes) play an important part in triggering events indicated by progression.

An Example From Real Life

The progressions referred to in the above example were simple two-planet combinations. It goes without saying, however, that the greater the number of factors involved in a combination, the more precise conclusions can be drawn. I will mention one case of a dramatically correct three-planet combination from my own experience. A few months before I learned of the technique under discussion, I was approached by a client whose planetary positions at birth (data withheld) were as follows:

Ketu	– 10-TA-05
Moon	– 29-TA-41
Venus	– 27-GE-59
Sun	– 13-LE-49
Jupiter	– 17-LE-47
Mercury	– 10-VI-56
Saturn	– 03-SC-45
Rahu	– 10-SC-05
Mars	– 28-AQ-01 Rx

His question was not one I was used to dealing with, nor could I (or any astrologer-friend I discussed the chart with) see the situation reflected in the birth chart according to standard Parashari rules. In short, his employer – a multinational company – had assigned him to buy a piece of property in a CIS country in order to establish a branch there. He had set up a deal with a

---

[4]This principle will be familiar to those who have studied the work of K.N. Rao.

land-owner; but after several initial difficulties, the final blow came when a third party – a friend who was supposed to act as an intermediary – disappeared with a large share of the purchase-sum. The two parties were now entering into litigation over the property, and my client wished to know the outcome. Simultaneously, but without reference to these events, he was being attacked and slandered separately by two female co-workers.

At the time, I resorted to Prashna (horary astrology) to answer the question at hand, but the birth chart kept haunting me: why couldn't I see the event? When shortly thereafter I learned of the Bhrigu Nadi technique, I went back to the chart, calculated the progressions of my client (who was near the age of forty), and at once found a number of significant hits. Most spectacular of these was the conjunction of the progressed Moon with natal Mercury, who in turn formed a perfect trine to natal Ketu. I quickly located this three-planet combination in R.G. Rao's Transit of Planets, which quite laconically stated: *"There will be land dispute, dispute with two women, and deceit to the native."*

This, in brief, is the predictive system of Bhrigu Nadi – a path unknown to most, little used and partly overgrown, but well worth the effort of clearing it. Salutations to Maharshi Bhrigu for illuminating this path!

Martin Gansten is a practising astrologer, devoted since fifteen years to the study of Indian thought. He has his academic training in Indology and Sanskrit from the University of Stockholm, and is currently planning a dissertation on Nadigranthas at the Department of Religious Studies, University of Lund (Sweden). Mailing address: Stora Kvarngatan 47, S-211 29 Malmö, Sweden. E-mail: mgansten@sbbs.se. Phone: +46 40 234436.

BREAKING THROUGH THE LANGUAGE BARRIER

Alan Goodman

Vedic astrology is a part of the very rich cultural history and spiritual tradition of India, a tradition going back thousands of years. For most of those millennia this knowledge was passed orally to the son who listened to his father tell the stories of ancient sages, great kings and mighty warriors. Only in the last 2,000-2,500 years was any of this knowledge written down, and then only as a memory aid since the real learning was done by the student listening to his teacher.

Much of the writings that have survived were written in regional Indian languages and in Sanskrit, a language that is today generally spoken and taught only by scholars in a few universities in India, and by Hindu priests. This limits the availability of the original material to those few scholars versed in these languages. There are also differences over how the words in the English translations should be spelled.

A westerner wishing to learn Hindu astrology would best begin by reading the few books written by other westerners who have studied in India. These explain the basics of the Hindu system, and this anthology is based upon the assumption that you may have read one or two of these. But to really learn more, one has to begin reading books from India.

While there are many good Indian astrology texts from India written in English, they are written in a style that is quite different from anything in the West and very confusing at times. Some of the simplest terms can sometimes throw you for a loop. An example of this might be their frequent reference to children as "issues" (presumably because they issue forth from their mother).

Many Sanskrit words are also used that have no direct English equivalent, and some common English words are used in ways never imagined in the West. Some authors express themselves much more clearly in English than others, and you will develop favorites in that regard. Some books have a brief glossary of technical (Sanskrit) terms, but they only cover a few of the potentially confusing terms in the book. Other books either assume that you know the terminology, or they let you figure it out yourself.

Parenthetically, one of the more comprehensive efforts I have seen by a Western astrologer to capture many of these terms is the 1,700 word glossary in the back of Richard Houck's *Astrology of Death*. This glossary also quickly reveals the multiple English spellings of numerous Sanskrit words. This essay will attempt to provide an introductory foundation for clarifying some basic terms unique to Hindu astrology.

The books from India can be divided into two groups: those written by modern Indian writers, and ancient classics that are translated by modern scholars. The books in the first group should be read first. They are easier to comprehend and frequently contain the important principles from the classics. The classics themselves are like encyclopedias. They are hundreds to thousands of years old, written in a cultural setting for which Westerners have no frame of reference, and they are filled with factual assertions but carry very little explanation.

The more understandable translations are those in which the translators have added their own notes and maybe even provided sample charts to illustrate the principles. Many translators are reluctant to add their own thoughts since the ancient sages are considered to have been enlightened beings. Consequently their works are not considered open to debate and criticism. It is also important to know that the quality of translations can vary widely in terms of clarity, idioms and explanation. So before you send quite a bit of money off to a distant mail order publisher or distributor, you should ask around about this matter within the community of Western astrologers who are studying these books.

Astrology is the study of how the lives of people are affected by planetary movements in space and time. But the measurement of these quantities is done differently in the East than in the West, and very little information is easily accessible concerning the eastern methods. One of the most controversial of these measurements is the ayanamsa, the difference between the tropical and sidereal zodiac positions. Astrologers have different opinions about when the two zodiacs coincided and how fast they are diverging, and this leads to arguments, sometimes heated, over planetary positions.

But it is when the choice of ayanamsa changes the Ascending sign, and therefore the whole focus of the chart, that the controversies are greatest. When reading a Hindu astrology book, one should be very aware of what stated or implied ayanamsa the author is using, particularly where charts are demonstrated, and how other choices might give very different results. Such charts are also fertile material for research into which is the "correct" ayanamsha.

Measurements of time in Indian books is also different than in the West. This can have a definite impact upon your understanding of a technique the book is trying to communicate. While the newer books use hours, minutes and seconds as we do in the West, the older ones use a very different reference scale in which:

- One Day is divided into 60 Ghatis. A Ghati is therefore 24 minutes.
- One Ghati is divided into 60 Vighatis or Palas. A Pala is 24 seconds.
- One Pala is divided into 60 Vipals. A Vipal is 0.4 second.

In traditional astrology, the Hindu day begins at sunrise, not at midnight as in the West. Since birth data in many texts will often be expressed in Ghatis and Vighatis, it must be kept in mind that this is quite likely in reference to sunrise and not to midnight. To cast such a chart in order to further study it, we must not only convert the Ghatis and Vighatis, but must also find the time of sunrise on that day at the birth latitude. Fortunately this task is easily performed by numerous astrological software packages. There is also needed in some techniques a measurement called Ishta-Kaala which is the specific elapsed time in Ghatis and Vighatis after sunrise of the birth or event in question.

Time zones are never mentioned in Indian books since all of India is in one zone. This is 5 hours and 30 minutes east of the Greenwich meridian. Also Daylight Saving Time has never been used in India except during World War II. This is true for all births in the 20th century except for some areas of eastern India before 1947.

Further, keep alert to the fact that event dates in Indian books are written the reverse of how they are in the United States. For example, 10-05-1995 is October 5, 1995 in the United States, but is May 10, 1995 in India. This conforms to European notation and apparently is a vestige of British rule.

Notation of zodiac positions is also different in most books that come out of India. A planetary position listed as 7 Leo 25 in a western book on Hindu astrology might instead be shown as 4s 7d 25m in an Indian book. Since Leo is the 5th sign, this notation is read as 4 signs plus 7 degrees and 25 minutes having elapsed to that planet's position. 0s would therefore indicate a position within the sign of Aries.

Since the Moon is of paramount importance in the Hindu system, much more so than the Sun, its position from the Sun is equally enhanced in importance. This generates more terminology. Some commonly used terms associated with the Moon are:

- Janma Rashi - The birth sign. In the West when asked "What's your sign?", it is your Sun sign that is being inquired about. In India, the Janma Rashi is always your Moon sign.

- Lunar Month - The time for the Moon to go from one new Moon to the next new Moon.

- Shukla Paksha - The waxing half of the lunar month, new Moon to full Moon.

- Krishna Paksha - The waning half of the lunar month, full Moon to new Moon.

- Tithi - One lunar day or 12 degrees of longitude. There are 30 tithis in each lunar month. Since the Moon can travel more or less than 12 degrees in a solar day, a day can have part of a second tithi in it, or be less than a full tithi.

- Karna - Half of a tithi.

Different effects are attributed to whether the birth occurs during the day or at night, and whether in Shukla Paksha or Krishna Paksha. Also each lunar month has a planetary ruler as does each weekday and each tithi. When choosing a favorable day to begin an important activity, having the correct ruling planets is one indicator of success. (Of course, other rulers, such as sign and nakshatra rulers, will also have to be factored in.)

The subject of many Hindu astrology books is not always apparent from the book's title until the reader knows the major divisions of Jyotish (astrology). The important point to note is that when one of the following words appears in the title of a book, it will give you a good clue about the general classification of its intent. These terms are:

- Jataka - Natal astrology

- Prashna - Horary astrology

- Murhurta - Electional astrology

- Tajika or Varshaphala - Annual horoscopy based on solar returns of the natal chart

- Samhita - Mundane astrology, specifically the interpretation of omens

This has been only a brief introduction to the array of Sanskrit words and other unfamiliar expressions found in many Indian astrology books. If you encounter something unknown which is not explained, just continue reading. The term is likely to come up again in another context, and the meaning may be deduced by comparing the two uses.

Clues can also be derived indirectly in another way. For example, the Sanskrit word for the sign of Sagittarius is Dhanu. We know that Dhanu is ruled by Jupiter. Therefore, if we see a class of yogas (special planetary combinations) cryptically referred to as Dhana yogas, we could assume that these are yogas for wealth and prosperity, as opposed to poverty and misery, if we had to make a snap judgment about the matter (by the way, it's true).

Trying to understand the Indian books, especially the classics, may seem difficult, but the rewards, the light that is revealed, makes it all worthwhile!

Alan Goodman is an officer in the Maryland chapter of the National Council for Geocosmic Research. He has been a serious and very active student of Vedic astrology for a number of years. He has written articles on the Vedic system and given presentations on the east coast with an emphasis on making Indian material more understandable to the western mind and ear. When not doing Vedic astrology, Al is a scientist with the US Government. He can be reached at 3819-B Longley Road in Abingdon, MD 21009. Phone: 410-679-0468.

CHOICE OF AUTHORITY IN VEDIC ASTROLOGY SOFTWARE

Das Goravani

Originally, Vedic knowledge was thought to be a unified, singular mass free from any divisions by superior knowledge, authority or opinion. Supposedly long ago there were also persons who, it is said, could memorize everything they were told. Whether you believe these things or not, and without regard to what you may believe concerning revealed knowledge, disciple succes- sions, or divine-human history, the fact is that we now have many differences of opinion, and these have split into all types of Vedic camps, spiritual as well as astrological.

In these modern times, when one goes to write Vedic astrology software, as I have done with my program "Goravani Jyotish," one is faced with this fact and must deal with it. This article covers the areas of choice as to the various interpretations one can apply in Vedic astrology, the reasoning behind some of the choices, and about how this affects the students and users of Vedic astrology software in this current era.

First let me suggest a useful consideration as we review some of these issues. Disputes over seemingly key astrological calculations definitely do exist, and each camp of believers claims remarkable results with their own chosen methods. Even Western astrologers often get significant results, and their planetary positions are "off" by 23 degrees! The truth is that we astrologers are readers of patterns, and by following a consistent system that evolves patterns based on planetary placements, one can get results.

The universe, and the karmic systems governed by it, consist of "patterned" dances of influential light or other types of rays, sectors, areas, and time periods. You are born into a swirling universe full of divine patterns of energy movement, but readers of patterns can find meaning in these patterns using a number of differing systems. Witness the effectiveness of Chinese astrology as one such example.

So the resolution is that many systems can work simultaneously, each one focusing on a true, existing wavelength or pattern, and thus they can all achieve some accurate predictive results. One pattern may be slightly more significant than others, but never able to actually negate the other patterns.

The Tropical zodiac is the one the seasons live by, so is it not important to what grows upon the earth—including us? It certainly is an important pattern of celestial reality in our lives, even if we are "Vedic" or "Sidereal" astrologers. By this same logic, the Vedic practitioner or student can understand that different patterns exist within "Vedic" reality; thus slightly varying approaches to a particular Vedic astrological technique can explore any special advantages that may be offered by this fact. In the end we need to approach these issues in a broadminded way.

First, let's review the important, or at least most well known, disputes. Some astrologers use the solar year to calculate the Dasas while others use a fixed 360 day year, while fewer still are interested in trying the lunar year, the sidereal year, and even other units of time. I have discussed this particular point with a number of astrologers who are competent in Sanskrit, and each is able to cite passages in "classics" which support one, or the other, position.

It's important to understand that "classic astrological scriptures" are, after all, books written by humans and sometimes later changed by humans. It's also important to know that what we can see, count and understand—and consequently program into computers—may not be the actual way it is in the heavens. What Hindu scripture ever said that Divinity, God, or the Gods are beholden to our small brains? Actually, quite the contrary has been stated many times. So, we must humbly assume that what has been revealed to us, or discovered by us, has necessarily been "rounded off" to fit our world view. And since we are "the created," i.e., the ones smaller than, and dependent upon, that which did the creating, then we necessarily cannot have subsumed the whole truth.

So, since this argument about the length of the Dasha year is so well known, and since there are followers on both sides who want to purchase software, most programs make this a variable option. The user then simply selects the one they believe and use.

It is not clearly stated in the cornerstone classic, *Parasara Hora Sastra,* which of these two is correct. Therefore, this issue remains a point of potentially irresolvable disagreement. I think that even if sophisticated research and testing could statistically prove which year is most often correct, quite clearly it still would not mean that the other is always incorrect.

The other main popular item of disagreement is the ayanamsa. There are a number of popular ones, the Lahiri being the most commonly used, followed by the Raman, Sri Yukteswar, Krishnamurti, and others. These different ayanamsas were arrived at using various levels of astronomical science and reasoning, in reference to previous citings, and spiritual or mystical inspirations. Again, each has it's devoted and convinced followers. Because of the complexity of "proving" astrology, due to so many overlapping influences, it would be very hard or impossible to ever demonstrate, clearly and scientifically, that one of these were superior. But again, since the followers of all of these ayanamsas purchase software, most programs provide these choices as an option.

Now what about those areas of disagreement where the programs tend to not give options? These include some of the bala calculations like Shad Bala and Ashtaka Varga. Is the average reader of this article aware that, in the books of different authorities, the calculations for these vary significantly?

For example, Dr. Raman has a very good and detailed book on Shad Bala calculations. I used these in my program. In this book however, in one part, he uses and replicates some calculations from the Vedic classic on astronomical calculations Surya Sidhanta. These replicated calculations "approximate" the positions of the planets in the zodiac at the time of the birth. Now: should I, as a programmer, use these calculations as given by Dr. Raman, or refine them with the more modern positions we have available to us in our programs already? What is more important here: remain true to ancient books, or go with technical adjustments we have data to suggest are better? A very tricky question, that. But did you know, as far as I know, no software program makes this particular issue an option?

I personally went with the book on this point. Another program will do it another way, resulting in slightly varying shad bala results. This same type of dilemma applies to other parts of shad bala and Bhava bala. I am not fixed in my position on this point. If someone were able to demonstrate in a convincing way that the other approach is more divine, i.e., clearly intended by the ancients, then I might switch or at that time program in the option. None of us Vedic astrology software programmers claim to be all-knowing masters. Rather, we are more the servants, the blacksmiths, who create tools for others to use. We are subject to input and correction.

When we go to create a new feature, say for example "Kala Chakra Dasha", then we open our books to find the calculations therein. Immediately we are able to find the calculations for this or any other technique replicated in a number of books, some "classics" and some by modern, living authors. But we find that the content of these books will vary. Which should we follow?

Some of these authors simply claim to be repeating what their Guru has taught them. Others will state that they are transparently translating a classic scripture which stands on its own merit as a "Classical Vedic Scripture," thereby implying unquestionable revealed truth as their argument for authenticity. Okay, they often back off a bit and say, "well, at least we have to be careful about disregarding this ancient work since it may be our only link to the original divine truth about the matter." So the question of authority definitely does affect, or at least tries to affect, our decisions on how to program various features.

So, speaking for myself, when I am faced with a variety of approaches to supposedly the same Vedic technique, I often ask living persons whom I respect what they have discovered about this technique. Often this helps to clarify the positions of the various authors in question. However, often these modern scholars disagree with each other still. So, ultimately, it is left to the programmer to decide how to implement the technique, whether to provide options, or go with the technique that seems to be the most mainstream and accepted.

To be honest, a large number of the supposedly standard Vedic techniques have, in fact, this dilemma behind them if you are well read enough or have talked to enough adherents of the various camps. So many features are therefore coming to you with the choices already built into the software you buy. The programmer decides what to include based on their own type of worship of Vedic things, their respect for various camps of thinkers or practitioners, and their own good, or misdirected(!), karmic thinking patterns. Ease of programming, and time constraints, also play their part in the decisions. [If you are starting to get the impression that software is not the "Voice of God" but the "Voice of Programmer X," then I should also mention here that I personally often have trouble just keeping my shirt tucked in!]

Consider just this simple dilemma: When astrological books say that a certain reading or interpretation requires the conjunction of "benefic" with some other planet, should you use the permanent, or the temporary, benefics? Very simply, the books of readings often do not say which they mean. However, your choice here will greatly affect the outcome of the readings you select from the book to apply to a given chart because the permanent versus temporary malefics and benefics are very different.

Consider further: when we approach the subject of temporary benefics, just start comparing the different tables provided by the different modern authors and the classics as what planets are temporary benefics and malefics for the 12 ascendants. You will find greatly varying opinions about how to reckon these. Therefore, do you know how it is being done in the software package you own and use? Are you aware that there is dispute on this important point and do you know which method you have been following simply by using a certain software package? Parenthetically, my own program deals with this point by allowing the user to specify the temporary benefics for each ascendant. You can set them all to the permanent settings, or various "temporary" settings.

I am always amazed at how little I am asked about the details inside my own software program which is used worldwide by hundreds of Vedic astrologers and students. Very rarely do I get asked questions on the deeper levels of detail. This means that many students and astrologers are not aware of the disputes or the affects of one choice over the other upon their learning or work.

For us tool-creating blacksmiths, as our client base becomes more aware and sophisticated, I expect that the main impact on our lives will be the need to install more and more selectable options in our programs!

Das Goravani was born in California in 1960. Raised a serious Catholic, he converted to Hinduism at 19, spent some years as a brahmacari monk, later married, and is raising some cool kids. He has been to India on four separate occasions to learn the ancient ways. He has written "Goravani Jyotish," a Vedic Astrological Software program which is both sophisticated and friendly. He owns and runs Goravani Astrological Services, which creates tools for spreading the Vedic Sciences including software, books, lecture tapes, videos, and web sites. He can be reached at Goravani Astrological Services: 1-800-532-6528 or 541-485-8453. Fax: 541-343-0344. E-Mail: goravani@aol.com. There are three web sites: www.goravani.com, www.vedic-astrology.com and www.vaisnavism.com. Or write: 211 Crest Drive in Eugene, OR 97405.

SIBLINGS IN THE HOROSCOPE

Teresa Hamilton

Matthew Quellas, a well-known Western Sidereal astrologer, presented a very interesting puzzle to on-line astrologers in June of 1994. He challenged astrologers to tell which of a set of twins died at the age of 13. The twins were born only four minutes apart. From the birth certificates, the birth data is as follows:

Male twins, believed to be fraternal (names are fictitious):

> DOB: 20 April 1973
> POB: Long Beach, CA (33N47 & 118W11)
>
> Dan (older twin) at   9:06 PM PST
> Leon (younger twin) at   9:10 PM PST

- One of the twins died in his sleep on September 14, 1986 between 4:00 and 4:30 AM CST at Azcapotzalco, Mexico (19N28 & 99W14). Although there is no clear proof, the family felt there was a possibility that he was poisoned by something he ate.

- Matthew Quellas presented this puzzle as a challenge to Vedic astrologers. Along with others, I took up the challenge based on Hindu theory. Because the results were correct, I present here the analytical process I used, so that other astrologers can test the principles.

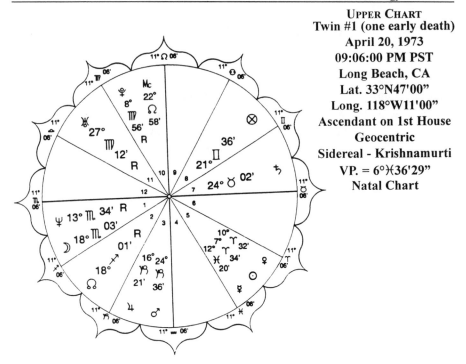

UPPER CHART
Twin #1 (one early death)
April 20, 1973
09:06:00 PM PST
Long Beach, CA
Lat. 33°N47'00"
Long. 118°W11'00"
Ascendant on 1st House
Geocentric
Sidereal - Krishnamurti
VP. = 6°)(36'29"
Natal Chart

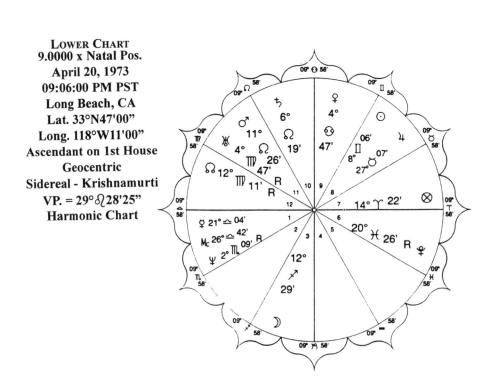

LOWER CHART
9.0000 x Natal Pos.
April 20, 1973
09:06:00 PM PST
Long Beach, CA
Lat. 33°N47'00"
Long. 118°W11'00"
Ascendant on 1st House
Geocentric
Sidereal - Krishnamurti
VP. = 29°Ω28'25"
Harmonic Chart

Horoscope of the Twins

Following is the rasi and navamsha for the twins:

I use Krishnamurti's ayanamsa for the calculation of the charts, as well as the Indian equal house system, which puts the Ascendant degree on the cusp of each house, the cusp marking the house center. After running all the charts, Tropical astrologers would note immediately that the younger twin's chart has the exact (a minute of orb!) square of Saturn to the MC. Tropical astrologers would go on to note aspects to house cusps, solar arc progressions at the time of death, midpoints, etc.

I asked myself, "With so little emphasis on precision, what would Hindu astrology do with this puzzle?" If the birth times are far enough apart then there are differences in the Navamsa, Dwadasamsa, and Drekkana (used for siblings) charts. But in this case, with only 4 minutes between the births, these sub-charts are also all identical. Even the natal Ascendant is in the same degree!

I reasoned that one twin was the younger brother of the older, and the other is the older brother of the younger. Traditionally, older siblings come under the 11th House while younger ones come under the 3rd House. So I studied the basically identical natal charts with this in mind.

– Virgo is on the 11th cusp, so Mercury rules older siblings.
– Capricorn is on the 3rd cusp, so Saturn rules younger siblings.

Analyzing these two planets, we observe the following in the Rasi (birth) chart:

Mercury rules older brothers:

- Mercury is in the benefic 5th - good.

- Mercury's dispositor Jupiter is conjunct an exalted Mars - good.

- Mercury's dispositor Jupiter is in its fall in Capricorn in the 3rd - mildly bad.

- Dispositor Jupiter is in the Moon's star (Sravana in Capricorn), and the Moon is strong in the 1st - good.

- In Navamsa: Ruling the benefic 9th, significator Mercury is strong in the 1st in Libra.

Saturn rules younger brothers:

- Saturn is placed at the juncture (Hindu equal house) between the 7th and 8th Houses - very weak.

- Saturn's dispositor Venus is combust the Sun in the 6th - unfortunate. Dispositor Venus is in the star of Ketu (Ashvini in Aries); Ketu is in the 8th House of danger to life and vitality.

- In Navamsa: Saturn is in the 11th which is a favorable position. But it is in its enemy sign of Leo and conjunct Mars, which rules the Navamsa 7th House of death. Saturn in a good house, but an inimical sign, gives support for Navamsa signs being more important than Navamsa houses. In traditional Hindu astrology, the signs in a sub-chart, such as the Navamsa, are emphasized.

Using the Drekkana or Decanate Chart (not shown)

The Drekkana, or decanate chart, is the traditional chart for siblings. If you run it, you will see that Pisces rises in this chart, placing Mercury-ruled Virgo on the 7th cusp of death. In this chart we consider the placement of the Dasa and sub-period rulers at the time of death. The Dasa (major period) ruler is Mercury. Jupiter is the sub-period ruler, and Ketu is the sub-sub lord.

Saturn rules younger siblings:

Saturn is placed in Capricorn, so Capricorn may be taken as the 1st House for younger siblings. Dasa ruler (Mercury) is in the 7th from Saturn, i.e., in the house of death. Jupiter is malefic for a Capricorn Ascendant since it rules the 3rd and 12th Houses. It is in the unfriendly sign of Taurus with Uranus. Taurus is the 3rd House from the Drekkana Ascendant, so it is also the house of younger siblings. Ketu, the sub-sub ruler, is in the malefic 8th House which afflicts the natural vitality. Saturn is in Capricorn, so disposits itself in the natal chart. I've already pointed out that Saturn's placement is weak at a house junction point.

Mercury Rules Older Siblings:

Mercury is in Cancer, so Cancer may be taken as the 1st House in the Drekkana chart for older siblings. Since Mercury is the Dasa ruler, its position in the 1st is strong. Sub-ruler Jupiter is benefic for a Cancer Ascendant. Mercury's Drekkana dispositor is the Moon. In the natal chart the Moon is strong in the 1st House.

Therefore, based upon the decanate chart, the Hindu progressions are unfortunate for the younger brother. This technique should be checked in other charts to see if the principles work consistently.

Closing Discussion

The question many Western astrologers would naturally ask is, "Do planets ruling houses really represent people in the horoscope?" Does the 4th house ruler really stand for the mother, for example? If planets represent people, this puzzle is fairly straightforward. "Planets as people" is a symbolic point worth looking into.

In astrology there is rarely a pure and clear picture of an event. Most often there are pointers in two or more directions, and it's up to the astrologer to choose the strongest pattern. In this puzzle planets in houses (either good or bad), and the planets they conjoin, overshadowed the more general placement of planets in natal signs, which clearly would affect all horoscopes over the life of the transits through signs.

Thus Mercury in a good house, its dispositor conjunct an exalted planet, and Saturn being weak by house with its dispositor combust pointed the way to solving the puzzle. Mercury (older brother) in its fall in Pisces, Saturn (younger brother) in a good sign, and Jupiter (older brother's dispositor) in its fall would have all pointed to the older brother's death rather than the younger brother's.

A former public school art teacher and professional therapist, Teresa Hamilton has degrees in psychology from UC Berkeley and San Francisco State University. She has studied and worked with astrology since 1965, first as a counselor using the Tropical zodiac, and later as a researcher and writer using the Sidereal zodiac and the astrological system of India. She has pub-lished articles in several journals in the United States, England and India, and is the current editor of the Vedic Voice *newsletter. Teresa is currently studying the parallels between Project Hindsight translations and the astrol-ogy of India. She is also preparing a book on the solar zodiac and the 27 Indian nakshatras. Contact the Institute for East-West Studies at 803 Rockfellow Drive, Mount Shasta, CA 96067. Phone/fax is (916) 926-4256. Or Eastwest @ showcrest.net or T.hamilton9 @ genie.geis.com.*

INTRODUCTION TO THE NAKSHATRAS

Dennis M. Harness, Ph.D.

To appreciate the depth and uniqueness of Vedic Astrology, one must encounter and explore the nakshatras. Nakshatra literally means "that which never decays." They reflect the primordial level of the zodiacal belt, which lies beneath the twelve basic signs. In comparison to the signs (or rasis as they are named in India), the nakshatras reveal the deeper, more profound effect of the constellations. While the rasis reflect a "mass or heap" of the twelve signs, the nakshatras further divide the constellations into 27 segments of equal length. Each nakshatra is 13° 20' in duration. Multiplying this length by 27 equals the entire zodiacal belt of 360°.

Each nakshatra has a rich mythology and powerful deities that reside within it. It is important to remember that "the basis of astrology is mythology." By exploring the myths and archetypes of the nakshatras, the constellations are brought to life. One of the best books on this subject is *Myths and Symbols of Vedic Astrology* by Bepin Behari. As Behari points out, "the Atharva and Yajur Vedas give complete lists of them (nakshatras) and associate them with the oldest Vedic gods." By befriending the particular god or goddess of a given nakshatra, archetypal healing becomes possible. As the great Swiss psychiatrist C.G. Jung once stated, we must "feed the gods."

The nakshatras represent the fields of activity or environment in which the creative powers of the planets can reveal their multi-faceted nature. They are called lunar mansions because the Moon "lives in" each of them for approximately one day. Each lunar mansion of 13° 20' length is further subdivided into four quarters of 3° 20' called padas (identical to a Navamsha division).

An ancient Vedic myth describes how the Moon god, Soma, was given 27 wives by the lord of creation, Prajapati. Each wife represented one of the lunar mansions which Soma, the Moon god, inhabited during his lunation cycle through the constellations.

Each nakshatra is associated not only with particular deities, but also with a specific planet which rules that asterism. It may fall completely within a particular sign or overlap between two signs. Thus, it is also influenced by the sign or rasi it resides within. Each nakshatra is male or female, as well as sattvic, rajasic or tamasic in nature. Sattva has a quality of spirituality, harmony, balance and purity. Rajas, which is dominant in human experience, signifies high-energy activity and somewhat "Type A" behavior. Finally, tamas has the basic quality of dullness, inertia, sloth and darkness. These are the three basic gunas in which life reflects according to the Vedas.

A specific animal species, sex, caste, temperament and primary motivation such as dharma (life purpose), artha (wealth), kama (fulfillment of desire) and moksha (enlightenment) is reflected through each nakshatra. Personality strengths and weaknesses are also correlated with the basic nature of each lunar mansion. Finally, a specific archetypal symbol is depicted for each asterism.

Because Vedic Astrology is a sidereal system, it is based on direct observation of the planets in the constellations. Thus when you observe the Moon at night near the fixed stars of Al Sharatain and Mesarthim, you know it resides in the first lunar mansion of Ashwini (0° to 13° 20' of Aries). In this respect the Vedic or sidereal viewpoint is more in line with an astronomer's picture of the cosmos than the season-based tropical zodiac many people use in the West

ARIES

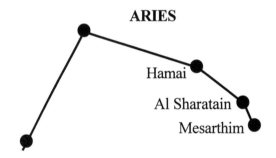

As an example of how Nakshatras are interpreted, let us focus on Ashwini. Note, however, that aspects made from other planets can greatly influence the quality of a planet in a particular nakshatra. The strength of the ruling planet of a nakshatra will also provide further insights into the nature of the planet residing there.

Ashwini (0 - 13° 20' Aries)

The first of the 27 lunar mansions is called Ashwini, which resides entirely within the sign of Aries the Ram, ruled by Mars. The nakshatra itself is ruled by Ketu, the South Node of the Moon. Thus, a Mars/Ketu mixture of energy is experienced by planets which inhabit it. Dynamism, tenacity, fierce activity and a thirst for life are reflected by this combination of forces. Activation of primordial energies with the awakening of consciousness is associated with this asterism.

The symbol of this nakshatra is a horse's head. It consists of three stars in the head of the Ram constellation. These fixed stars are Mesarthim, Al Sharatain and Hamal. These stars lie just a little north of the ecliptic. This lunar mansion is called "the star of transport." In her wonderful book, *The Circle of Stars*, Dr. Valerie Roebuck reveals that Ashwini also means "the horse-woman," "possessing horses," "yoking horses," and "she who yokes horses." Interestingly, famous horse lovers Prince Charles of England and Jackie Onassis have their natal Moons placed in this nakshatra. The power and stamina of the horse as well as its "headstrong" nature are found within this asterism. The grace and beauty of a horse in flight may also be witnessed through Ashwini.

A playful and childlike nature can also be experienced through Ashwini. A dauntless spirit that likes to explore new lands may be observed. As Bepin Behari writes, "If a rider is able to break and subdue a wild horse, he can use it to travel far." The love of just "horsing around" may also be present. For example, the famous comedian Jerry Lewis has his natal Moon in Ashwini.

The Sun is exalted in this nakshatra. There is therefore a thirst for leadership, authority and honor associated with Ashwini. The great Hindu deity Shiva is said to inhabit this lunar mansion. The primary motivation of this nakshatra is the principle of dharma or righteous deeds and activity. Law, duty, religion, and ethical conduct are all emphasized.

The myth of Ashwini is also connected with Surya, the Sun god in Hindu lore. The story goes that Surya was so brilliant and hot that no one could bear to be in his presence. To help him, his father divided him into twelve parts, each a Sun with its own universe. Bits of solar energy that were whittled away in this process provided the material used to create Shiva's trident, Skanda's spear and Vishnu's discus. The Sun in our own universe was then married to the daughter of Vishwakarma, the divine architect. Her name was Sanjna which means intellect. But due to the heat and intensity of even this division of the original Sun, she needed to spend time away from Surya even though, in a sense, his divine light represented her true nature.

During one of Sanjna's absences, she asked her housemaid, Chhaya, to take care of her husband. Interestingly, Chhaya translates to mean "shadow." Surya fell in love with Chhaya while his wife was away. When Sanjna returned, she found out about this betrayal and became so angry she turned herself into a mare and galloped away. Surya, realizing the grave mistake he had made, turned himself into a stallion and galloped after her. He finally caught up to her in a beautiful meadow and they made love, conceiving the Ashwin twins, the two horsemen. The Ashwins are pictured as divine, mystical doctors who ride in a golden chariot, bringing their healing energy down to the earth plane. They bring light, happiness and bliss to everyone they touch. They are known as the "physicians of the gods."

The Ashwins can be invoked to bring about healing and rejuvenation of the body, mind and spirit. They assist in childbirth and can restore youth to the old and even life to the dead. A Greek equivalent to the Ashwins is Asklepios, the father of healing in ancient times. Miracles are experienced within this nakshatra.

The shadow side of Ashwini is impulsiveness, aggression, a stubborn and arrogant nature. Adolf Hitler had his exalted natal Sun placed in Ashwini. Passion, lust and lack of discretion may be present if afflicted planets are placed in this nakshatra. Venus placed here may bring difficulties with sexuality. Dissatisfaction, disappointment, lack of mental quietude, and fear of criticism may appear if Saturn resides in this lunar mansion.

Ashwini at a Glance

Range: 0° - 13°30' Aries
Symbol: Horse's Head
Ruling Planet: Ketu
Nature: Deva (god/goddess)
Primary Motivation: Dharma
Animal Symbol: Male Horse
Direction: South
Sounds: Chu, Chey, Cho, La
Deities: Ashwini Kumars, Shiva, Surya

Ascendant in Ashwini

Graceful, handsome appearance
Brilliant eyes, magnetic look
Respected, prominent, modest
Wealthy, efficient
Controls diet

Famous People

Martin Luther King
Carlos Castenada
Robert F. Kennedy
Elvis Presley

Moon in Ashwini

Intelligent, bright mind
Attractive, beautiful appearance
Happy mood, gives hope to others
Healing gifts, nurtures others
Fond of music and the fine arts
Love of travel
Attracted to spiritual life
Believes strongly in God
Sincere love of family
Marriage usually occurs
   between the ages of 26 - 30
Struggles until 30th year,
   then progress occurs

Famous People

Prince Charles
Jackie Onassis
Jerry Lewis
Alfred Adler
Rick Tarnas
Aldous Huxley
Ingrid Bergman
Geena Davis
My wife Laura

Sun in Ashwini

Regal, proud nature
Excellent business skills
Aggressive, militant
Leadership, authority positions
Desire for power, fame

Famous People

Al Pacino
J.P. Morgan
Adolph Hitler
Charlie Chaplin
Shirley Maclaine

Ashwini Career Interests

Psychologists, therapists
Physicians, healers
Mystics
Military personnel
Police
Criminal courts
Merchants, salespeople
Musicians
Horse trainers, jockeys

Health Issues

Head injuries
Headaches
Mental Illness
Small Pox
Malaria

Dennis Harness,who holds a doctorate in Counseling Psychology, is Director of the Institute of Vedic Astrology in Sedona, Arizona as well as Vice President of the American Council of Vedic Astrology.   He is a full-time Vedic astrologer, a frequent lecturer, and is currently writing a book about the nakshatras.   Dennis can be contacted at P.O. Box 2149, Sedona, AZ 86339. Phone: (520) 282-6595.

MOKSHA: ESSENCE OF MIND AND HEART

Edith Hathaway

Moksha is spiritual liberation, and any inquiry into the nature of Moksha necessarily means an inquiry into the nature of birth and death. A deeper inquiry yields the reality that birth and death reside in the mind. And though the mind is our cognitive capacity, it is all too often weakened by a profoundly conditioned sense of self. Thus, the mind is the beginning and the end of all suffering. This truth is central to the Vedic teachings.

The 4th House in the Vedic chart is the first of three Moksha houses (i.e., the 4th, 8th and 12th). The 4th House is also the place where the soul discovers it is both embodied and disembodied, just as Brahman (the cosmic force) is both "the formed and the formless, the mortal and the immortal, the stationary and the moving, the actual and the yon" (Upanishads, II, iii.).

It is well-known that among the Moksha houses the 8th and 12th, and their karakas and house rulers, are capable of inflicting the greatest degree of earthly pain and loss. Through such pain and loss—the so-called "churning of the ocean"—Moksha comes. To varying degrees, this also depends on our willingness to see suffering as a friend and teacher, as well as the fruition or completion of the effects of past karma.

However, since the 4th House is the first Moksha house, it is both the beginning and ending of all suffering. The reason is that the 4th House also contains the seat of consciousness, of pure awareness, and of the workings of the mind—both the Absolute mind and the relative mind, also called Big mind and small mind in Buddhist thought. You may already know that from the 5th House we judge the level of intelligence and creative capacity.

Moon and Mercury

The 4th House has two karakas, or astrological significators, which are the Moon and Mercury. Along with the ruler of the 4th House we look to these planets as key indicators of the workings of the mind and heart. The mind should not be top-heavy with intellect (Mercury working overtime) nor awash in a sea of emotions (Moon working overtime in its role as conduit of the past). At the extreme, afflictions to the Moon and Mercury in the Vedic chart establish a potential for insanity.

In fact, when the Moon and Mercury aspect each other it impairs the ability to detach from over-influence of the conditioned mind. Mercury is debilitated in a water sign (Pisces), and it is generally thought to not do well in either Cancer or Scorpio (especially Cancer) or when in a mutual reception to the Moon. The pull of past conditioning and the conditioned mind (Moon) is too strong, and this weakens Mercury's ability to think and communicate clearly.

Mercury symbolizes the intellect and the nervous system, and is a planet of discrimination. The Moon is the planet of emotional connections, and it highlights the capacity for creating ease, peace and harmony within ourselves and with others. Even with severe problems in life, a well-placed Moon, indicating an ability to return to the Absolute nature, can create the necessary peace and serenity to overcome all obstacles.

As karakas of the Seat-of-Consciousness House, the Moon and Mercury might seem, at first, too fickle to carry such weight in the chart. After all, they are the planets that move at the greatest speed, especially the Moon, and they have the greatest reputation for changeability. But in Vedic astrology, mutability and the mutable signs are given the capacity for the greatest openness to change, and this is a quality which can lead to spiritual evolution.

The Myth of Soma and Tara

The Moon and Mercury are both carriers of consciousness, something all too often bogged down by the vicissitudes of daily life. In the Puranas, the mythical teachings of the Vedas, there is an important myth which unites the Moon and Mercury as parent and child respectively.

In this myth, the wisdom goddess Tara is married to Jupiter, a high priest and leader of ceremonies. They are unsuccessful in producing a child together. Eventually Tara is seduced by Soma (the Moon) who is a male in this story. Soma and Tara go off on a tryst, and their union produces a child called Mercury. Mercury becomes such a charming child, witty and endearing, that Jupiter is persuaded to take him and raise him as his own.

The wisdom of this teaching myth is that Jupiter's knowledge, though vast and precise, is too concerned with the correctness of the ceremony; it is not fertile enough to ignite the heart. Only the Moon (Soma) can give this to Tara, an important Hindu goddess in her own right. She is the power of sound and its current, the Divine Word. Her creative vibration underlies the energy of time, the Word being the consciousness of time.

Together, the Moon (Soma) and Tara produce a child who is capable of communicating between the kingdoms of the heart and the mind, thus bringing them together. Soma's humanness and humane compassion are the keys in this matter. He can help bring Tara's wisdom down to earth. Soma has the necessary nectar.

In the Shvetasavatara Upanishad (II: 6-7), there is another description of the dawning of the mind: "Where the fire (Agni) is enkindled, where the breath (Vayu) is controlled, where the nectar (Soma) overflows, there the Mind is born."

When two opposites unite, in this case Agni (fire) and Soma (water), an offspring is created: Vayu (wind or air), epitomized in the Puranic myth by Mercury. So we see how the cosmic male and female forces keep interchanging. Agni is fire, yet Shakti, a cosmic female force. Soma is water, yet Shiva, a cosmic male force. In maleness is contained femaleness, and vice versa.

In the Tantric teachings, which evolved from the Vedas, Mercury is an embodiment of Prana (breath or Vayu). Prana is Air, Life and Being. Tara brings the fire of her wisdom to the union which creates Prana (Mercury). Her fire represents Light and Consciousness. In Tantric literature fire is Tejas. Soma, the Moon, brings his water (Ojas, in the Tantras), and this is Love and Bliss.

The Tibetan Book of Living and Dying

Buddhism is a further outgrowth of the Vedic teachings. A major concept in *The Tibetan Book of Living and Dying* is that of Ground Luminosity and Path Luminosity, also called respectively Mother and Child Luminosities. There is a tremendous parallel to the moksha 4th House in the Vedic astrological chart. Also, remember that, among other things, the 4th House identifies the mother, the ground, and one's family foundation in life.

The Tibetan Book repeats the teaching that "life and death are in the mind itself." That Ground Luminosity consists of Clear Light: "this self-originated Clear Light, which from the very beginning was never born." It is "where consciousness itself dissolves into the all-encompassing space of truth." It is sound, color and light.

If Ground, or Mother Luminosity is the Absolute nature of mind that pervades our whole experience, then Path, or Child Luminosity is the key which will open us up to the total knowledge so that our Absolute nature can become our everyday reality.

Linking back to Moksha, and its development through the houses, Ground Luminosity can be seen as the 4th House and its karakas, while Path Luminosity can be seen as the 8th and 12th Houses. True to form as water houses, their rivers all flow into the same ocean. Similarly, in The Tibetan Book, Ground and Path Luminosities (Mother and Child Luminosities) are seen as merging together, that their union is, in a sense, the final fruition.

From these the Bardo (transition) teachings of The Tibetan Book comes the awareness that the most important qualities in life are love and knowledge, compassion and wisdom.

Thus, from the Vedic chart, how we evolve from and into our Absolute nature is the key to our soul's highest nature. How to reach that state of pure awareness is the subject of another discussion, but the Vedic literature always points to meditation and spiritual practices as leading to a Sattvic, or balanced and harmonious, way of life.

The heart is said to be beyond the physical organ of the body—both inside and outside, yet neither inside nor outside. The Vedas speak of consciousness alone as the heart of all being, and that only a mind freed from all conditioning can flow into pure consciousness. Knowledge of the Self as pure consciousness, merged with the infinite consciousness, frees us.

In closing, the Chandogya-Upanishads have this instruction for passing from darkness into light: "When the senses are purified, the heart is purified; when the heart is purified, there is constant and unceasing remembrance of the Self; when there is constant and unceasing remembrance of the Self, all bonds are loosed, and freedom is attained."

A full-time professional astrologer since 1980, Edith Hathaway has a national reputation as a consultant, writer, teacher and lecturer. She is currently one of a small group of practicing astrologers who are well grounded in the best predictive and delineation methods of both East and West. Her book, Navigating by the Stars, *was published by Llewellyn in 1991. She has a regular column,* The Vedic Connection, *in* The Mountain Astrologer *magazine. She is a certified Astro*Carto*Graphy interpreter, holds a certificate as Qualified Consulting Astrologer from the NCGR, and is a Qualified Teacher and Founding Member of the American Council of Vedic Astrology. Edith is also a 1996 recipient of the Jyotish Kovid title from the Indian Council of Astrological Sciences in Madras, India. Contact: P.O. Box 9609 in Santa, Fe, NM 87504. Phone: (505) 989-8465.*

THE UNIQUENESS OF EACH FIXED DEGREE

Richard Houck

Western astrologers who are interested in migrating to the stronger perspective of Vedic astrology sometimes feel as though they are wading through a lot of strange books of dubious usefulness and distinction. Doesn't it seem that for every 100 pages we read, we hope to find about 10 generically clear and useful ones? Sometimes this is a problem with the writer, but of course sometimes the problem is with the reader who is often struggling to adapt to significant differences in history, language, culture, learning styles, and so forth.

So it was with some delight that I ran across a little book by Manik C. Jain titled *The Stars and Your Future* published by Sagar Publications in New Delhi. In the US it can be easily ordered for about $5.00 from either of my favorite two specialty outlets (i.e., nothing but books from India): either Vinnie at *Nataraj Books* in Virginia (phone: 703-455-4996), or Deepak at *JDR Ventures* in Ohio (phone: 330-263-1308). *The Astrology Center of America* in California also carries it online with quite a good selection of Vedic astrology books (phone: 805-641-2157 or www.astroamerica.com).

The purpose of this article is to tell you what this little book is, and why I think it's worth your time. As part of my argument, I'll quickly cite about a dozen random cases of how it works. I'll then expand on one client case to show how it can be applied to enhance your analysis. Note that Mr. Jain was perfectly happy to subsume a range of materials that are not necessarily part of Vedic classical tradition at all—as long as the materials could be demonstrated to work. His link to Kozminski's work needs further explanation.

The Stars and Your Future is simply a series of brief commentaries (only about 3-4 sentences) on each degree of the sidereal zodiac. Now I have a fair number of tropical degree books, but I've found most of them to be too vague and "flowery." You can see in them what you want to see. And, of course, within one average lifetime all tropical placements will slip out of position by a full degree relative to the fixed stars. Since I am now anchored fundamentally in the sidereal zodiac, I've assumed it is commentary in the Western books that will slip out of position and not the Eastern books. Further, my experience suggests that this is so.

Like many other souls of marginal evolution, the first thing I do when I pick up a book like this is to look up myself! *"Moi,"* I whisper, "what about *moi?"* If its comments are flattering, I'm prepared to conclude that it is potentially accurate! Isn't that how it works? For my Sagittarius Lagna degree the book said many swell things, but it also added that "...he has uncommon knowledge which concerns the coming into and going out of earth conditions." Now the odd thing is that I didn't pick up this book until *after* my first book, titled *The Astrology of Death*, was in publication! So this seemed like quite an objective reference. James Butler, the main editor of that book, also has his Midheaven exactly on this degree.

I looked up my 7-Bindu 1st House Moon. Jain referred to this degree of Sagittarius as the "Degree of Eloquence." This is again objectively demonstrable (and not just through the reviews of my book, etc.). Exactly 30 years ago I was president of my college debating team and won a competitive divisional award as the outstanding speaker and debater on the Atlantic coast (the ACC Conference).

[As a parenthetical aside, both of these degrees are in Purva Ashadha. Hart deFouw, in his excellent new book, *Light on Life*, refers to this as the "undefeated" or "invincible" nakshatra. He writes, "when the Lagna or Moon appears in this nakshatra it often indicates a good debater." And here is a final twist: Venus rules my wife's 7th House, and her Venus is also in Purva Ashadha between my Lagna and Moon. Where did we meet over 30 years ago? On the college debating team!]

The prior paragraph might suggest that there is a link between the nakshatras' characteristics and Jain's commentary. But that is generally not true at all. Also, planets in fallen places will often receive quite constructive commentary; planets in exalted places will often get quite negative commentary. And Libra degrees can be quite war-like, etc. It just seems to depend upon the degree alone. By the way, from 0-1 is considered the 1st degree and from 29-30 is considered the 30th degree. Except where noted, all commentary in this article is based upon exact degree hits with no orb. But Jain suggests allowing just a tiny bit of slack since the sky is not always that digital.

I started looking up clients to see if the demonstrable objectivity of his comments held up (i.e., where no subjective judgment is required on anyone's part). Considering how brief his comments are, and their generic nature, nevertheless they typically did. Here are just a few random examples, and I'll give the data so you can check it yourself. In all cases, there is essentially no orb.

- Female (b. 9/21/56 @ 15:40 EDT 39N17 & 76W37). Sun is in 6th degree of Virgo in her 10th. In addition, she was in Sun Dasa from 1989-1995. During that entire time her occupation was selling perfume. Jain says: "He loves the beautiful in form and colour. Scents and perfumes fascinate him."

- Male (b. 10/14/48 @ 00:58 CST 35N28 & 97W31). Moon at 16th degree of Aquarius rules his 1st. He runs a conglomerate of enterprises in Texas primarily related to oil exploration. Jain says "this degree has something to do with gasoline, and vocationally it is connected with oil producing."

- Female (b. 11/23/55 @ 13:39 CST 46N53 & 96W47). Mercury and Saturn exactly conjunct at the 2nd degree of Scorpio in the 10th. She has a Ph.D. in an advanced area of chemistry and is very highly respected. Jain emphasizes the powers of concentration associated with this degree, then he adds, "vocationally this degree is often associated with chemists and scientists."

- Male (b. 8/6/57 @ 10:05 EDT 38N43 & 75W04). Virgo rises with its ruler Mercury in the 18th degree of Leo. He joined the Air Force during his Mercury Bhukti. Jain calls it the "aviator's degree." If he had not been thrown out of the Air Force for dangerous stunting, it probably would have been his career. Now he is a space consultant.

- Female (b. 12/31/46 @ Noon CST 44N59 & 03W16). Lagna at 19th degree of Pisces. She is a trained motivational speaker. Jain says the 20th degree "gives pleasure to many and will meet with great applause." Note that 1996 Academy Award winner Nicholas Cage has Sagittarius rising and Jupiter at this exact same degree. Indeed, he won the Best Actor award during his Jupiter Dasa.

- Female (b. 12/19/62 @ 14:25 PST 34N01 & 118W29). Moon is in the house of work and health at the 16th degree of Virgo. Jain says, "with regard to health, it is connected with the back, and a slight curvature may develop." She is a very successful chiropractor.

- Boy (b. 01/13/77 @ 4:27 CST 29N46 & 95W22). Saturn is in his 9th of the father, at the 22nd degree of Cancer. He found his father hanged (suicide) in their basement. Jain calls this the "degree of extinction... (and one who) goes down to a watery grave." This is one degree away from Marilyn Monroe's Lagna; it is said that she also committed suicide. Further I had another client with Jupiter exactly on this degree (in his 2nd and allegedly "exalted") who nevertheless has been subjected to a life of many bankruptcies with little other suggestion of this in his natal chart. He also persistently claims to have had no good luck in his entire life.

- Client in prison (b. 4/1/58 @ 7:19 EST 42N59 & 70W57). Arrested/convicted for illegal drug production during Moon Dasa (Moon is 3 degrees from Pluto, and he was arrested in California exactly on his Pluto/Descendant line). The Moon degree is 11th of Leo. Jain says, "the time may come when he will be forced to pause... (and) he risks being the inducer of his own dangers." I've noticed that this chronically shows up as really quite a weird degree. The strange stories I have on this degree...

- Male (b. 4/21/63 @ 11:57 EST 39N45 & 07W33). Was once in a truck cab dangling over the side of the bridge above a river. Another time a bullet went completely through his neck. There is more. It's true that Mars is one degree from his Asc and the Sun is one degree from his MC. But his MC is at the 7th degree of Aries. Symbol: "A man saving himself from falling into a deep cavern by clutching a wild rose tree with thorns." Jain says, "this is the degree of life and death accidents." Also review this chart to see why he was *completely unhurt* in all these cases (The bullet did not touch his windpipe, an artery, a muscle nor a nerve). Should have been a stunt man.

- Female (b. 6/3/39 @ 15:57 -8ST 31N14 & 121E28). At age 52 she sold her successful jewelry business in a very elegant location, and at age 54 moved to the mountains to join an ashram where she is to this day. The 13th degree of Libra rises. Jain calls this the Degree of Abdication. Jain's symbol: "A woman in a dark blue costume entering a convent door, her head erect and her arms raised." Jain says, "She will be blessed with worldly gifts, but will in the midway of his life know how weak worldly wealth is and how important to satisfy the craving of the spirit." By the way, her MC is on the 17th degree of Cancer, and for this Jain says, "she will accumulate by or through merchandise of universal demand."

Jain calls President Bill Clinton's Lagna the Degree of Tribulation whose symbol is a "large black cloud around which are bright silver lights." He writes, "...denotes one who will endure much sorrow and strange suffering. He is well and strangely gifted, and will leave his mark on the world. He should be cautious in his choice of companions and should beware of allurements. If Neptune is there [*Editor's Note: Neptune is there, one degree away by longitude and within only a few minutes by declination.*] it will be the degree of a player on the stage." Clinton's Midheaven is the Degree of Deceit, "rushing from place to place and denies the ability to make up his mind." (Perhaps by "deceit" Jain more generically means "politics?")

For billionaire Ross Perot's Lagna, the symbol is "a blind giant in full armour hitting out wildly with a huge battle axe at nothing. Denotes one who overestimates his power and who rushes into quarrels from which no good can be obtained. After trouble and waste of energy he may find to his chagrin that he has gained nothing by his adventures but the reward of folly. The motive power for this proud and ambitious native is the money chest."

I could go on and on. Tonya Harding's Moon/Saturn conjunction is on an "enmity and competition" degree. I have a friend who is a nationally recognized psychic; his Moon is exactly on 11-Sagittarius which Jain says, "denoted a psychic of ability and reputation." I have a professional composer client whose Jupiter, as ruler of his 1st and 10th, is at 18-Aquarius. Jain says this degree "gains recognition in music." See Hitler's Libra Lagna degree. Jain says, "attains influence and power through aggression, force and fighting... endures a wound for the glory of getting it... artistic, but with a powerful disposition." You may know that Hitler did paint, and he wrote one of the best selling books in history.

As usual, to process these indications, everything else must be woven in. For instance, a difficult pattern that is sitting on a very good degree is greatly offset. As an example, I have a client whose Moon is exactly conjunct Saturn and in a very tight square to Pluto. Sounds really rough, no? But the Moon is on an excellent degree. He is an M.D. and lawyer with high political connections. He is of a powerful, industrious and very fine character. Conversely, another client has a "good" chart but it's sitting on a whole series of bad degrees. She is very successful but in a very materialistic way. So you can start to see how all this might work out.

I'll close with a more detailed look at a client case (used with permission) to show how this information might be more usefully applied. The client is a full professor born 10/8/43 @ 5:18 EDT 42N38 & 83W17. She had surgery for an acoustic neuroma on 3/13/96 (benign brain tumor) after several years of gradual hearing loss. Surgery necessitated severing the nerve for hearing and balance on the right side. The right side of her face is now paralyzed although the nerve may regenerate. She must keep her right eye lubricated and can't see well out of it. A spinal leak developed requiring a second operation on 4/4/96. Now they want to do another procedure to put a weight on her eyelid. Naturally she is balking at this.

What's happening here? She has Leo rising so is ruled by the Sun. Further, we are told that the eyes are generally ruled by the Sun (although sometimes we read that the Sun rules one eye and the Moon rules the other), so we look up the degree of her Sun. It's between the 21st and 22nd degree of Virgo. Jain says that both of these degrees have to do with "visual defects, eye injuries, blindness, or at least defective vision." Her Sun is also weakened by being in the same house with Neptune. There was an eclipse exactly opposite her Sun right before the first surgery, and the second surgery was on the exact day of another eclipse (!) again exactly conjunct her natal Sun on this terrible degree. This is quite incredible.

Her natal Sun has only 2 bindus (of a possible 8) in a sign with only 21 (vs. an average of 28). This is her 2nd House, and transiting Saturn was in her 8th during this period fully aspecting the 2nd. She was also in a Saturn Dasa and Bhukti. And note that Saturn was basically stationary at birth, so very strong. Notice how this started as a nerve (Mercury) problem, and her stopped Saturn is exactly 90 degrees from her natal Mercury. Where is Mercury? - also in the 2nd house with the Sun and Neptune. And they want to put a weight (Saturn) on her eyelid!

Many things confirmed the Sun as the focal point, but Jain put the icing on the cake by confirming that it would be as bad as it is, and that all these hits would relate to the eyes. So now we can give her some detailed timing concerning the Sun (for example, transiting Saturn had not even exactly opposed it yet!) including Western progression methods. We can assure her that when transiting Saturn gets out of her 8th House that things will improve for sure. We can suggest remedies to strengthen the Sun. We can suggest locations for recuperation (unfortunately, where she lives further aggravates the strength of Saturn on the Sun). We can define the strongest possible recuperation cycles for any further necessary surgery, and so forth.

I have industrialist clients in Hong Kong who tell me that Chinese astrologers rectify birth times based upon exact degrees (relative to what has already manifested in the client's life). Maybe we should give this some closer modern research. For example, I have two clients who are both very successful, highly compensated marketing VP's. One has her Lagna at 10-Taurus, and the other has his Midheaven at 10-Taurus. Jain refers to this 11th degree as having to do with "the unity of human aims," so you can see how this might be modernized as a marketing/ advertising degree. People with strong placements at 10-Taurus want to make us all drink Miller Lite!

Well, I hope I've made a potential believer out of you. And I hope Mr. Jain's publisher proposes just the tiniest kickback on every future book that he sells. After all, profit is just a matter of *degree*!

Richard Houck was the sole sponsor of the largest Hindu Astrology Conference ever held on the East coast of the US. To leverage off his extensive prior business background, Rick's focus is upon optimizing the practical timing requirements of corporate, political and professional clients (guaranteeing political elections, business ventures, litigation support, marketing programs, employment/staffing, medical research, augmentation of therapies, etc.). His astrological work has been featured in investment magazines, on radio, cable and a prime time network TV special, twice on the cover of what Paul Harvey has called "the world's most exclusive magazine," and more. His newsletter ("The Clock") is available only to retainer clients. He has an excellent public forecasting record that has been meticulously documented. He publishes a Special Sidereal Ephemeris, *and his first book,* The Astrology of Death, *received many constructive reviews, including from the traditional medical community. His next book will be titled* Digital Astrology. *Write: P.O. Box 8925 Gaithersburg, MD 20898. Phone/fax: 301-353-0212. E-mail: RichardHouck@worldnet.att.net.*

KALA SARPA YOGA: CAUGHT IN THE KARMIC AXIS

Linda Johnsen

The much dreaded Kala Sarpa Yoga reveals a soul trapped within the karmic axis. This sobering planetary configuration is generally understood to occur when all the classic planets (sidereal Sun through Saturn) fall between the Moon's nodes. It signals a lifetime of more than usual karmic significance, a "make or break" life in the cycle of a soul's incarnations.

Kala Sarpa Yoga ("the Serpent of Time") is considered highly inauspicious. It is sometimes associated with physical or moral deformity, severe difficulties, reversals of fortune, and betrayal. Perhaps its most common association is with a sudden quick rise in life, followed by a disastrous fall. When the planets lie between Rahu and Ketu, great material success followed by a precipitous downfall may be indicated. When the planets fall between Ketu and Rahu, a serious spiritual crisis is possible.

Probably the most spectacular recent example of a Kala Sarpa Yoga in action is Donald Trump (June 14, 1946 at 9:51 a.m. EDT in Queens, NY*). This yoga was fully activated in Trump's chart because he was born so near a lunar eclipse, the nodes palpably signaling their power. In Trump's natal chart Rahu lies a bare two degrees from his Sun, and Ketu a scant fraction of a degree from his Moon which is fallen in the inauspicious nakshatra of Jyestha.

As Trump entered his Sun Dasa (major planetary cycle) in mid-1976, he began his meteoric rise in the real estate business. Note that his natal Sun/Rahu lie in the 11th house of gains and profits. By the middle of his Moon Dasa he was a self-made billionaire, as well as a world-renowned celebrity. However, the Kala Sarpa Yoga played itself out by the conclusion of the Moon cycle in July 1992. By that time Trump's vast financial empire had collapsed, leaving him $900,000,000 in debt. Debilitated Moon/Ketu in the 5th house of financial speculation gave major losses and terrible mental anguish.

In October 1989, just as Trump entered the Ketu Bhukti (planetary sub-cycle) of his Moon Dasa, three of his top executives were killed in a helicopter crash. Trump himself had originally been scheduled to be on that flight. The shock of this brush with death precipitated Trump's break with his wife Ivana a few months later, as he struggled with deep depression and reevaluated his course in life. Never under-estimate the impact of powerfully placed nodes!

What do you say to a client when you see this configuration in his or her chart? First, before you sound the alarm, remember to read the yoga against the chart as a whole. In my personal collection of several thousand Vedic charts, Kala Sarpa Yogas, while not common, are also not rare. In some charts the yoga stands out, in others it is nearly subsumed by more prominent astrological factors. It takes one second of analysis to determine that the Kala Sarpa Yoga is the defining configuration in Donald Trump's chart. In another horoscope, however, this yoga may play out far more subtly.

Secondly, never, ever frighten your client. When clients consult you, even if their attitude seems nonchalant, a part of their subconscious is relating to you as an oracle, a voice through which the cosmos itself is speaking to them. It sometimes horrifies me how vividly many people recall a negative remark an astrologer thoughtlessly made to them years previously. As Vedic astrologers we are literally karmic counselors. Our job is to help direct our clients to the most auspicious fulfillment of their destinies possible through their dedicated and inspired self effort, not to a sense of fatalism and futility.

When you note a powerfully activated Kala Sarpa Yoga in an individual's chart, advise them that, from a Vedic perspective, they are living out a particularly pivotal lifetime in which they may be given the opportunity, perhaps more clearly than their peers, to move forward in their karmic development. Immense blessing can result if they are willing to allow the nodal axis to propel them to a higher state of awareness, much like an electron being hurled into a higher "orbit" around an atom. Because this is a special incarnation, it is especially important that they conduct their affairs with the highest ethical standards, as well as with humor, detachment and common sense.

Mention the positive qualities associated with this yoga, such as the increased capacity for concentration and hard work which can lead to exceptional success in their fields. Then direct them to look beyond material success for personal fulfillment, explaining that it is important to keep life events in a wider perspective. Because an extraordinary opportunity for spiritual growth is being presented, they need to look at their successes and failures not just as personal challenges, but as important lessons for the soul. Look to the houses along which the nodal axis lies to delineate how this spiritual opportunity is most likely to unfold.

If your client is currently suffering the rude effects of Kala Sarpa Yoga, help them place these events into a spiritual evolutionary context. In terms of remedial measures, mantras to Rahu and Ketu can be prescribed, as well as appropriate planetary pujas (rituals). I have seen astonishingly positive results from pujas when each of the following conditions are met: (1) the pujari conducting the ritual is both technically competent and mentally pure, (2) the client is spiritually receptive to the ritual transmission, and (3) the client is willing to change the self-destructive patterns that are precipitating the current problem. When the third condition is missing, the ritual may cause a dramatic breakthrough, but after several weeks the unsatisfactory situation returns. The puja provides the breakthrough, but the individual must provide the follow through.

As for the Kala Sarpa Yoga in my own natal chart, I treat it with respect, endeavoring to conduct my affairs with some degree of self awareness, chanting my mantra, and reminding myself not to take anything in life, including Kala Sarpa Yoga, too seriously.

* Data Source: *Data News*, April and June 1992, "reliable personal source," per Lois Rodden.

Linda Johnsen's book, Daughters of the Goddess: The Women Saints of India, *received the publishing industry's 1995 Midwest Book Achievement award for "Best New Age Book of the Year." Her many articles on Vedic Astrology have appeared in* Yoga Journal, The Mountain Astrologer, *and* Yoga International. *Linda is a Board Member of the American Council of Vedic Astrology. Contact: 522 Joaquin Drive, Sonoma, CA 95476-5953. Phone: (707) 939-1787.*

INTRODUCTION TO THE KRISHNAMURTI SYSTEM

Sat Siri Khalsa

What is the "Krishnamurti Paddhati," i.e., system, and why should anyone care about it—especially astrologers coming from a Western background, curious about reports of fabulous treasure awaiting trusty diggers into the dusty lore of the Vedas, but soon daunted by the vast task of finding a foothold in this particular infinite ocean? Why take on one more interpretive system in a sea of fathomless study already so awash in cross-currents of alternative methodologies?

To feel truly comfortable with Jyotish, you already have to know about ash-takavarga, shadbala, Vimshottari Dasas, Chara Dasas, Yogini Dasas, Parasari aspects, yogas, the equal house system, the Sripati house system, avasthas, vargas, and so much more. Why also learn about nakshatra lords, sub-lords and "ruling planets?" And why, after you have simplified at least one area, i.e., having thrown overboard the baggage of the various Western house systems with all their complications and controversies, and having begun to enjoy the bold reduction of the classical Jyotish practice wherein one sign equals one house, not counting where the sign begins or ends, why go back to the most common "Western" house system, known as the Placidus system, with its troublesome irregular cusps? Indeed why... well, maybe we should just put this Krishnamurti system, this KP, on the shelf and get on with memorizing some more yogas, eh?

The fact is that the KP system, sometimes referred to by its enthusiasts as "advanced stellar astrology," works. The answer is always there, the only question being our ability to discern it. And so this method boosts astrology's reputation for doing what it has, since the beginning of history, been meant to do, its adherents have longed for it to do, its detractors have ever debunked its ability to do, as the so-called scientific method, originally invented by astrologers, has forged ahead in specialized directions fortified by heavy encasings of materialistic prejudice. Mystics also have demeaned the full promise of this "science of light," with talk of tendencies and vague influences and possibilities that mask their cloud of unknowing.

Ketu 18:00	Saturn 20:14 Jupiter 20:45		
			Lagna 15:16
Moon 01:18	JOHN LENNON (rectified)		Venus 09:22
		Mercury 14:34	Mars 09:10 Rahu 18:00 Sun 22:31

People have also feared Professor K.S. Krishnamurti's sometimes harsh declarations that accurate predictions can always be found in properly drawn charts, whether natal or prasnas (known as "horary" charts in the West). People have found it morally incumbent to alight on one side of the "fate versus free will" debate, a never-ending game of duality that is as meaningless as trying to declaim that light is either a wave or a particle (or that light is superior to dark)—one only and not the other. But people could not disregard the evidence of Krishnamurti's record of amazing pinpoint predictions of events from moments to years in the future, and so his circle of students has grown, and their ability to make pinpoint predictions is attested to in ever-growing numbers of documented case studies.

In fact, the Krishnamurti system doesn't introduce anything not able to be found somewhere in the astrological classics, but the system pulls together scattered elements and organizes interpretation in a user-friendly hierarchy that simulates the greater leverage that highly detailed logic does (as, for example, in computer programming or in working up living organisms from the four DNA components C/G/A/T).

For purposes of this very brief overview, I can just highlight two of three broad areas of concern in KP and give a schematic outline of a third. The three areas are 1) assigning significators in a hierarchical way to the houses of a chart; 2) determining the effects of a house by a study of the house cusp's sub-lord; and 3) using the ruling planets, at the time of judging a natal or prasna chart, to rank the significators and exactly time the event being considered.

In assigning significators to the houses (a more technical term for houses is "bhavas") KP uses a hierarchy that takes into account the familiar Sun signs, as well as the 27 lunar mansions or nakshatras, that ancient system of division which forms the basis of the Dasa cycles, which many Westerners, upon first encountering Jyotish, immediately recognize as a profound advancement over the tools currently known to them through Western astrology.

Using a rectified chart of John Lennon as the example chart, I'll now begin to explain how this hierarchy works. The comments that follow are based upon a chart of: 9-Oct-1940 at 00:59:32 a.m. in Liverpool, England.

The lowest level of the hierarchy is the sign ruler. Lennon's 1st Bhava starts in Cancer. The ruler of Cancer's sign ("rashi") is the Moon. (Notice how Lennon's early bowl-shaped haircut, later his perfectly round granny glasses, his pale visage, and his famous song-statement "Imagine" all exhibit the lunar qualities of a Cancer ascendant aspected by its lord the Moon.)

The next level up the hierarchy is planets that occupy a nakshatra ruled by the sign ruler. All nine planets used in Jyotish (the seven traditional planets plus the two nodes, Rahu and Kethu) rule the 27 nakshatras, each planet controlling three nakshatras. See related discussions elsewhere in this anthology. John Lennon's 1st Bhava is ruled by the Moon. The Sun occupies the nakshatra Hastha, ruled by the Moon. Rahu occupies Hastha also. So the Sun and Rahu become stronger significators of Lennon's 1st House than the Moon. The Sun, lord of Lennon's 2nd House (of speech containing Venus, karaka of music) is conjunct Rahu, the hypnotic worldly serpentine force of the subconscious, made him a glittering icon of mass culture.

The third level, in the order of the increasing strength of significators, is the occupant of a Bhava. Jupiter and Saturn occupy Lennon's 10th Bhava. Being in the 10th, they describe the depth and dimension of his career. "As the only Beatle to have...acquired a serious taste for things avant-garde, Lennon reacted to the group's astonishing commercial success with a bitter sarcasm that created considerable tension between him and the others," comments popular music historian Martha Bayles in her book Hole in Our Soul: The Loss of Beauty and Meaning in American Popular Music. This sophisticated sensibility goes with the Jupiter and the bitter sarcasm with the debilitated Saturn.

The fourth, and highest, level of strength for Bhava significators is that of the planets which belong to the nakshatras owned by the Bhava occupant. Lennon's 2nd House is occupied by Venus. Jupiter is in the nakshatra Bharani, which is ruled by Venus. Therefore Jupiter becomes a stronger significator than Venus of the 2nd Bhava. Jupiter in Aries, the leading-edge sensibility that informed Lennon's career actions, expressed itself in the form of music (Venus, karaka of music, located in the 2nd House of speech).

Another meaning for these planets was also fully expressed by the piling up of Jupiter (karaka of wealth) in a nakshatra of Venus (karaka of money) in the 2nd House of income. Still another meaning was expressed as the 2nd House (of foods) became an avenue of escape (Jupiter and debilitated Saturn in the nakshatra of Venus) via illegal drug abuse.

In Jyotish all the meanings come through; one doesn't repress the other. How else to account for Yoko, John's second wife, also shown by the 2nd Bhava in the horoscope? (This usage, still unfamiliar to Western astrologers, takes its logic from the fact that, in the event of death or divorce of the first spouse, we shift eight houses away from the 7th House of marriage, eight being the number of discontinuity, break, death and resurrection, thus bringing us to the 2nd House for the second spouse. Note also that the 2nd House is generally also the house of the kinship circle, those in our immediate family and in solidarity with us.)

Yoko again compresses the meeting-of-the-extremes symbolism of the Jupiter-Saturn conjunction working through the 2nd House Venus (karaka for wife): a relatively untalented "perverse modernist" acting out, Bayles suggests, "every musician's nightmare: the star's tone-deaf girlfriend getting up to sing with the band." Bayles gives some hilarious examples of the effect of Yoko's absurdist style on Lennon's rock and roll roots. And, as Bayles goes on to point out, the Saturnian perversity Lennon's second wife displayed in her art was the precursor of a whole new generation of crude and clangorous modernist rock that would practically drown out the Jupiterian purity of the original rock and roll which Lennon loved.

So far we've seen some examples of how the significators pile up to weave the meaning ever thicker in each Bhava. The next major area in which the Krishnamurti system brings out unique insights concerns the timing of life events or a horary question. For this we use cuspal sub-lords and ruling planets. Our limited format only permits us to touch on a subject on which many books should be written. Very briefly: The point shown as the cusp of each Bhava, reckoned as in the Placidus house system (the arguments for which is an article for another day) is assigned a starlord, i.e., its nakshatra ruler, and a sub-lord. Subs are the next level down in the fractional division of the zodiac into nakshatras.

This fractional division is already exemplified in the standard Dasa system, where the larger Dasa cycles are mirrored in smaller Bhukti cycles and even smaller antara cycles. The sub or sub-sub cycle is a circle within a circle identical to the larger except in its length. Krishnamurti divided each nakshatra into 9 sub-cycles following the order of the Dasa system, and he found that these subs have unique power to indicate the timing of events.

Take as an example the assassination of John Lennon. Longevity is shown by the first house cuspal sub-lord. Lennon's 1st House sub-lord is Jupiter. To the extent that sub-lords symbolize a long or short life this will ultimately reflect in the actual length or life. The three main houses of short life are the 2nd and 7th Houses, known as marakas or death inflictors, plus a third house known as the bhadaka (or trouble-causing) which varies according to the type of rising sign.

For Lennon the bhadaka House is his 11th. Lennon's Jupiter signifies his 2nd House, as we have seen, and also his 11th because its nakshatra lord is the 11th House ruler. Jupiter closely joins Saturn, the sole significator of the 7th House, so all three houses which Jupiter signifies are houses of short long evity.

The ruling planets play in here as well. Ruling planets, which hold some of the most amazing secrets of the Krishnamurti theories, are the planets of power which preside over every chart (natal, event or question). They are the sign and nakshatra lord of the Ascendant, the sign and nakshatra lord of the Moon, and the lord of the day of the week. Every event that occurs is in an intricate implicate relationship with the ruling planets. Major events in life will occur when the current Dasa and Bhukti cycles coincide with ruling planets at birth. The sub-lord of the 1st House is always a ruling planet and will always be activated at the time of death. Thus Lennon's four levels of Dasa at the time he was murdered were Jupiter/Jupiter/Venus/Jupiter. The cuspal sub-lord indicator of a short life was realized tragically in the Dasa of Jupiter.

Sat Siri Khalsa is a long time student of Yogi Bhajan and a practitioner of the Way of the Sikhs. She began with Western methods but now concentrates exclusively on Jyotish specializing in the Krishnamurti system. Sat Siri, a Harvard graduate, has over 20 years of experience teaching astrology. Contact: P.O. Box 486 Santa Cruz, NM 87567. Phone: 505-753-6521 or fax: 505-753-7898.

CAUTIONS ABOUT THE USE OF GEMSTONES

Alfred & Dawn King

How can it be that a tiny gem might affect you for good or ill? Our understanding must begin with a consideration of the very root of creation. Scientists and seers alike tell us that all we know of creation came from the same source. Scientists call that instant of creation the "Big Bang."

For a microsecond of time the same material that forms the very atoms of your body, the core of our earth, the other known planets, the Sun and the myriad other parts of creation, all existed as a single first "cell" which instantly exploded, divided and eventually became everything we consciously know, and don't know, in existence. We are truly star born and, indeed, related in a mystical, as well as a very physical way, to the stars and planets.

The invention of the radio began as a quartz crystal wired to an amplifier. Such a simple device can render vibrations in our atmosphere as audible. But how many more types of vibrations are received by crystals across the broad-band electro-magnetic spectrum? And are different types of crystals not attuned to different types of vibrations?

Operating like the first crystal radios, gems tune in the music of the planetary spheres. When we wear a gem it brings us greater attunement with unseen sources. The seers of antiquity knew the relationship of gems to planets: ruby and red spinel crystals for the Sun, blue sapphire crystals for Saturn. Emerald was known as a messenger of Mercury's mental acuity, and so on.

A planetary ruler of each week day was recognized. Various parts of the body and even the hand are ruled by particular planets. Thus palmistry began and appropriate fingers were designated for particular planetary gem materials. Ancient teachings specify gem clarity, shades of color, complimentary metals and more. From the earliest times, gems were revered, and enhanced as well as imitated by both craftsmen and con men. Gems altered by high heat, modern radiation, dyes and fracture filling are to be avoided for astrological use, as are all synthetics. This has many practical reasons as well as preserving the natural integrity and power of the materials.

Today we are rediscovering this wonderful wisdom through Jyotish. An astrologer may observe the client's need for improved relationships and suggest a gem for propitiating Venus or, for easing emotional turbulence, a gem to soothe an afflicted Moon. However, sometimes a gem improves one area in the native's life, only to harm another.

We have gathered numerous accounts of the benefits of wearing properly prescribed gems. Occasionally we are told a story that is remarkably illustrative of the opposite case: ill effects from wearing the wrong gem.

An example is our friend David, who wanted to further his career. His astrologer recommended a gem for Mercury. As he began to wear his new green tourmaline ring, David felt empowered to speak up for himself. He asked his boss for a raise. The raise was granted. The cost of his new ring was quickly recovered. It seemed the gem was just what he needed, but within a few weeks David began having kidney problems. As soon as he took off the tourmaline ring, his kidneys recovered.

Blue sapphire is a powerful gem material. It focuses the vibrations of Saturn, including discipline, restrictions, responsibility and longevity. We recommend that clients try out Saturn gems before committing themselves to a purchase. Any gem can be taped to the body with medical tape, placed in the pillow case at night, held while meditating, or worn in a pouch or secure pocket. However, with blue sapphire, if ill effects will be experienced they usually happen so soon that most of these trials aren't required.

If you decide to experience blue sapphire's effects, but your astrology chart is indicating Saturn should be left well enough alone, the following may happen: You hold the gem for five minutes and find yourself getting a headache. You put the gem in your pillow case and have nightmares. You wear the gem on your person and find you feel depressed for no apparent reason.

With Saturn and Rahu in her natal 12th House (Gemini), during Rahu Dasa/Saturn Bhukti, Dawn was stressed. She decided it might help to honor Saturn by wearing an amethyst bracelet. (Amethyst is an alternate material for Saturn.)   After 30 minutes her arm began to ache. She suddenly realized it was the bracelet. Dawn attempted to open the clasp but found it was stuck.   She couldn't get the bracelet off.   In her mind horrible images formed of   drastic measures being needed to remove the painful shackle.   Panic (Rahu) was taking over when Al came to the rescue and wrenched the clasp open.   A word to the wise.

Mars has a wonderful, hot driving energy that can motivate one to action or anger.   It can also alleviate anemia.   If red coral is worn by someone who is already a "hot head" — look out! It can cause overwhelming impatience, accidents and injuries.

Want to be overly generous, optimistic and expansive—or overweight? Wear yellow sapphire or topaz when your natal Jupiter is already extremely powerful.   Few of us have this problem, but we know several people for whom Jupiter gems would be disastrous.

A gem for the Moon (pearl or moonstone) is very frequently prescribed. When inappropriate a Moon gem can cause water retention, congestion or excessive emotional attachment.   Too much desire for sensual pleasures and opulence can be a negative effect of diamond or white sapphire. Venus should not be strengthened with these gems in such a case.

Gomeda is boon or bane.   Worn for Rahu, it can be soothing, or it can increase materialistic desires and tendencies.   Cat's Eye Chrysoberyl, which is worn for Ketu, has been reputed to cause bleeding, fever, headaches and eye pain when wrongly worn, although it also has been credited with bringing wealth and spiritual insight.

Indian lore has many stories of Ruby causing heart trouble, fever or bleeding.   The Sun is important to our self-esteem, or impact in the world, and our health.   But enhancing Sun can also cause an over-inflated ego or excess ambition.

It's also important to realize that when a gem is recommended for a particular Dasa, it should not be worn indiscriminately forevermore. In the end the key is balance in prescribing and wearing gems. Maybe for a short-term career boost one can risk kidney problems, but ultimately the right gem for the right planet, and for the right period of time, is critical.

Al & Dawn King have been giving presentations on gems and filling the astrological gem prescriptions of Vedic astrologers since 1989. They are co-authors of Secrets of Gems for Love, Health and Prosperity—Jyotish, Ayurveda and Vedic Lore In Action Today. *Dawn is also author of* Did Your Jeweler Tell You? *— an insider's guide to facts you need to know about your jewelry and its care. King Enterprises is at 1305 North H Street (A-289) Lompoc, CA 93436 Phone: 805-693-0911.*

SEVEN TIPS FOR USING VARSHAPHAL
(THE PROGRESSED ANNUAL HOROSCOPE)

ROY KIRKLAND

Of the many techniques available to the student of Jyotish, one of the most useful, yet often ignored, is the Varshaphal, or annual horoscope. This annual chart can greatly aid in the analysis of Natal horoscopes. The indications are usually very clear if one follows Tajika Padhatti, a set of North Indian techniques that give good results in prashna ("horary") horoscopes as well.

Two excellent books by Dr. B. V. Raman *(Varshaphal,* published by IBH Prakashana) and Dr. K. S. Charak *(A Textbook of Varshaphala,* published by Bharatiya Prachya Evam Sanatan Vigyan Sansthan) explain the calculation of Varshaphal in full. Additionally, I can tell you from personal experience that correct predictions can be achieved only by following the method of Dhruvakana (this refers to the rate of progression of the annual chart, and it approximates the Sidereal year). Note that, unlike western solar returns, all charts are based upon the birth place including Varshaphal.

TIP #1: After calculating the chart, you should make an assessment of the strength of the planets. Our texts show how to determine the balas used in Tajika, but it is more efficient to "eyeball" the strength of the planets and not get too involved in the details.

Look at the planet's sign position in Rasi and Navamsa. See how far (in either direction) they are from the exaltation position. They lose about one "point" per sign, i.e., Moon in Libra is stronger than Moon in Scorpio.

Look for the Dasa lord. It will tend to give more pronounced effects (than other planets) according to its karakatwa (defined as that which a planet represents) and according to its temporary benefic or malefic nature in the Varshaphal.

Look at the planets' house position in the Varsha chart. Those in Kendras are stronger. Any planet conjunct or opposite within 2-3 degrees to a planet in the Natal chart will have pronounced effects during the year.

	Moon 27:12	Rahu 25:05 R	
	CHART 1 BILL CLINTON Natal		Saturn 09:00 Mercury 14:30
			Sun 02:54
	Ketu 25:05 R	Jupiter 00:07	Lagn 12:23 Mars 13:15 Venus 18:01

	Moon 09:12	Mars 21:49	Ketu 05:04 R
	CHART 2 BILL CLINTON Varshaphal		Lagna 10:10 Mercury 14:36
Saturn 20:29 R			Sun 02:54 Venus 21:11 Jupiter 25:05
Rahu 05:04 R			

At this time, let's look briefly at two charts that can show some of these principles: the 1992 Varshaphal and the Birth chart of current U.S. President Bill Clinton. We can see that the Moon, Venus, Mercury and Saturn all have some strength in the annual chart. The Sun is strong naturally, being exalted in the Navamsa, and well placed in the 2nd House of the Varshaphal chart. Venus has its own sign in the Varsha-Navamsa, but it does not hold angular position in the Varsha itself.   Saturn is Swakshetra and angular in Varsha, and angular in 10th in Varsha-Navamsa. The others gain strength from Kendra Bala.

TIP #2: The Moon is never Vareshwara (Lord of the Year) unless none of the other planets qualify. Even if it has little strength, the planet with the closest "aspect" (by this we mean the Tajika aspects which, like Western aspects, are measured as angular separations of the following degrees: 0, 60, 90, 120, 150 and 180—see tip #3 below) to the Varsa Lagna is the Year Lord. The stronger the Vareshwara, the better its results.   In this chart, Mercury, his natal Ascendant Lord, is Lord of the Year.

TIP #3: The main Tajika yogas are similar to western aspects, counted by angular separation. They are considered as multiples of 30 degrees, with the 2/12 and 6/8 house positions considered unfavorable, the 5/9's and 3/11's favorable, and the 4/10's and 1/7's neutral but intensify the planets' effects.

In the Varshaphal, the Moon's 120-degree aspect has moved past the Sun and is too far from Venus. But its 90-degree aspect is approaching Mercury, making a strong Yoga called Ithasala. To explain further: each planet has a range within which its aspects operate: Sun - 15°; Moon - 12°; Mars - 8°; Mercury - 7°; Jupiter - 9°; Venus - 7°; and Saturn - 9°. Half the sum of any two ranges is the Deepthamsa of aspect. For example, Venus = 7° and the Moon = 12°. So half the sum = 9.5°. Therefore the Moon does not make Ithasala with Venus. But the Venus/Mars Ithasala is exact, thus bringing the results of houses 4, 5, 10 and 11.

Considering the 5th house, and its Lord Mars, as an indicator of Prarabhda Karma (that which manifests in this period), we can see gain of position and new residence due to its aspect with Venus, Lord of the 4th, and its position as Lord of the 10th (Karma) in the 11th. Saturn, the 7th and 8th lord, having Ithasala with the Vareshwara (Mercury) indicated surprise (8th) to the opponent (7th). Note further that Rahu in the 6th is helpful in any chart in which the person faces a challenge.

Other important Tajika yogas are formed when a faster planet carries the aspect between two slower planets, or a slower planet grounds an aspect between two faster ones. Look at Sun and Mercury; the Moon falls within range of both planets. The Moon represents a 3rd person who will bring about matters concerning houses 3, 12 and 2 (ruled by Mercury and Sun). Remember that the 12th represents Sanchita Karma (the accumulated Karma that binds us to rebirth), as well as losses. This probably resulted in his better speech-writing, and popular running mate, but is a powerful indicator that his most important karma was at work—that this campaign was his "destiny." The fact that he faced a hostile congress and his own past is also seen here.

When a Malefic aspects a point between two planets, it acts like a "purse snatcher," stealing the aspect power. Look at how Venus will reach exact aspect with Mars before Venus aspects to Jupiter. This ruins the yoga between them, making those periods (Venus/Jupiter) problematic according to the Karakatwa, ownership and position of these planets. But the Yoga is good between Mars and Jupiter, probably explaining the ease with which he brushed off attacks about his alleged amorous adventures (5th, 6th, 9th and 10th), but why he is still haunted by the real estate scandal (4, 6, 9 and 11).

TIP #4: Use the Patyinti Dasa system, which is based on the relative planetary (and Lagna) positions within the Varshaphala. It is specific and reliable. The planets that have Ithasala will give the powerful results in their Dasas. When the Ithasala is broken by a degree or more (e.g., the faster planet is ahead) then the houses they rule give challenging results in their Dasa and Antaradasa. The other yogas will manifest in the combined periods, but when a planet carries or grounds energy as above, the carrier will often manifest the results of the two planets it joins. Lots of other reliable rules can be easily derived after looking at a few charts. Full instructions for its calculation are given in the books by Dr. Charak and Dr. Raman. It is also calculated properly by several computer programs.

TIP #5: The Muntha (progressed Ascendant) should always be studied with a Varshaphal chart. It is calculated by adding the number of elapsed years of life to the number of the Lagna sign in the Rasi chart. Divide the total by 12, and the remainder gives the Muntha sign (and it takes the degree of the birth Lagna). If the remainder is 0, the Muntha falls in Pisces. The Muntha can have 2.5 degrees added to it per month (1/12th of 30) in order to get more accurate predictions.

Since Mr. Clinton was 46 years old at the time of the Varshaphal, the number of elapsed years is 45. Adding 6 (for the Virgo Lagna) we get 51. Dividing by 12 leaves a remainder of 3—putting the Muntha in the 3rd sign (Gemini) at 12:23. Although this falls in the 12th House, it receives 60-degree aspect from the Moon (good for popularity), and after 3 Months, will fall into the 60-degree aspect range with Saturn (Lord of 7th and 8th, competition and surprises), Venus and Jupiter (natural benefics and lords of 6, 9, 11 and 4; enemies and overcoming them, fortune, gain, home and comfort). However Muntha is with Ketu, so some sort of scandal, mischief or intrigue is indicated.

TIP #6: Always pay attention to the Masaphala (monthly charts). They are created by striking a chart for the exact moment the Sun reaches any multiple of 30 degrees from the Varshaphal Sun. The Masaphala that covered the election period featured Venus and Rahu in Scorpio Lagna, Mercury and the Sun in the 12th, Jupiter in the 11th, Moon in the 9th, Mars in 8th, and Saturn in the 3rd.

Certainly in the debates, he seemed to maintain a level of composure. He called for discussion of the underlying issues facing the nation, and to put aside bickering between the political parties. This certainly speaks for the Venus in the Ascendant with Rahu—which in this position gives great charisma. Saturn and Moon in their own signs and auspicious houses (Saturn is generally favorable in the 3rd house), coupled with Jupiter in the 11th, emphasized the favorable position of Venus. Mars in the 8th is good for impressiveness, but coupled with Sun and Mercury in the 12th, we have a hint of the pressure he is about to face. Possibly some of the campaign promises that were not kept are represented by the fallen Sun in the 12th with Mercury as well.

You could also consider Venus as the Month Lord, and put the progressed Muntha in its proper place (it moves 2° 30' per month), but that is not really necessary. Some practitioners derive daily charts in this fashion, but I do not find them important or accurate enough to employ regularly. More than enough detail should be revealed by the Natal and the Varshaphal charts.

TIP #7:   The Varshaphal is meant to be studied as an adjunct to the Natal chart.   Any prediction available through Varshaphal should be confirmed by Rasi, Navamsa, at least one Dasa system, and by transit. The Varshaphal will often point to a sure-fire prediction, but the verifying phenomena must be present in the birth chart.   Never give a prediction based on the Varshaphal alone.

Roy Kirkland has been studying astrology since 1968 and Vedic astrology since 1972. A Jyotish Kovid, he began his professional practice in 1987 and has since appeared on radio and television numerous times. His private practice includes private consultations, teaching classes and writing. At this time he is perfecting a set of techniques to optimize the results of commodities and options trading. Roy has a national clientele and is preparing a series of books on astrological techniques. Contact: 570 Athol Avenue, Oakland, CA 94606. Phone: 510-444-2773.

PRACTICAL APPLICATIONS OF JAIMINI ASTROLOGY

Robert A. Koch

It is not by accident that the sage Parasara included the methods of Jaimini astrology in his great work, *Brhat Parasara Hora-sastra.* In fact, chapter 48 of that text deals specifically with the calculation and use of 31 different Dasa systems, ten of which are Jaimini Dasas. Exactly who Jaimini was still remains an enigma among historical scholars of Vedic astrology. Yet what is clear is that Parasara specifically intended the methods of Jaimini to be used alongside the typically Parasari techniques, although they appear to be unique and very different in their form and application.

This article will discuss some of the very basic and fundamental areas of Jaimini astrology since these form the structure upon which the predictive systems inherent in it are founded. The information here is far from complete, yet it should provide some useful guidelines for students interested in this branch of astrology. We will look into three important areas of Jaimini in this article: (1) karakas, or planetary significators, (2) aspects, and (3) we will provide some hints regarding Dasa interpretation.

Karakas

Karakas, or planetary significators, play a very important role in Jaimini astrology. For each chart, and excluding Rahu and Ketu, the seven planets from the Sun through Saturn are arranged, in order, from the one with the highest degree in its sign down to the one with the lowest degree. Thus each planet in order becomes a *karaka*, or significator, for specific matters. In degree order they are briefly described as follows, but keep in mind that there are also more liberal interpretations when using them in chart interpretations:

1. Atma-karaka (AK): This is the most important planet in Jaimini astrology, and should be examined very carefully. It is akin to the fixed Parasari Karaka, the Sun, for the 1st House, and thus concerns the self and self-assertion, health, physical constitution, destiny, and the capacity to realize destiny in the current lifetime. Given its relevance to the lagna and 1st House, the AK has been shown to be very important in longevity determination using Jaimini methods. Like all the karakas, it should be examined in the Rasi, as well as Navamsa and other divisional charts. The Navamsa sign of the AK is the Karakamsa lagna, which is equal in importance to the natural Ascendant of the birth chart.

2. Amatya-karaka (AMK): Parasari Karakas related to the 10th House, viz. Sun, Saturn, Jupiter and Mercury, are akin to the AMK. Thus, career, status or reputation, influence, and societal contributions are to be seen from it. The AMK is very important in the charts of famous persons, and in this regard significant results have been shown in the research work of Mr. K.N. Rao and his associates. (See *Advanced Techniques in Astrological Prediction*, edited by K.N. Rao). Rise, as well as fall, in career will be found respectively in Dasas when the AMK is either strong and involved in powerful yogas, or weak, poorly aspected, or involved in Arishta yogas. This will especially be true if the AMK is poorly placed relative to the current Jaimini Dasa.

3. Bratri-karaka (BK): Bratri means brothers, yet in this context siblings of both sexes, as well as father, are to be included. Father is logically included here as the 3rd and 9th houses form a natural axis. According to some scholars, the Pitri-karaka is given for father, yet this does not seem to be the method followed by the majority of Jaimini astrologers. Also see the BK for other 3rd House matters such as mental firmness, determination, decisiveness, and competitiveness.

4. Matri-karaka (MK): Apart from its obvious relevance to the mother, it should also be looked at for all 4th House matters, viz. home and residence, property, fixed assets, family and personal associates, as well as the natural happiness or contentedness of the native. Of course, everything related to the mother is examined from the MK. Look to the Rasi Dasas related to the MK, either by conjunction, occupation, or aspect, in order to get a hint on the times when change of residence can occur. The specific planet becoming the MK, along with its associations with other planets, can describe the types of residences that the native may enjoy. The direction ruled by this planet can also be considered in deciding which geographical direction would be most suitable as a residence for the native.

5. Putra-karaka (PK): It describes the native's children, or lack of them for the most part, in addition to all 5th House matters. Since the 5th House covers a broad range of matters, especially the past life Sadhana, or spiritual practices, it is in fact a very important significator in Jaimini astrology. In the same way that the Ascendant, 5th, and 9th are Dharma houses in Parasari astrology, the PK can also be considered as relevant to Dharma, and the karmic inheritances of the individual in the present lifetime, since all the Dharma houses are 5th and 9th from each other.

As will be mentioned later in our discussion of Jaimini yogas, the relation between the PK and the AK should be examined very carefully in assessing the overall strength of the horoscope. The PK is also important for education; thus educational degrees and career directions can be determined from it.

6. Gnati-karaka (GK): This is said to relate to relatives since the 6th planet in order of degrees has relevance to the 6th House—thus aunts, uncles, cousins, etc. Since we have other important matters to look at with regard to the 6th House (debts, disease, enemies, obstacles and adversity, competitors, etc.), Dasas connected to the GK should be examined very closely. An afflicted lagna lord, or the AK in conjunction, association, or aspect with the GK can forewarn against illness or other hardships experienced by the native.

Usually, the GK plays an important role in bringing forth financial setbacks, as well as delays due to unforeseen obstacles such as accidents, when it is associated with the current Rasi Dasa by occupation or by connection to its lord. See Dr. K.S. Charak's excellent book, Subtleties of Medical Astrology, for extensive illustrations on the use of GK in medical astrology.

7. Dara-karaka (DK): It is primarily concerned with the spouse, whether husband or wife, although the literal meaning of Dara in Sanskrit is the wife. Anyway, the DK is equally as important as Venus, or the lord of the 7th House, when determining the times for marriage (through Dasas connected to the DK), the nature of the partner, the career of the spouse (take the 10th House from the DK), the mind and intelligence of the spouse (5th from the DK), and so forth. Look for other 7th House matters from the DK also, such as the public, public contacts, or business partners.

Even if you do not make an extensive study of Jaimini astrology, I still strongly recommend that you use the Jaimini Karakas as summarized, in combination with Parasari karakas, in order to get a more thorough grasp of the horoscope. You can also use the Jaimini karakas in judging the results of Vimsottari, and other Parasari Dasas. As with the Parasari karakas, judge the matters connected to each house from the relevant karaka in order to know greater details about what that Karaka represents.

For example, look at the 10th from the PK for the child's career, the 4th from the MK for the grandmother's nature (the mother's mother), or the 6th from the AMK for further descriptions on the career of the native him or herself.

Use the Jaimini karakas in judging health matters also, based on the houses they link to. For example, a weak or afflicted PK may suggest heart problems (a 5th House matter), or an afflicted AK (1st House matter) may indicate migraine headaches, vulnerability to face or head injuries, or health problems in general.

Aspects

In Jaimini astrology, all cardinal signs, and planets in them, aspect the fixed signs (adjacent ones excluded). All mutable signs, and planets in them, aspect the other mutable signs. This scheme suggests that the origins of Jaimini astrology may have been south Indian, as the aspecting signs are most easily visible when used with the south Indian chart diagram. All the signs at the corners of the square diagram, which are the mutable signs, are both opposite and equidistant from each other. All the rest either aspect the sign directly opposite (Aries to Scorpio, or Taurus to Libra, for example), or the one "around the corner" from it, i.e., Taurus to Cancer, Leo, to Libra, Scorpio to Capricorn, and Aquarius to Aries.

Four Matters To Consider

1. "So when do you use Jaimini aspects, and when should the Parasari ones be used?" is a question frequently asked by students. In practice, you will generally find yourself using the Jaimini aspects when judging the results of Rasi Dasas, or in other interpretative Jaimini methods. Still, if both methods are described in the Parasari writings, and both are valid and useful, then why should there by any restrictions as to when, or under what circumstances, one should use one or the other?

If, for example, a Jaimini Rasi Dasa comes under the 8th House (Parasari) aspect of Mars, this should never be overlooked in your interpretation of that Dasa just because Mars may not aspect the concerned Rasi according to the Jaimini system. I personally have found the Jaimini aspects to be significant when judging a horoscope for medical or longevity issues, although these particular areas are not exclusively singled out in the books for judgment with Jaimini aspects.

2. None of the aspects in Jaimini are inherently considered either good or bad; this is determined by the nature of the signs and planets aspecting, as well as their house relationship with each other. Particular note should be made of the signs which aspect from the 6th and 8th location to each other.

So if, for example, malefic planets, or ill-natured ones, are in Aries and Scorpio, and thus mutually aspecting, it could bring disaster to the native if either sign happens to be the currently running Rasi Dasa. Benefics contributing to such as situation, of course, could modify the results.

3. It will also be found that when planets in mutable signs are mutually aspecting, they tend to bring events and experiences to the native more dramatically because such planets are in mutual kendras, or angles, from each other. It is well known that angular planets stimulate events more quickly and dynamically than those in either a trinal relationship, or 3/11 relationship.

4. In conformity with general methods of chart interpretation, review the aspectual relationship between planets in the birth chart as well as the Navamsa chart. For example, mutually aspecting 6/8 planets in the birth chart may find a more harmonious expression later in life if, in the Navamsa chart, they are found to be aspecting from 5th and 9th sign locations. Or see if mutually hostile planets (aspecting from the 6th and 8th locations in the birth chart) are harmoniously related in other divisional charts. If such occurs, then whatever that divisional chart represents, will be an area where these planets can work together more smoothly.

Suppose the lord of the 10th House in the birth chart is in the 8th from the lord of the ascendant and mutually aspecting it? In that case the native may encounter obstacles to the fruition of his or her profession. But then the same two planets may be favorably related and aspecting (say, for example, 5th and 9th from each other) in the Drekkana chart which would suggest that the native's sibling(s) may help him in finding his career in life.

Rasi Dasas In Jaimini Astrology

Chara and Sthira Dasas are generally preferred over other Dasas among astrologers, although there are at least 44 Dasa systems in Jaimini, and they are all Rasi Dasas. This means that signs are used in the calculation of time cycles—not planets. Certain Dasas are considered for particular purposes, while others, especially Chara dasa, are universal in their application. Brahma Dasa, for example is used in determining disease, while timing the moment of death is determined making use of Nirayana Shula Dasa.

Sthira Dasa is also very key in longevity studies since the Dasas are fixed in years. Thus through Sthira Dasa one can divide the lifetime into three khandas, or sectors, each lasting for an average of 32 years. Therefore if, according to the standard methods of ascertaining the term of longevity, one were to have madhyayu, or the middle term (32 to 64 years) then death will happen during the most powerful maraka Dasa during the second Khanda, or middle third of life.

In any case, Mr. K.N. Rao has advised that Sthira Dasa can be used for all purposes, apart from longevity studies, in much the same way as Chara Dasa is used. (*See Predicting Through Jaimini's Chara Dasa*, by K.N. Rao, for further details regarding the calculation and use of Chara Dasa.) In my upcoming book on longevity, I will give many practical illustrations of how, and under what circumstances, Sthira Dasa can be used.

Five Other Matters To Consider

1. Jaimini Dasas establish time cycles according to sign and not according to the lunar nakshatra method of Parasari Dasas. Rasi Dasas are thus useful because they give further timing for results of the inherent yogas that are present in the birth chart. Yogas, whether Raja, Dhana, or Arishta (greatness, wealth, or misfortune respectively), show the destiny of the individual, and are observed relative to the lagna of the natal horoscope. Now, the Jaimini Rasi Dasas, since they operate relative to certain signs of the chart, are, in effect, the birth lagna progressed to a certain point in the person's life. Thus the natal yogas, when viewed in relation to the current Rasi Dasa, will either operate fully, or will be modified, depending on the house of that Rasi, and the relation of the natal yogas to that house.

Let's take an example. Suppose in the birth chart that the 10th lord were in the 8th, thus indicating delays or setbacks in the fruition of that person's career objectives. But then suppose the Rasi Dasa of the 10th House were to become active. In this case, since the 10th House now becomes the lagna for that period in life, the lagna lord (10th lord from the birth lagna) is now in the 11th House, thereby indicating the possibility of progress, gains, or new connections so far as career is concerned. So you have a static promise shown in the birth chart, and ultimately that promise can either be fully or partially manifested, or maybe experienced in different ways, depending on the relation between the current sign and house (Rasi Dasa) and the natal yogas.

2. Strong planets by house rulership, or as karakas, will bring forth their positive results when Rasi Dasas connected to those planets become active. The same is true for weak or afflicted planets.

3. Karakas which are in a 6/8 or 2/12 relation to the current Rasi Dasa, will suffer during the times such Dasas operate. This will be especially true if such karakas are weak or afflicted natally. The opposite will be true for karakas which are in mutual kendras or trikonas from the Rasi Dasa, and which are otherwise strong and well-aspected.

4. Functionally benefic planets in strong association or mutual aspect with the following, or if the following are connected with each other, will bring Rajayoga results when associated with the current Rasi Dasa: AK, AMK, PK, DK, and 5th lord.

5. When the Moon has many aspects to it, especially by benefic planets, then Rasi Dasas connected to the Moon will be very auspicious. The same will be true if the Moon and Venus are in conjunction, and if they occupy or aspect the Rasi Dasa sign.

As with all branches of Vedic astrology, there are many details included in Jaimini astrology which cannot be discussed in a space-constrained format such as this. In any case, the above should provide some clues on how Jaimini can be applied, in practical ways, to the judgment of any horoscope. In my forthcoming book on the subject of longevity in Vedic astrology, I will give many more details, as well as examples, on the use of this system of Vedic astrology.

Robert A. Koch has been a practitioner of the predictive art of Vedic astrology for more than 10 years. His work draws upon experience gained from having spent 20 years as a Vedic monk, and having journeyed to India six times in the late 1970's. His full-time professional practice of Vedic astrology began in 1987, at which time he left the monastic way of life in order to devote full attention to Vedic astrology which is what he considered to be his chief mission in life. At present, Robert is a full-time Vedic astrological consultant, as well as teacher, in Seattle, Washington. He is currently in the process of completing a book entitled Life and Longevity, As Seen Through the Vedic Horoscope, *which is currently scheduled for publication in 1997. Contact: 317 N 188th St. Seattle, WA 98133. Phone: (206) 542-6688. Fax: (206) 546-5352. Email: 103137.133 @ compuserve.com.*

KEYS TO THE USE OF THE NAVAMSA CHART

R. G. Krishnan

In Sanskrit there is a saying which runs thus: "Grahanam Amsakam Balam," which literally means that the real strength of planets is to be ascertained from the Navamsa (or Navamsha) chart. In other words, the Navamsa chart holds the True Key in regard to the strength of planets. For example, if a planet is exalted in the Rasi chart but debilitated in the Navamsa chart it is to be considered as debilitated. Conversely if a planet is debilitated in the Rasi chart but is exalted in the Navamsa chart then it is to be considered as exalted. Similarly if a planet is placed in an enemy house in the Rasi chart but placed strongly in its own house in the Navamsa then it is to be considered as strong. The converse will also be true.

The best situation in the Navamsa chart is to be *Vargottama* (the literal meaning in Sanskrit is: the best situation in the Varga chart). In this situation a planet occupies the same sign in the Navamsa as in the Rasi. This is said to confer on the planet very good strength, as if the planet is placed in its own house. It is further stated in the classics that if a native has only his Ascendant placed in Vargottama then he is bound to make a mark in life. If more than one planet is Vargottama then the native will become prominent in one field or another. In the extremely rare case that all seven planets (here excluding Rahu and Kethu) are Vargottama then the native will become an "Emperor" (or the current equivalent such as President of a nation, etc.).

The classics also discuss the placement of planets in exaltation signs, debilitation signs and own signs in a Navamsa chart. Extreme cases are often used to give the flavor of this. For example if, in a native's horoscope, all seven planets were to occupy their own signs in the Navamsa chart then the native will become a "King" (or its modern equivalent such as a Governor). If, in a native's horoscope, all seven planets occupy exaltation signs in the Navamsa then the native will become very rich and famous along the lines of a big business tycoon such as the Chairman of IBM, etc. And if, in the native's horoscope, all seven planets were to occupy debilitation signs in the Navamsa then the native will become cruel and notorious, and he will also be a tyrant, like the Boss of the Underworld or a Vice King, etc.

Navamsa and Tulya Rasi

We have just reviewed the results of planets being exalted in the Rasi chart but debilitated in the Navamsa chart, and vice versa. There is yet another method for arriving at the strength of planets using both the Navamsa chart and the Sarvashtakavarga ("SAV") chart in juxtaposition. In this method, we superimpose the bindus in the SAV chart, based on the Rasi chart, into the corresponding signs in the Navamsa chart.

[This discussion assumes that the reader is familiar with the fundamental concept of SAV which, in brief, is that 337 points are available for distribution into the 12 houses. Therefore each house "should" average about 28 points. The procedure by which individual houses end up higher or lower than this average will not be addressed here.]

The logic is simple. The bindus of the SAV chart (of the Rasi chart) are superimposed on the Navamsa chart sign for sign. If a planet occupies a sign with a low number of bindus in the Rasi chart, but in the Navamsa chart it occupies a sign with a high number of bindus, then the planet is, in fact, considered strongly placed. The converse will also be true. For the purpose of illustration, let's take the horoscope of former U.S. President Lyndon B. Johnson. He was born on August 27, 1908 at 4:18 AM (CST) in Texas (at 30-N-16 & 98-W-25). His horoscope is given below. From left to right is the Rasi, the Navamsa, and the SAV bindus.

RASI			
Saturn			Rahu Venus
	RASI		Asc
			Sun Moon Mercury Mars Jupiter
Ketu			

NAVAMSA			
		Jupiter	Venus Mars Ketu
	NAVAMSA		Sun
			Moon
Asc Rahu	Saturn		Mercury

The following will be seen from these charts. The Rasi Ascendant is Cancer, and the Navamsa Ascendant is Sagittarius. In other words, the sign of Sagittarius becomes "Navamsa Tulya Rasi" meaning it becomes the Rasi equivalent of the sign occupied by the Ascendant in the Navamsa chart. We thus tabulate the bindus in the various signs, and the equivalent signs in the Navamsa chart, as under:

PLANET	Asc	SU	MO	MA	ME	JU	VE	SA	RA	KE
RASI **Bindus**	Ca 24	Le 23	Le 23	Le 23	Le 23	Le 23	Ge 42	Pi 25	Ge 42	Sa 28
NAVAMA **Bindus**	Sa 28	Ca 24	Le 23	Ge 42	Vi 24	Ta 37	Ge 42	Sc 23	Sa 28	Ge 42

From the table above it will be seen that the Ascendant occupies the sign of Cancer in the Rasi where the total number of bindus is only 24. However in the Navamsa chart the Ascendant occupies the sign of Sagittarius where the total number of bindus (as superimposed from the Rasi) comes to 28. Thus the Ascendant occupies a sign in the Navamsa chart with higher bindus as compared to its position in the Rasi chart. The conclusion is that the Ascendant is strengthened by picking up the stronger bindu status of its "new" (Navamsa) sign.

Using the same analogy, looking at the seven planets we see that the Sun is rendered stronger, the Moon is the same in both cases, Mars is rendered very strong, Mercury is rendered a bit stronger, Jupiter is rendered very strong, Venus is of the same strength in both, and Saturn is rendered a bit weaker. From Ashtakavarga theory we know that the Dasa and Antar Dasa period of a strongly placed planet will be better, and that the Dasa and Antar Dasa period of a weakly placed planet will be bad. To check this idea, let's analyze some key events that happened in President Johnson's lifetime.

Mr. Johnson was elected as a Senator in 1960 during Rahu/Venus. In his chart note that Venus is Vargottama and also in a sign with 42 bindus. He was sworn in as vice-president during the duration of the Venus Antar Dasa which ended on Oct 13,1961. He became President of the USA after President Kennedy was assassinated in late November 1963. At that time Rahu/Moon was on. Although the Moon occupies a sign with only 23 bindus, here his special boost was due to the Moon being Vargottama.

The Antar Dasa of the Moon was followed by Mars which was very powerful period for him because Mars occupied a sign in the Navamsa Chart having 42 bindus. During this period he was soundly re-elected as President
defeating a formidable rival, Senator Barry Goldwater, with the largest percentage of popular vote ever accorded to any US President. But during 1968,
when his Jupiter/Saturn period was on, he declined to accept re-nomination
for Presidency due to exceptional unpopularity related to the Vietnam war.
Note that Saturn has very low bindus (23 only) in the Navamsa Tulya Rasi.
No wonder he left the White House in the Antar Dasa of Saturn.

It can be seen from the above how easy it is to forecast results using Navamsa
Tulya Rasi in combination with SAV.

Effects of Malefic Transits over the 64th Navamsa

What is the 64th Navamsa? It is the first Navamsa exactly eight signs reckoned from the positions of the Ascendant, Moon and Sun. This Navamsa arc,
covering a length of 3 degrees and 20 minutes, is a highly sensitive area in
anyone's horoscope. Whenever any malefic planet transits over these arcs the
native will be prone to health-related problems, accidents or injuries, and in
some cases, where too many adverse factors coincide, it may even indicate
death.

How do we reckon the 64th Navamsa in any horoscope? As an example, if
the native has an Ascendant at 10 degrees of Aries then the 64th Navamsa will
commence at 10 degrees of Scorpio and extend over an arc of 3 degrees and
20 minutes from this point. Similarly we can reckon the 64th Navamsa from
the Moon and also the Sun in any chart.

How is this used? As already noted, the 64th Navamsa is a very sensitive
area over which if there is an adverse transit of a malefic planet then the
native becomes prone to some health-related problem, or accidents, or
injuries, or some sort of setbacks. Sometimes there can be some bad news
regarding bereavement or some major illness to a close family member
which will cause mental agony to the native. In some cases, this adverse
transit of malefics may coincide with the Dasa or Antar Dasa or
Pratyantar Dasa of *Chidra Grahas* (meaning harmful planets). These are:

1. The lord of the 8th House.
2. Planets posited in the 8th House.
3. Planets aspecting the 8th House.
4. Planets conjunct the lord of the 8th House (merely by sign).
5. The lord of the 64th Navamsa from the Moon.
6. The *Atisatru,* or bitter enemy, of the lord of the 8th House.

In a case where a difficult transit through the 64th Navamsa (reckoned from the Ascendant, Moon or Sun) coincides with the Dasa, Antar Dasa or Pratyantar Dasa of Chidra Grahas then the native will be prone to major health setbacks and even death. In my 40 years of experience I have noticed that, in such cases, the native either gets hospitalized due to major illness, or undergoes surgery, or faces a life-threatening situation (major auto accident, plane crash, etc.). In some cases death has taken place due to drowning in a swimming pool.

Chandra Navamsa Rasi Transited by Saturn

What is Chandra Navamsa? It is the sign occupied by the Moon in the Navamsa chart. One of the classics on Vedic Astrology, called Deva Keralam, states thus in Sanskrit:

> "Chandramsa Rasi Harabya
> Gochare Twashtame Sanow
> Rahu Daye Mahat Kashtam
> Yoga Bhangam Vinirdiseth"

Translation: When Saturn transits the 8th sign from the Chandra Navamsa Rasi the native will experience calamities, and if Rahu Dasa or Antar Dasa is operative during the time of this transit, then it will nullify good yogas that are present in the horoscope. In simpler terms, this means that whenever Saturn transits the 8th sign from the sign occupied by the Moon in the Navamsa chart the native will undergo many problems including calamities.

Let us apply this principle to the charts of a few celebrities:

In the case of Mr. O. J. Simpson born July 9, 1947 at 8:08 AM PST in San Francisco, CA 32-N-47 & 122-W-25 (chart not shown), we find that his natal Moon occupies Cancer in the Navamsa. From the ephemeris we note that Saturn transited Aquarius (8th sign from Chandra Navamsa Rasi namely Cancer) from January 1994 onwards, and it remained in this Sign until June 1995 (and again from August 1995 Saturn transited Aquarius until February 15, 1996). Everyone is aware that his ex-wife,

Nicole was murdered in June of 1994, and since then a criminal case against Mr. Simpson made major headlines around the world. A close link can be seen between Saturn's transit of the 8th sign from Chandra Navamsa Rasi and the calamity faced by Mr. Simpson.

Returning again to the case of former US President Johnson, his natal Moon occupied the sign of Leo. It was Vargottama since it occupied Leo in the Navamsa also. His Chandra Navamsa thus becomes the sign of Leo. From 1965 through 1967 he was undergoing Rahu/Rahu. Coincidentally Saturn was transiting the 8th sign from his Chandra Navamsa Rasi in those years (the same situation described above in the classic Sanskrit verse). Those who remember those years will recall the agitation all over the USA against the Vietnam War. On March 31, 1968 LBJ made a snap decision and declined the re-nomination of his party for the Presidency.

Among other things, this article is meant to help clear up the misconception held in many minds that Navamsa charts are meant only to ascertain information about one's spouse. The information given above highlights only a few uses of the Navamsa chart as culled from the classics which, in fact, contain other practical applications of the Navamsa. Your further research is invited.

OM-TAT-SAT.

When he was 12 years old, R. G. Krishnan was initiated into Astrology by his Guru, the late Raja Iyer, a renowned Vedic Astrologer of yesteryears. Mr. Krishnan has been honored with several awards in India and in the US for his contributions to the science of Astrology. He was awarded "Outstanding Teacher in Vedic Astrology" by the AFA at their 1992 Chicago convention. His book, titled Ashtakavarga Made Simple for the Western Astrologer, *is available directly from him. He also offers a correspondence course (in English) on Vedic Astrology. Mr. Krishnan writes a column on Astrology in* Asian News *(published in Dallas) and the* India Herald *(published in Houston). Contact: P.O. Box 852892, Richardson, TX 75085-2892. PHONE: 214-783-1242.*

"REVERSED" RAJA YOGAS

Sandeep Kumar

Viparita raja yoga is a peculiar and fascinating type of raja yoga. The word *Viparita* means "contrary, reversed or inverted." It has been stated that during a Kali Yuga period—and we are in one now—it is even more effective than the usual raja yogas.

Viparita raja yoga is formed by the Trik (Dusthana) lords, i.e., the rulers of the 6th, 8th and 12th (this is not to be confused with the trikona house lords). If any lord of a Trik house occupies any other Trik house (other than his own), or interchange their houses (thus also forming Parivartana Yoga), or have mutual aspect, or are posited together in any of the Trik houses, they become powerful and form Viparita raja yoga.

But in all these cases they should not be connected with, nor aspected by, any other planet. They should also not be debilitated. It is sometimes also observed that this yoga will bring about an unexpected improvement in circumstances, often right after some period of great difficulty.

Raja yogas are normally caused by a relationship between the lords of Kendras (1st, 4th, 7th and 10th) and the lords of Trines (5th and 9th). The Trik lords are traditionally observed to be harmful with little capacity for good. But these evil lords give good results if they are crippled of their bad lordship by being posited in bad houses. They seem to become beneficial—perhaps on the basis of the mathematical proposition that two negatives make one positive.

Kalidasa, in his work *Uttara Kalamrita,* refers to these Viparita raja yogas. He says that these yogas confer good opportunities like a king, and they provide the native with immense wealth and fame. If Viparita raja yoga is present in a horoscope then the person achieves many good results in his lifetime.

Besides the Viparita raja yoga, an evil lord can also form other good yogas in a horoscope. When the lords of the 6th, 8th and 12th occupy any of the 6th, 8th and 12th houses, including their own houses, then they produce Harsa, Sarala and Vimala Yogas respectively. But these lords should be free from aspect by, or conjunction with, any other planet in the horoscope.

Harsa yoga makes one fortunate, happy, invincible, physically strong, wealthy and famous. *Sarala yoga* makes a person long-lived, fearless, learned and prosperous. *Vimala yoga* makes a native frugal, happy, independent, and possessing noble qualities. So when the evil lords cause any of these yogas they overcome the evil nature attributed to them, and they give good results such as winning over enemies, long life, salvation and many other good effects.

Let me now give five illustrations of this:

Moon Jupiter Rahu			Mercury Saturn
			Lagna Sun Venus
	CHART 1		
		Mars	Ketu

Horoscope 1 is that of Bala Gangdhar Tilak. In his chart the 8th lord Saturn is in the 12th House. This causes Viparita raja yoga and Sarala yoga. The 12th lord Mercury is in his own house. This causes Vimala yoga. He was a scholar, a great leader and famous. You will see that there are other good yogas in this chart.

Mercury Mars	Saturn Lagna Sun Venus		Rahu
Moon	CHART 2		
Jupiter Ketu			

In horoscope 2 the 6th lord Mercury and the 8th lord Mars are together in the 12th House. They are not aspected by, nor conjunct with, any other planet. This is a case of pure Viparita raja yoga. This person was a scholar, wealthy, famous, and had no enemies. There are also other good yogas in the chart.

	Rahu	Mars	Sun Mercury Jupiter
			Venus
	CHART 3		
Saturn Lagna	Moon	Ketu	

Chart 3 is the horoscope of the great musician Dr. M. Balamuralikrishna. Here the 6th lord Venus is in the 8th, the 8th lord Moon is in the 12th, and the 12th lord Mars is in the 6th causing Viparita raja yoga, Harsa, Sarala and Vimala yoga. He is also a well known composer of songs. He has received many awards and thrilled millions of music lovers.

	Mars Lagna		Sun Mercury Ketu
			Venus
	CHART 4		
Moon Rahu	Saturn		Jupiter

Chart 4 is the horoscope of Guljarilal Nanda. The 12th lord Jupiter is in the 6th causing Viparita Raja yoga and also Vimala yoga. He was twice Prime Minister for brief periods, and he was also a Cabinet Minister. Besides his fame, he has a good reputation as an honest person and is endowed with noble qualities.

Venus		Mars	Lagna
	CHART 5		Ketu
Sun Mercury Rahu			Jupiter
	Saturn		Moon

Chart 5 is the horoscope of Dr. Zakir Hussain. The 8th lord Saturn is in the 6th, and the 6th lord Mars is in the 12th causing two Viparita raja yogas and also Harsa and Sarala yogas. He was a scholar, held many important positions like vice-chancellor, Minister, Governor and President of India. There are also many other good yogas in this chart.

Sandeep Kumar is General Secretary of the Faridabad Chapter of the Council of Hindu Astrological Sciences. He is a science graduate with a B.E. degree which has facilitated the systematic and simplified presentation of astrological topics via his books and many articles. His book, The Easy Way to Learn Astrology, *uses a step-by-step method to help serious students get past the inconsistencies in the classical texts. The titles of "Jyotish Shiromani" and "Jyotish Pracharak" have been conferred on him by the Astro Science Research Organization and the Indian Council of Vedic Astrology respectively. He may be reached at: Jyoti-Dham 2E/36, N.I.T. Faridabad - 121001 Haryana (India). Phone: 0129-213539. Fax: 0129-287920.*

WEATHER PREDICTION AND VEDIC ASTROLOGY

Michael Laughrin

Ancient astrology is obviously allied with the weather. Otherwise, why would there be air signs, water signs, earth signs, and so forth?

The traditional seven planets all relate to one or more of the elements (earth, air, fire, and water), although we won't get involved here with Vedic "ether." The Sun and Mars are hot, fiery, dry planets. The Moon and Venus are soft, watery, feminine planets. Ayurveda, the ancient Indian medical system, provides further correlations of the planets to the elements.

Saturn is a Vata (airy), dry planet—not watery at all. Rahu resembles Saturn in its actions and significations; it is dried up and dark in color. Also Rahu and its partner in weirdness, Ketu, can bring very sudden changes in the weather. Ketu is similar to Mars in its qualities—hot and dry. Whenever one finds Mars and Ketu together in a Fire sign, one will tend to find unseasonably hot and dry weather. Mercury, being a very mutable planet, tends to pick up the qualities of the planets it is conjoined with or aspected by. When it is with the Moon or Venus, it also is a watery planet. Jupiter is also a semi-watery planet, especially when posited in water signs or in some relationship with Venus or the Moon.

So, using a little bit of logic, which is certainly allowed in astrology, if we find watery planets in water signs (Cancer, Scorpio or Pisces), strongly placed in a chart—especially in the angular Houses (1,4,7 and 10)—it would certainly be reasonable to predict precipitation for the period covered by the chart. On the other hand, if hot planets (Sun, Mars and Ketu) and dry planets (Saturn and Rahu) are found in fire signs (Aries, Leo and Sagittarius) in a strong position in the chart, and if indications for rain are weak, one is pretty safe in predicting very hot and desert-like conditions.

Warning: the budding weather astrologer must never forget the normal weather distribution for the geographical region he is predicting for, and he must always remember the season. For example, indications of precipitation for Los Angeles in the Summer and Seattle in the Summer, using the same exact chart, will be rather different since L. A. is basically a desert area, and Seattle is more or less a rain forest. Again, allow some common sense to prevail.

With these bare-bone basics, when and how does one cast a weather prediction chart to be able to predict the weather for a given day? The best way to approach this is by way of an example. I'll use my wedding as an example because I did a great deal of work on this chart, and in the process, discovered a number of classical principles from the ancient Vedic texts on Jyotish.

The wedding (meant to be only a reception—it became my 2nd wedding to the same woman) occurred on Saturday, June 18, 1994, at about 2:30 p.m. EDT in Cleveland, Ohio. The special consideration that is recommended by *Prasna Marga,* an ancient Sanskrit text on astrology, to predict weather is to set up a chart for the exact time of the entry of the Sun into a new sign in order to predict the weather for the appropriate period. This is referred to as the solar ingress in Western astrology, but of course, here we are speaking sidereally.

	Mars 22:39 Ketu 29:36		Sun 00:00 Mercury 14:25
Saturn 18:34			Venus 05:59
		CHART 1	Moon 08:01
Lagna 22:21		Jupiter 11:25 Rahu 29:36	

For example, the Sun's ingress into sidereal Gemini (see Chart #1) will show the general weather patterns for the whole month of "Sun in Gemini" (approximately June 14 to July 14) for where the chart is cast. Notice that we have Sagittarius, a very hot and fiery sign, on the Ascendant, aspected by that hottest of all planets—the Sun. And since Mercury is with a hot and dry planet, it becomes hot and dry itself.

The two most watery planets (Moon and Venus) cannot promise us much rain because the Moon is in Leo (a hot and dry sign), and Venus, although in the very wet sign of Cancer, cannot much increase precipitation because of its weak position in the 8th house. Also, it neither aspects, nor is it aspected by, any other watery or semi-watery planet. Furthermore, in the Navamsha chart, Venus is found in the hot sign of Leo.

The hot and dry influences win out over the rainy ones for this 30 day period. An important rule of thumb that I have evolved is to count the number of planets (including the Ascendant) in odd (masculine or dry) signs versus those in even (feminine or wet) signs and see which side is greater. Be sure to also count the planets and Ascendant in the Navamsha chart. In this case we have 9 out of 10 planets in odd signs in Rashi and 8 out of 10 planets in dry signs in the Navamsha chart. This rule of thumb is never sufficient to be used by itself, but it can add weight to the argument for or against rain. Here we have a clear case of the Sun in Gemini being a very hot and dry month.

Mars 05:36 Mercury 13:32	Sun 00:00 Venus 21:10	Ketu 00:10 Moon 01:53	
Saturn 14:53	**CHART 2**		
	Rahu 00:10	Jupiter 18:02	Lagna 18:23

The Sun's ingress into Aries is used to predict the weather both for the year ahead and the quarter ahead, i.e., until the Sun enters Cancer. See Chart #2. Here we have a mixed prediction as far as rain is concerned. Six out of 10 planets are in wet signs in the Rashi chart, and five out of 10 planets are in wet signs in the Navamsha. However, there are no unafflicted watery planets in a strong position in the Rashi. Mercury, being conjoined with hot and dry Mars, becomes a hot planet itself.

The Moon, although exalted and posited in the 9th house, is with Ketu, a hot and dry influence. Venus cannot promise too much rain being with the Sun in Aries, and in the 8th house—although it will give some precipitation because it is in its own sign in the Navamsha. My conclusion of the effects of this Aries ingress chart on rain for the three months from April 13 to July 13 is that there will be normal rains, or a little less, with somewhat hotter than normal temperatures.

	Mars 25:19 Ketu 29:36		Sun 03:30 Mercury 13:21
Saturn 18:36		Venus 10:17	
	CHART 3		
		Jupiter 11: 15 Rahu 29:36	Lagna 16:07 Moon 29:06

Last, but definitely not least, see Chart #3, the chart of the day of the wedding itself. This chart should carry the most weight for weather for that day—about 40%. The monthly ingress chart (Sun into Gemini—Chart #1) is 2nd and gets 30%; the yearly chart (Sun into Aries) is 3rd and gets roughly 20%. Other factors, such as the Sun's entry into the Nakshatra Mrigashira, and the Sun's entry into the quarter of a particular Nakshatra, receive the other 10%. As this monograph is designed to be only a brief overview of weather prediction, we will not go into these numerous subtle factors here.

Some authorities assert that one should cast a chart for the exact moment of sunrise, i.e., the exact conjunction of the Sun with the ascending degree, for the chart of the day. I use the chart either with the Moon as the Ascendant, or I don't use the Ascendant at all. In the latter case I just determine the strength of the planets from their sign placements, the aspects they receive, and their Navamsha placement. This is the method I am illustrating here.

Let's first examine the watery planets, and then the hot and dry planets, and see which group is stronger in this chart. Yes, the Moon is vargottama in Virgo, indicating possible moisture. But it is in the last degree of its sign, and this is traditionally considered very weak. Also, and perhaps more important, the Moon neither casts, nor receives, an aspect from any other watery or semi-watery planet. Venus is in the watery sign of Cancer in the Rashi and in its own sign of Libra in the Navamsha. But again, is not reinforced by a relationship with any other watery planet. Both Jupiter and Mercury are nullified as watery planets as Jupiter is aspected by Mars, and Mercury is conjunct with the Sun. Both of them are also retrograde.

Now let's review the hot planets: the Sun, Mars and Ketu. The Sun is in the masculine sign of Gemini in the Rashi, and it is in the Nakshatra of Mars, another hot planet. Mars is triply hot and dry in this chart. First, it is in its own sign of Aries. Second, it is conjoined with Ketu. And third, in the Navamsha chart it is in its own sign and conjunct with the Sun. Mars is at full strength as an extremely hot and dry indicator.

Ketu has four factors that contribute to its heating effect: First, it is in Aries. Second, it is conjunct Mars. Third, it is found in a star ruled by the Sun. And fourth, in the Navamsha it is in Sagittarius, a fire sign. It is clear that the fiery planets are much stronger than the watery planets in this chart. In fact, the day was so hot and dry (in the 90's!) that it was almost uncomfortable—BUT NO RAIN!

The clincher was the conjunction of Mars and Ketu in Aries. While this conjunction existed (from around May 15, 1994 to around June 25, 1994) there was, in fact, very little rain and the temperature was unseasonably high. As soon as Mars entered Taurus, and the Sun entered the Nakshatra of Ardra, ruled by Rudra, the Lord of thunderstorms, there were huge thunderstorms and very heavy rains for about 10 days.

This example provides us a pretty good method to determine, with about 75% accuracy, what the weather (at least as far as precipitation is concerned) will be like on any given day at any given place.

To sum up, here's what we must do:

1. Cast the chart for the day you want to predict for.

2. Cast the chart for the exact minute of the Sun's entry into the sign it currently occupies.

3. Cast the chart for the Sun's ingress into either Aries, Cancer, Libra or Capricorn (whichever quarter of the year is applicable).

4. (Optional) Cast the chart for the Sun's entry into Aries if it has not been done at point #3 just above.

Apply the methods I have outlined to determine whether the hot planets (Sun, Mars and Ketu) or watery planets (Moon, Venus, and sometimes Mercury and Jupiter) are stronger and predict accordingly. If the two groups of planets are equal, predict normal precipitation and temperature for the appropriate time period and geographical location.

For further study, I recommend:

• *Astrology in Predicting Weather and Earthquakes* by Dr. B. V. Raman.

• *Applied Astrology* by K. N. Rao and Meenakshi Raut.

• *Prasna Marga*, a classical text whose author is unknown.

• *Brihat Samhita* by Varahamihira. This work is the greatest compendium I have found on subtle and obscure aspects of Jyotish and Nimitta (the study of omens).

Michael Laughrin is a full-time Jyotishi who has studied several thousand charts. He was a speaker at the First East Coast Hindu Astrology Conference in Washington, DC in September 1994. He has developed a special interest in weather forecasting. He can be reached at 11101 Donmar Rd. in N. Royalton, OH 44133-6004. Phone: 216-582-9848.

WHAT IS A PANCHANGA

William R. Levacy

This article is fundamentally about planetary almanacs and has three main objectives. First, it will explain how the Western ephemeris differs from the Vedic or Hindu panchanga. Second, the purpose and meaning of the Vedic panchanga will be explored. Finally it will provide some other reasons why all ephemerides/panchangas will differ due to different authors' or publishers' choices of planetary theory.

Most Vedic astrologers use a panchanga, which is a type of ephemeris or planetary almanac. A majority of information in the panchanga is derived from calculations based on the Moon. In addition to astrological calculations, a significant percentage of the panchanga data is used by priests and religious devotees to determine a correct time to celebrate traditional Hindu religious events.

The word "panchanga" means "five limbs" in Sanskrit. It describes five ways to divide the span of a day. That day is marked from sunrise to sunrise. In the days before clocks, people would rise with the Sun and keep track of time by using hourglass-like devices called "Ghati-Yantras." There were 60 Ghatis, or time intervals, in a day. Today most Hindu panchanga makers still use the sunrise to sunrise convention (5:30 am to 5:30 am). Some even continue to mark time in Ghatis.

A confusing convention used by traditional Hindu panchanga makers is that the time past midnight, and up to the 5:30 am threshold, is still counted as the previous day. In an attempt to reduce confusion, most publishers will add 24 hours to the time past midnight and up to 5:30 am. Thus 1:00 am will be listed as 25 hours (24 + 1) and will still be counted as the previous day, again up to 29 hours and 29 minutes, the 5:30 am new day point. There are some panchangas being made today that have converted to the midnight time change convention. They usually will state that they mark the time change at midnight. You need to watch for this so you don't get confused and list the wrong day.

A significant difference exists between Western and Vedic planetary almanacs. This is due to different conventions for calculating the start of a new astrological year. Vedic astrology is sidereal, or star based. Each new year starts from a fixed marker star (Spica in Alpha Virginis). In the West, the new astrological year is measured from the vernal equinox. However, this first moment of Spring is not fixed. The equinox point drifts westerly at a rate of about one minute per year or about one degree every 72 years (this is the precession of the equinoxes).

The effect is that today, when the Sun rises at the equinox, it is actually, speaking astronomically, about 24 degrees back into about 6 degrees of the sign of Pisces (using the star-based Vedic convention) and not at zero degrees of Aries (Western convention). At the equinox, the measured difference of arc between the two systems is called the "ayanamsa."

Another Hindu convention is to mark the change of signs in the second week of the month, rather than the third which is the Western convention. Yet another convention in a traditional Vedic panchanga is to list the planets from Mercury through Saturn and to include the north and south nodes of the Moon (Rahu and Ketu) where eclipses occur. The outer planets of Uranus, Neptune and Pluto are not widely used, but they are now inserted by many panchanga makers

From the panchanga elements described below, most Vedic astrologers make the greatest use of the Nakshatra data, and the Tithi is next in priority. The Vara is used occasionally, often for prasna (horary) or muhurtha (electional), while the Karana and Yoga is used mostly for religious event calculation and infrequently, if at all, for astrological interpretation. The information provided below is limited. A good source for panchanga information is the *Kalaprakashika,* and the *Prasna Marga* which deal extensively with Nakshatras, Tithis, and the like.

Vara

The Vara is the day of the week. A specific planet is designated as the ruler of that day. The rulers are as follows: Sunday or Ravivara is the Sun, Monday or Somavara is the Moon, Tuesday or Mangalavara is Mars, Wednesday or Budhavara is Mercury, Thursday or Guruvara is Jupiter, Friday or Shukravara is Venus, and Saturday or Shanivara is Saturn. Each day is considered for the influence brought about by its ruling planet.

Nakshatra

The Nakshatra is the "Moon sign." There are 27 Nakshatras and their names are given in several other articles in this anthology. Each Nakshatras accounts for 13 degrees and 20 minutes of the 360-degree annular "path" of the Sun. Each Nakshatra is further divided into four sub-sections of 3 degrees and 20 minutes called a *pada* ("foot"). A pada is similar in length to a navamsa or 1/9 division of a 30 degree Sun sign. Nine Nakshatra padas make one Sun sign.

Note that different panchanga publishers will spell these Nakshatras differently since there is no standard used in translating the Sanskrit terms into English sounds. For example, some spell Moola as Mula, or Purvaphalguni as Pubba, and so forth.

Tithi

A Hindu lunar month starts from the day after the full Moon (purnima) and ends on the next full Moon. The 30 day lunar month is divided into a dark half (Krishna Paksha) and a bright half (Shukla Paksha). Each half is sub-divided into 15 parts which are called lunar days or "Tithis." A Tithi is the span of time the Moon will cover in 1/30th of a lunar month (full Moon to next full Moon). A lunar year is about 11 days shorter than a solar year. To synchronize the lunar year with the seasons, an extra month is added approximately every third year according to specific rules. In the long run, the solar and lunar years stay synchronized.

Mathematically a Tithi marks the daily spread of the distance between the Sun and the Moon, which is approximately 12 degrees. The amount of space covered by a lunar day does vary from time to time, so Tithi lengths will differ. Also, due to time, latitude/longitude and different horizons, most panchanga data is correct only for the city for which it is calculated. Users have to adjust for their current location. An ancient Vedic text called the *Narada Purana* indicates that one counts a Tithi from its end point to be in tune with the forces of nature (devatas).

The names of the Tithis, starting from the first day of either the waxing or waning Moon are: 1. Pratipada, 2. Dwitiya, 3. Tritiya, 4. Chaturthi, 5. Panchami, 6. Shashti, 7. Saptami, 8. Ashtami, 9. Navami, 10. Dasami, 11. Ekadasi, 12. Dwadasi, 13. Trayodashi, 14. Chaturdashi, and 15. Prunima (Full Moon). This cycle repeats from 1-14 with the next 15th being Amavasya or New Moon.

Karana

There are 30 lunar days or tithis; after dividing them in half we have 60 Karanas. Karanas gives us a more exact description of the nature of the favorable or unfavorable influences occurring around us at a specific time of day. In fact, most astrologers make little use of the Karana.

Yoga or Nityayoga

In this instance, the word "Yoga" means the union or spatial relationship between the longitudes of the Sun and the Moon. There are 26 Yogas and a specific interpretation is allotted for each of them. The Yogas are generally not much used for astrological analysis or prediction. These These Yogas are not to be confused with the many astrological planetary combinations which are also called Yogas.

Why Ephemerides Differ: Beyond Western vs. Eastern

Having just explained some of the differences between Western and Eastern planetary catalogs, it is important to know that you will find differences between ephemeris and panchanga makers that go beyond the basics of as trology. In the development of an ephemeris certain decisions must be made in selecting theories of planetary motion. Not all ephemeris makers make the same choices or even include all the variables. In many cases, what could appear to be discrepancies between different panchanga works may be due to different choices. This is, in fact, much more likely than errors in calculations.

On top of this list of variables must be added the various ayanamsas. The major ayanamsas being used today are those established by Lahiri, Raman, and Krishnamurthi. As mentioned earlier, an ayanamsa is the number of degrees separating zero degrees of Aries from where the Sun actually rises in Pisces at the Spring Equinox. The difference among the ayanamsa creators listed above is with reference to the exact degree where they place the sidereal marker star. There have been many articles written about these various ayanamsas, and they are available in the general Vedic astrology literature. The effect of these variations becomes very apparent when you calculate the slower moving outer planets and the faster moving Moon and the rising signs, when you find planets positioned on the cusp of signs, or when you are looking at the many more sensitive sub-charts called varga charts.

Another choice in planetary theory leads us to consider whether to judge the planets from where the are truly positioned in the sky or where they appear to be. *Apparent* effects result from the bending of light due to gravitational deflection, correction for light-time, annual aberration, diurnal aberration, and astronomical refraction—all very foreign sounding to the average astrologer. Apparent effects are included in the *Astronomical Almanac* since this publication is meant for observational use, such as navigating ships at sea.

The Vedic convention, at least for sunrise, is to judge the position of the Sun as it is truly positioned above the horizon (i.e., half the diameter of the Sun above the horizon). The atmosphere makes the Sun *appear* to rise about 2-3 minutes before it actually does rise. This convention causes us to consider whether this rule should apply to all planets. There is only one U.S.-based panchanga maker currently using this convention (Educational Sciences Corporation of America) along with one panchanga maker in India (B.V. Raman has just started to use this as of the end of 1996).

Another variable between ephemerides is in the accuracy of calculations. Most ephemeris makers are within one minute (60 seconds) of arc. This appears to be accurate enough for a sound reading. Some claim to be accurate within a second of arc.

Regarding fractions of a degree (less than 60 seconds or one minute of arc), most ephemerides will round the minute to the next minute if the seconds are 30 or more; if they are 29 or less then the degree will stay the same. If rounding is not consistently done then planetary placements will differ.

Regarding the degrees of the slow moving outer planets, it should be noted that some ephemeris makers use tables instead of direct computer calculations. These manual tables are not as accurate as some computer-based applications. This convention can make the positions of the outer planets vary quite a bit.

More details concerning ephemeris and panchanga construction, and the meanings of the various panchanga divisions, has been limited by the constraints of this brief article. There are many sources of material in print that can explain the meanings of the panchanga information. Hopefully you can nevertheless use the information provided in this article to guide you in the selection of a good ephemeris or panchanga. You will find that a close study of these books will enhance the success of your practice as an astrologer.

Bill Levacy holds a BA degree in English and a Masters in Creative Intelligence. Working as a Vedic astrologer since 1982, Bill has a busy practice in the Los Angeles area, where he teaches workshops and consults with clients from around the world. Bill is also a consultant in the aerospace industry. This professional role has led him to work with many experts in the field of astro physics and celestial mechanics. The outcome of these contacts has resulted in his development of very accurate Vedic astrology ephemerides and the development of a computer-based expert system that interprets the natal chart. Bill has appeared on television and has been awarded the title of Jyotish Kovid by the Indian Council of Astrological Sciences. Contact: 6365 Green Valley Circle (#219) Culver City, CA 90230. Phone: (310) 670-2360. Fax: (310) 670-SKYE.

NIMITTA, LAKSHANA AND SAKUNA:
THE ART & SCIENCE OF READING SIGNS

Paul Manansala

The art of reading omens simultaneous with reading of the birth chart is a practice that has been somewhat ignored by modern day astrologers. The ancient texts of India make copious mention of this technique, so there can be no doubt about its helpfulness in making correct readings. Varahamihira dedicates large sections of his monumental *Brihat Samhita* to the interpretation of signs, and in his instructions on prasna (horary astrology) in various works, he advises the astrologer to take into careful consideration the signs that are manifest.

Likewise, Maharishi Parasara, the great authority of Indian astrology, details the use of certain omens and bodily signs in his *Brihat Parasara Hora,* the bible of classical Hindu astrology.

The interpretation of signs is not limited to prasna, yatra (travel), etc., but is also recommended for personal astrology, or hora. The terms usually used in sign interpretation are *sakuna* (omen), *lakshana* (sign) and *nimitta* (cause). Sakuna usually refers to warnings given before a particular event is about to begin. In the case of particularly bad omens, the astrologer is advised to be very cautious and to take remedial measures. In extreme cases, the whole reading would be called off and rescheduled.

Lakshana generally refers to signs which occur during the reading or query, but also includes the bodily marks and disposition of the native. *Nimitta* also refers to the signs accompanying the reading or query including the disposition of the astrologer in terms of the "direction" of his breath.

Although many types of sign interpretation are given, primarily in the prasna works, the author has found that these are also useful in personal birth chart readings. They can be used along with the omens mentioned specifically for use in hora. Among the important factors are the breath of the astrologer, the direction and nature of the place occupied by the native, the object touched by the native upon meeting the astrologer, the first words uttered by the native, the physical and emotional condition of the astrologer, the mood and behavior of the native, and the signs that manifest themselves around the astrologer and the native.

The time that a person comes to have a reading is important, and I like to use the Lagna of the time as an Arudha (event Ascendant) alongside the Janma Lagna (birth Ascendant). If the indications from the two Lagnas agree, then the results should be more strongly felt. If doshas exist such as bad yogas, nakshatras, ghatikas, muhurtas, etc., then the bad effects may be stronger while the good ones will be weakened. On the other hand, if the various divisions of time at the start of the reading are favorable, then the good results should be augmented and the bad ones minimized.

Examination of the time of the reading or query is known as *samaya*. In *Prasna Marga,* the times to be noted for prasna are nakshatra, Gandantha, Ushna, Visha, Riktha tithi, karana, sandhi, gulikodya Kala, Vyathipatha, Eclipses, Sarpasiras, Ekargala, Mrityu and Dagdha yoga, planets rising and aspecting the rising sign, the 13th tithi, Pradosha, Nishi, Ravi Darshana, and sankranti.

It might be impractical to consider all of these in regular readings, or even in Prasna sessions. However the astrologer can choose which time periods are most important. Personally, the author likes to check the 27 daily yogas (Nitya Yoga), the karana, the weekday (Vara) and the planets rising in, or aspecting, the Ascendant. The most inauspicious periods are Visti karana and Vyatipatha yoga. Visti Karana occurs during the first half of the 5th, 12th, 19th and 26th tithis, and the last half of the 1st, 8th, 15th and 22nd tithis. Vyatipatha Yoga starts when the combined longitudes of the Sun and Moon divided by the duration of a nakshatra (13d, 20m) equals 16. It ends when the quotient is 17. It should be noted, though, that in situations where the astrologer makes the appointment for the native, the effect of samaya should not be taken into account.

The astrologer's study of his or her own breath is known as *swarayu.* If a query about sickness is made when an astrologer inhales it is a positive sign; if the astrologer is exhaling during a query the omen is not so good. The astrologer is to judge in the morning whether the breath is stronger from the right or left nostril. If the breath is stronger in the right nostril, and the querent, while asking a question, favors the right side (the querent's left side) by, for example, leaning or turning toward that direction, it is auspicious. If he favors the left side when the breath is stronger in the left nostril, it is inauspicious. If on the opposite side of the nostril with the stronger breath, good results can only occur with some effort.

Generally the right breath is considered favorable for bathing, eating, sexual relations, business, debates, gambling and fighting according to Prasna Marga. The left breath is good for travel, dress and ornaments, marriage, reconciliation, making a gift and visiting someone.

The *avastha* of the astrologer is also important. If, at the time of the reading the astrologer's mood is negative, then this may affect the reading. Of course, the astrologer will need to understand their own inner condition rather than any superficial reaction to the native. Likewise, the condition of the querent is valuable in reading good or bad into the chart. If the native is in good spirits, then it will add good, while it will have a negative influence when the mood is bad. If shabby or soiled clothing, excessive anxiety or similar conditions exist then it would have a negative affect. Red and blue clothing are considered negative, while yellow and white are fortunate.

Prasna Marga states that when person is looking with eyes open wide at auspicious objects, good results can be predicted, but if the eyes are half-open while looking at inauspicious objects then the results will be negative. The physical appearance of the native is also very important. Varahamihira states in *Brihat Samhita* that the lustre, voice and other physical characteristics of a person can help determine whether a Panchamahapurusa Yoga will come to fruition or not.

Even the nature of things surrounding the astrologer at the time of meeting the native are important. For esample, seeing a pair of birds fighting at the time of meeting may mean that the native is prone to conflict, or is having marital difficulties. If the native is holding auspicious objects it is good, and the reverse holds if the objects are inauspicious. In the old days, objects like a conch, lotus, etc., would be considered auspicious. These days the astrologer will often have to construct his own judgment to decide whether an object is fortunate or otherwise.

If the person is asking about the possibility of marriage and the astrologer sees two people bidding each other farewell, it is negative; it is positive if two people are greeting each other at the same time. Of course, with all these signs, one must integrate them with the indications provided by the birth chart. For example, if one sees a couple parting at the time the native asks about marriage, but the chart shows that marriage is strongly indicated, then the prediction can be that marriage will come only after some difficulty, or after initial failure.

The objects touched by the native at first meeting, or when asking a question, can also be taken into consideration. Analyzing the objects touched is known as sparsa. For example, if the native touches his chest or an auspicious object at the time of meeting, then good effects will occur. If the direction of a male querent is to the east, south, west or north, it is favorable; if toward the northeast or southeast, it is bad. The directions are reversed for a female. The direction here is that in which the querent is situated at the time of first meeting the astrologer. For example, if upon meeting the astrologer the querent is to the south, from the astrologer's viewpoint, it is good.

Generally it can be said that any type of inauspicious activity or appearance is relevant during the reading, particularly those that occur simultaneously with the subject's arrival or queries. C. G. Jung explained the principle of omens and similar phenomena as synchronicity. In this view, events have a type of coincident interdependence and are not governed simply by chance. This, however, is not necessarily the Eastern view. Here there is an element of causality in which the spirit world takes part in our own mundane plane. Either way, the author believes this science works harmoniously and productively with the reading of the stars.

Paul Manansala contributes articles to The Times of Astrology. *The renowned editor of that journal, Sri R. Santhanam, is also publishing the author's first book on astrology titled* The Sakadweepa System of Astrology. *The author's first book,* The Naga Race, *was published by Firma KLM Ltd. in Calcutta. He is co-author of a book on* hilot, *the system of massage and bone setting practiced in the Philippines. The author has also had works published in peer-evaluated, or scholarly, journals such as the* Indian Journal of History of Science, The Tibet Journal, International Journal of Dravidian Linguistics, Modern Review *and* Language Forum. *Numerous articles have been published in ethnic and international newspapers such as* The Statesman, The Philippine Pacific Examiner, Philippine News, Arab News, The Saudi Gazette *and* Kayhan International. *Contact: 3633 Comanche Way, Antelope, CA 95843. Phone: 919-348-9550. E-Mail: polmansl@ix.netcom.com.*

THE SOUNDS OF MONEY

Mimi Mukherjee

Introduction

The word "Jyotish" is very familiar to me from my childhood in India, yet it still remains full of mystery and magic. Unlike visiting a western astrologer, to see a jyotishi is to have a glimpse into the future. "Will I get this job?" "When will I get married?" "Will my brother get well?" For all its reputation as an ascetic pursuit, jyotish is very much a worldly practice.

Not only is a jyotishi expected to tell the future, but should the future be deemed unfavorable, he is to prescribe ancient remedies to mitigate its severity. It is this aspect of jyotish that conjures up images of burning incense, ghee, chanting of mantras, and the power of charms and amulets. This is all a part of the practice of jyotish. It is interesting to note that even though jyotishis predict the future as if written in stone, inherent in the practice of yagyas and such is the tacit admission that the future, in at least some cases, remains malleable. This I like. After all, why go to the doctor if there is no chance of a cure? *[Editor's Note: Please see James Braha's related discussion of yagyas.]*

Hindus also inherently believe in what is call "kripa" or blessing. With God's kripa anything is possible. And indeed, in a yagya or prayer service Hindus routinely ask for just that: blessings that will improve life. Kripa, however, is not granted to all who ask; not all prayers or remedial measures give the desired outcomes. Hart deFouw addresses this issue in his book *Light on Life*. He states a number of reasons why the use of yagyas, mantras, and gems might fail to give desired outcomes. According to deFouw, one such reason is that a certain class of karmas is so "fixed" that their effects are unavoidable.

Should one be too disheartened by this, he need only listen to the story of my grandmother. We called her "Dunu." Close to 80 years old and toothless, her name still tattooed on her wrist, she recalled the homa she attended when she was in her late 20's: ghee being poured into the fire, incense wafting in the air, the priest belting out rhythmic incantations. All the while, awed and prayerful, she sat silent with her hands clasped on her lap. Finally, the priest beseeched her: "Ask the Lord to give you. Ask... *ask*... **ask**."

But for all the things we want there is a price to be paid commensurate with our desire to possess it. After a miscarriage and then a still birth, followed by ten years of no pregnancies at all, she was still earnest in her desire to have a child. So along with the money to the priest, she vowed to give up meat, onions, and eggs (all these being dear to her) from that day forward... *for the rest of her life!* Breaking this vow would mean great harm to her children should she have any. In the autumn of the following year a son was born; a couple of years after that came a daughter. They named their first child Jyotirmay ("Full of light"). Such is the power of jyotish, "Creator of light."

Knowledge of jyotish may be used in many ways to improve different aspects of one's life: one's health, wealth, marital happiness, or begetting progeny, for example. Hart deFouw introduced an intriguing method at the Sacred Astrology Symposium in Seattle in 1995. Let me say now that what follows is: (1) my understanding of deFouw's method, (2) presented in a condensed format, and (3) my personal application of this method to the natal charts of individuals when selecting stocks for their portfolios to maximize profits.

The Method

This method is based on the assumption that each planet represents certain sounds. Following is a list of the planets and the corresponding sounds they represent:

SUN	all vowels
MOON	ya ra la sa ha
MARS	ka kha ga gha
VENUS	ca cha ja jha
MERCURY	ta tha da dha (nasal version)
JUPITER	ta tha da dha na
SATURN	pa pha ba bha ma

As this system is based on Sanskrit, it does present a few limitations when applied to English. For example, making use of the nasal tones is next to impossible. This information may be used for various purposes including, for example, to pick someone's name or the name of his company. To pick the most beneficial name for a person, one should use the sounds of the best-placed planet in his natal chart. The sounds of the weakest or most malefic planets should be avoided.

A similar but more complicated method is employed to pick the name of a company. This takes into consideration additional factors such as the type of business it is, and the natal charts of other partners involved in the business. Due to the complexity of this process, and the limitations of this article, further discussion of how to apply this method is left for another time. *But:* there is a fairly simple...

Application of this method to investing

Using even the very basics of this method one should be able to improve his financial gains in the stock market. The following is my implementation of Hart deFouw's teaching. I offer this method only as an experiment; an experiment that has yielded very favorable results for my personal financial account. The observations that I provide to support my thesis are only anecdotal; they do not qualify as a formally valid scientific method of testing.

Along with this, please also keep in mind the following:

- The natal chart must indicate some capacity for material prosperity. If the natal chart indicates poverty, this method of picking stocks will prove futile.

- If the person is under a very difficult Dasha, this method will probably not yield very good results during that period.

- When evaluating the performance of a stock one must keep in mind the classic phrase "all else being equal." This is a crucial point. If the broader market is up, with the Dow breaking records and so forth, and yours is one of the few stocks not performing well then we can definitely lament the selection of your stock. However, if the market is severely down but your losses are relatively minimal then, in my opinion, we have picked well, even though we have incurred a loss. Along this same line, we must not compare the performance of a Netscape to that of a Walmart. The former is an extremely volatile, small cap growth stock that can continue to increase earnings at a rapid pace whereas the latter is a full grown giant who finds it difficult to grow that fast and traditionally trades at much lower multiples.

With these caveats in mind, the next step is to study the natal chart. Consider the 5th House, the house of investments. If there is a fallen planet in that house, avoid companies with the sounds of that planet. If a well placed benefic is in the 5th, then choose companies with the sounds of that planet ("all else being equal"). In another words, if you have two companies, both with good fundamentals, similar P/E ratios, increasing earnings, etc., but only one of them represent the beneficial planet, then choose that one. If you have a natural malefic in your 5th, you should avoid the sounds that correlate to these planets, unless these planets are very well disposed in their own houses or form a rajayogakaraka for your ascendant. In those cases, they will most likely yield favorable results.

Try to find a confluence of indicators. If, for example, in a natal chart one certain planet is consistently favorable to the artha houses, then use the sounds represented by that planet—even though that planet might not be directly linked to the house of investments.

If there are rajayogas in the chart, especially in the artha houses, then you need not worry about this method at all... because money will find you! If instead the chart has malefic yogas, especially in the artha houses, then avoid the sounds of the planets contributing to those yogas.

The following examples from my own trading history illustrate the application of this method. Before I employed this method, my trading record had some gains but many losses. This was even at a time that the Dow was breaking records. Interestingly, the stocks that I did make money on at that time would be consistent in supporting this jyotish theory.

After many losses in options, I became adamant about investing in solid companies. I subsequently bought IBM at about $100 per share after it had plunged from $120 or so in a short amount of time. Following the street advice, and my own judgment, I thought this was a bargain. I soon came to understand the real reason they called it Big Blue! After the passage of a year, and the shedding of 50 more points, I sold IBM at less than $50 a share. This was precisely at the time when I should have been buying more to lower my cost basis. As if this was not bad enough, I realized at tax time that this transaction was in my IRA account; thus I was unable to write off the loss.

It was as if God himself was screaming in my ear, "Do not invest in companies with vowel sounds. You have a fallen Sun in your 5th House conjunct malefic Mars!"

But I could not hear. My time had not yet come to hear the wisdom of Mr. deFouw, so I proceeded to invest in companies with vowel sounds. Though the severity of IBM's disastrous results didn't follow, the stocks I selected gave minimal results. I held Washington Mutual Bank for over two years for an annual return of 4%. Again, this was at a time when the Dow, and stocks in the northwest sector of the US in general, were doing exceptionally well. Walmart gave almost equally dismal results. Both of these had done well both before and after I had bought and sold. But for me, with my fallen Sun in the 5th, they were not very beneficial.

In December of 1995, after reviewing my chart and my past trading history in relation to this method, I decided the most beneficial planet for me was Saturn. Its sounds are "pa", "pha", "ba", "bha", and "ma". I then remembered that in my earlier trading days I bought Bethlehem Steel just because I liked the name, and the fundamentals were not bad. I bought it at 12 and sold at 18 within 7-8 months: a return of 50% in less than a year.

In 1986, when the average investor was frantically buying Microsoft, I chose to buy Microsoft puts; even then I made money. Within a couple of weeks, I made $700 on a gamble of about $1,700: a return of about 41%. This suggests that whether one is long or short the market is less important than choosing a stock that is compatible with one's natal chart. These are just two examples selected from similar transactions that indicated to me in actual practice that Saturn was favorably disposed toward my investments.

Conclusion

Using this method since December of 1995, I have consistently realized positive results with such stocks as Philip Morris, Micron Technology, Merck, Finova group, and Burlington Resources. These all represent the sounds of Saturn, my most benefic planet. Investors who align their stocks with their stars guided by this method should find themselves navigating onto richer shores.

In closing, I would now like to express my personal thanks to Hart deFouw. His wealth of knowledge is only matched by the simplicity and generosity with which he teaches and shares this.

Mimi Mukherjee is a graduate of the University of Washington. She became a licensed broker in 1985 and still remains involved in the market. Her interest in astrology started in childhood, and thanks to James Braha and the publication of his book, Ancient Hindu Astrology For The Modern Western Astrologer, *she has become an avid student of jyotish. She may be contacted at: PO Box 95476, Seattle, WA 98105. Phone: 206-217-0825.*

THE LUNAR MANSIONS IN NATAL ASTROLOGY
(AN ORIGINAL TRANSLATION FOR THIS ANTHOLOGY)

Valerie J. Roebuck

The Vriddhayavanajataka of Minaraja[1], dating probably from the late 4th century of the Christian Era, provides the oldest account we have of the significance of the lunar mansions (nakshatras) in natal astrology, though there are earlier works which refer to them in other contexts[2]. Book 60 of Minaraja's work is concerned with the characters of women born under the different mansions, Book 63 with those of men. Although the subject matter anticipates that of Varahamihira, Brihajjataka, Chapter 16, the actual characters allotted to the mansions are widely different.

The Sanskrit text is frequently ambiguous and occasionally corrupt, and I have often had to choose between several possibilities as to what might be meant. For example, the woman born under Krittika is *virakta*—either "dispassionate" or "very passionate!" From the rest of the description of her character, the latter sense, though less usual, seems more likely.

The interpretations are intended to apply to the mansion in which the Moon is placed at the time of birth—see Book 63, verse 26 below.

---

[1] The title means *The Great (or Old) Greek Natal Astrology.* For the original text, see David Pingree(ed.), *Vrddhayavanajataka* of Minaraja, 2 vols., Oriental Institute, Baroda, India, 1976: Vol. 2, pp. 335-7, 350-353.

[2] The 3rd century astrologer Sphujidhvaja used them for military astrology (yatra): see David Pingree (ed. and trans.), *The Yavanajataka of Sphujidhvaja,* 2 vols., Harvard University Press, Cambridge, Mass., 1978, (text) Vol. 1, pp. 464-7; (translation) Vol. II, pp. 174-5.

Book 60: Lunar Mansions in the Charts of Women

1. A woman born under *Ashvini* will be[3] attractive, have much treasure, and be lovely to look at, pleasant in speech, all-enduring, delightful, pure, and devoted to gods and elders[4].

2. One of the female sex who is born under *Bharani* will be malicious and fond of quarrels, have very wicked thoughts, be devoid of riches, have her pride hurt, and always be badly dressed.

3. A woman born under *Krittika* will always be full of anger and keen on fighting, excessively passionate, a hater, without kinsfolk, phlegmatic[5], resilient of body.

4. A woman born under *Rohini* will have a beautiful body, be pure, not wanton, putting her husband first[6], devoted to her father and mother, with fine sons and daughters, endowed with wealth.

5. A woman born under *Mriga[shiras]* will be worth of honor, beautiful, pleasant of speech, fond of ornaments, and keen on all kinds of possessions, clothes and food, will have fine sons, rely on *dharma,* and be radiant of body and affectionate.

6. Under *Ardra,* a woman will have her pride injured, have a wicked nature, be both phlegmatic and choleric, will have a character like that of the king of the gods [Indra], will know the weak points of enemy factions, will have great losses, and be shrewd and wise.

7. Under *Punarvasu,* a woman will have a guileless nature, be devoted to sacred knowledge, intent on gaining merit, of good nature, intent on *dharma,* attractive, and greatly honoured, and always have a [living] lord.

---

[3]The Sanskrit throughout uses the optative form of the verb, implying probability rather than certainty. However "would be," "would have," "should have" sound rather awkward in English when constantly repeated.

[4]*Guru,* either as a spiritual teacher or more generally as a parent or other person worthy of respect.

[5]This refers to the theory of the three humours: *shleshman* or *kapha* (i.e., "phlegm"); *pitta* (i.e., "bile" or "choler") and *vata* or *vayu* (i.e., "wind" or "air").

[6]Or, her husband's chief (love)—as Rohini is of the Moon-god.

8. A woman born under *Pushya* will be beautiful, will accomplish her duty, be fortunate [in marriage] and have fine sons, be devoted to gods and Brahmins, will have a fine mansion, and be happy and dear to her relations.

9. Under the mansion of the *Serpents* [*Ashlesha*][7], a woman will be ugly, beset by troubles, neglectful of her duty, harsh of speech, dishonest of action, guileful, delighting in concealment, and ungrateful.

10. Under *Magha,* a woman will be worthy of honour, have a great faction of enemies, be surpassing in splendor, free from evil, devoted to her elders, respectful to Brahmins, and linked with the happiness of princes.

11. Under *Bhaga's* mansion [*Purvaphalguni*], a woman will be a conqueror of enemies, be fortunate [in marriage], have fine sons, be skilled in conduct,[8] skilled in taking the right action, devoted to the sciences (*shastra*), sweetly-speaking, gaining merit by her own actions, grateful.

12. Under *Aryaman's* star [*Uttaraphalguni*], a woman will be of steady mind and wealth, eminent in conduct, skilled in household duties, devoted to virtue, free from misfortunes, and free from illness.

13. Under *Hasta,* a woman will have fine hands and splendid eyes and ears, will be patient and rich in virtue, will know the rules of behaviour, and will have an extremely lovely face, and a body which brings growing bliss.

14. Under *Citra,* she will be brilliantly adorned and beautiful unless born on the fourteenth or first [of the fortnight]: then, if it is the dark fortnight, she will be a poison-girl[9], and if in the bright fortnight, poor and a prostitute.

15. Under *Svati,* a woman will always be virtuous and rich in offspring, wealthy, rich in truth, drinking a little, famous, with many friends, a conqueror of enemy factions.

16. Under *Vishakha,* she will be very soft-spoken, with a soft body, endowed with riches, devoted to pilgrimages, skilled in vows and *dharma*, lovely and dear to her kin.

---

[7]For the deities of the mansions, see Valerie J. Roebuck, The Circle of Stars: An Introduction to Indian Astrology, Element Books, Shaftesbury, Dorset, UK, and Rockport, Mass., 1992, pp. 102-111.

[8]Or "politics."

[9]A *femme fatale* believed to cause the death of any man who makes love to her.

17. Under *Mitra's* mansion [*Anuradha*], she will be free of conceit, have good friends, be pleasing of form, endowed with power, modest in dress and ornament, have a fine waist, be devoted to her elders, and always with a [living] husband.

18. Under *Jyeshtha,* a woman will be lovely, proud, very sweet-spoken, of good conduct, with much treasure, fortunate [in marriage], rich in offspring, dear to her relatives, and truthful.

19. Under *Mula,* a woman will have little happiness, be a widow, poor, afflicted with illness, with a great faction of enemies, deprived of kinsfolk, overcome by enemies, of low and proud speech.

20. Under the mansion of the *Waters* [*Purvashadha*], a woman will be agreeable, supreme in her family, most honourable of action, of unequaled energy and courage, with long eyes, of astonishing beauty, even famous.

21. A woman born under the mansion of the *All-Gods* [*Uttarashadha*] will be attractive, well-behaved, famous in the human world, endowed with various kinds of wealth and enjoyments, eminent, of contented mind, her husband's darling.

22. A woman born under *Hari's* [i.e. Vishnu's] star [*Shravana*] will be of great beauty, very intelligent, devoted to the sciences, of great power, ever delighting in giving, very truthful, and always devoted to helping others.

23. A woman born under *Dhanishtha* will be fond of stories, will enjoy plentiful food and fine clothes, be a giver of all kinds of wealth, relying on compassion, virtuous, and practicing good qualities.

24. Under *Varuna's* star [*Shatabhishaj*], a woman will be self-disciplined, respected, most worthy of honour in her family, devoted to the worship of the gods and to the best people, always good to those who are fond of her.

25. A woman born under the mansion of *Ajaikapad* [*Purvabhadrapada*] will have much treasure, delight in her offspring, be devoted to truth and praised in assemblies, wise, very wealthy, and famous.

26. Under the *penultimate* mansion [*Uttarabhadrapada*] she will be devoted to the good of her husband, patient, pleasing to her elders, a pacifier of hostility, linked with the happiness of her offspring, perceptive, ever intent on duty.

27. Under *Pushan's* mansion [*Revati*], she will be beautiful, have a great faction of friends, be pure by nature and keep her vows, be endowed with energy, very rich in four-footed [beasts], a destroyer of enemy factions, and lovely to look at.

Book 63: Lunar Mansions in the Charts of Men

1. A man born under *Ashvini* will always be pleasant of speech, intent on truth, proud, fortunate [in marriage] and dear to women, with a mind attached to fine ornaments.

2. A man born under *Bharani* will be cruel by nature, very harsh, ungrateful, fickle, thin of body, attached to the wives of others, malicious in action, greedy for others' wealth.

3. Born under *Krittika*, he will be afflicted by hunger, of evil mind, malicious, eating much, devoid of honest wealth, wandering astray, one of those who serve others, harsh of speech.

4. The male born under *Rohini* will be intent on dharma, skillful, of good conduct and pleasant in speech, will delight in the sciences, be rich in happiness, preeminent in his family, and perceptive, and will delight in pleasure.

5. A man ruled by *Soma* [i.e., born under *Mrigashiras*] will be rich in beds, seats, clothing and enjoyments, often in difficulties, very handsome, skilled in the duties of kings, always attached to the virtues of the virtuous.

6. A man born under *Ardra* will be of low character, without radiance or fame, devoted to his own kin and dominated by women, overcome by anger, ungrateful, and given to rashness.

7. A man born under *Punarvasu* will be generous, powerful, and skilled in the sciences and stories, will have many friends, always be proud, energetic, clever, and dear to princes.

8. A man born under *Pushya* will be complete in body, fortunate [in marriage], calm, intent on his own *dharma*, devoted to his father and mother, rich in four-footed [beasts], and respectful to Brahmins.

9. A man born under the mansion of *Serpents* [*Ashlesha*] will be evil by nature, a seizer of others' wealth, a robber, addicted to attacking living beings, wandering astray, his body tormented by desire.

10. A man born under the mansion of the *Ancestors* [*Magha*] will be ungrateful, masculine by nature, devoid of wealth got by good actions, skilled in illusion, his body afflicted by diseases of the anus, always harsh, but perceptive about living beings.

11. Under *Bhaga's* mansion [*Purvaphalguni*] a man will be fierce by nature, extremely angry, one who always desires to hurt, of terrifying expression, of cunning character, amorous, with countless enemies, but content.

12. A man [born under *Uttaraphalguni*] will be truthful, very proud, intelligent, eminent, generous, very compassionate, extremely clever, fond of guests, and increasing in fame.

13. A man born under *Hasta* will have merit and clothing, be fond of [wedded] bliss and of music, a knower of conduct, of noble thought, liked by the king, devoted to working for gods and Brahmins.

14. A man born under *Citra* will enjoy many-coloured clothes and jewels, will humble enemy factions, will be famous for his voice, thoroughly knowing conduct, of peaceful mind, always knowing the rules of behaviour.

15. A man born under *Vayu's* star [*Svati*] will be prosperous, handsome, greatly liked by women, making great gains, foremost, grateful, attached to learning, always knowing the rules of behaviour.

16. A man born under the mansion whose gods are *Indra* and *Agni* [*Vishakha*] will be attached to fire ceremonies, a speaker of reason, skillful, desirous, attached to bad women, devoid of good sense, helpful to his enemies, and fearful.

17. Under *Mitra's* mansion [*Anuradha*], he will be wise and a wanderer, have steadfast friends, will live in foreign countries, be unhappy through hunger, enjoy all kinds of jewels, pleasures and riches, be preeminent by birth, fame and energy, have both dharma and worldly gain, and be one who turns enemies into friends.

18. Under *Shakra's* [i.e., Indra's] mansion [*Jyeshtha*], a man will have wealth won by heroism and be of good character too, will have a body adorned by the gods, be daring, ever proud, well-built, and a terrifier of foes.

19. Under *Mula*, he will be very proud, as wealthy as a king, addicted to enjoyments, free from troubles, fond of his children, loved by women, rich in offspring, a conqueror of enemy factions, destroying a mass of evils.

20. Under the mansion of the *Waters* [*Purvashadha*], he will be fond of drinking and pleasure, energetic, great, wise, to be revered by his foes, knowing, attached to people who benefit him through improper means, a subduer of the senses, of extreme power.

21. Under the mansion of the *All-Gods* [*Uttarashadha*], a man will be merciful and passionate, will win fame in battle, will be generous, a lord, intent on duty, and will have wealth, a good place, and cattle.

22. Under *Shravana*, a man will be devoted to sacred knowledge, always attached to asceticism and hymns of praise, loved by the good, a giver of cattle and sons, devoted to the good of his dependents, and kind to the humble.

23. A man born under *Dhanishtha* will be wealthy, unstriving, humble in the world, intent on dharma, truthful and compassionate, with many dependents, and ever generous.

24. A man born under *Varuna's* star [*Shatabhishaj*] will be predominately airy combined with the phlegmatic [humour], hard to approach, fearful, very ungrateful, serving foreigners, with relatives of his own.

25. Under *Aja's* mansion [*Purvabhadrapada*], a man will be a conqueror of his enemies and a conqueror of a mass of evil, finding happiness in sacred knowledge, attached to his own wife and avoiding the wives of others, modest in dress, freed from enemy factions.

26. A man born when the Moon is in *Ahirbudhnya's* mansion [*Uttarabhadrapada*] will be preeminent among his family and noble in action, have most excellent food and drink, have a character of good dharma, and be very tall.

27. A man born under *Pushan's* mansion [*Revati*] will be famous, a minister of kings, always joyful, fond of gardens, ponds and woods, living wisely among wicked people.

Valerie J. Roebuck, MA Ph.D. (Cantab), author of The Circle of Stars: An Introduction to Indian Astrology *(Element Books, 1992), is a Sanskritist and scholar of Indian art, culture and religion. At present she is working on a translation of the Upanishads for Penguin India. She may be reached at 10 Lynwood Avenue, Whalley Range, Manchester M16 8JZ, England, UK. Phone: 0161-860-4716.*

TIMING FINANCIAL MARKETS
WITH HINDU ASTROLOGY

Barry William Rosen

It is a little known fact that W. D. Gann, perhaps the world's most legendary market timer and trader, went to India and studied Indian Sidereal Astrology. In his notebooks we find sketches of astrological symbols on his charts, and in his memoirs he discusses his journey to India. In fact, the famous Gann wheel was first used by tea merchants in 17th century India.

Gann also discussed the importance of using the date when the futures contract for a commodity first began trading for predicting the future of that commodity. To my knowledge, there are very few individuals who use these starting dates to successfully time the markets. However, it is my experience, using Indian Sidereal astrology, that these charts are invaluable. If one can verify the starting date and time of the first futures contract for a commodity, and run an Indian Sidereal natal chart from that data, then that chart can provide absolutely valid information for predicting, quantifying, and labeling the major and minor cycles that ultimately govern the major trends in the markets.

Following is:

- A brief introduction to Indian Sidereal Astrology

- How I became acquainted with it

- A brief review of the Vimsottari Dasha system (which I will usually refer to as "Indian time cycles")

- The practical application of using Indian time cycles for predicting the major movements, and changes in the direction of those movements, in the stock market, and

- A forecast for the future of the stock market based upon Indian astrological time cycles.

Early Research Beginnings

I first became interested in Indian astrology in 1985, when a Jyotishi (Indian astrologer) told me that I was finishing up a 20-year Venus cycle, and that my life would completely change in one year when I would enter a new six-year

Sun cycle. I was told that I would become famous, make great advances in my career, change professions and locations, and emotionally change from a depressing period, into one that was more jubilant and optimistic.

One year later, that is exactly what happened. I went from being an instructor in film studies in Bloomington, Indiana to studying Indian astrology, investments and commodities, and I moved to southeastern Iowa. My ability to very accurately forecast my own life, and those of my friends, led me to apply Indian astrology to the markets. This connection became especially exciting when a friend of mine, who was a Gann expert, told me of Gann's interest in Indian astrology.

The Western vs. Indian Zodiac

Indian astrology is over 5,000 years old and has its foundation in ancient science. Parashara, a great seer or ancient scientist, intuited the laws of space and time responsible for the evolution of human consciousness, and he recorded his findings in a book called the *Brihat Hora Sastra*. As with all ancient knowledge in book form, over time the knowledge became fragmented and lost as it migrated to various other cultures and became distorted. In its purest form, however, Indian astrology has always been acknowledged for its predictive abilities, whereas Western astrology (with the notable exception of Medieval astrology) has excelled in its analytical and psychological insights.

The first major difference between Indian and Western astrology lies in the calculation of the longitude of the planets. Ancient Indian astrologers observed that the equinoxes and solstices moved backward by one degree every 72 years, an astronomical phenomenon now known as precession. Over time this has resulted in a difference of slightly over 23 degrees between the tropical zodiac, used by Western astrologers, and the sidereal zodiac used by Indian astrologers.

In essence, the two systems differ in their choice of a zero point for Aries. The Western system uses the position of the Spring Equinox, while the Indian system uses a fixed star. Thus when the Sun is moving into Aries according to the Western system, it is still at six degrees Pisces in the Indian system. (For a further discussion of the differences, please see my article in the Winter 1989 *NCGR Journal*.)

Planetary Periods: Beyond Transits

A Dasa is a period of time during which one's life is influenced or governed by a particular planet. For example, the shortest period, the Sun period, lasts for six years while the longest period, Venus, lasts for 20 years. These cycles unfold in a fixed sequence and comprise 120 years before they repeat and

Ketu (Moon's South Node)	-	7 years
Venus	-	20 years
Sun	-	6 years
Moon	-	10 years
Mars	-	7 years
Rahu (Moon's North Node)	-	18 years
Jupiter	-	16 years
Saturn	-	19 years
Mercury	-	17 years

begin again. The order of the cycles is:
Where the cycle begins is based upon what lunar mansion (or constellation) the moon is in at the time of birth. For example, when soybeans started trading in 1936, the Moon was in the constellation (nakshatra) of Orion, which is ruled by the planet Mars. Thus a sequential unfoldment of cycles began, starting with (part of a) seven-year Mars period, followed by Rahu for 18 years, Jupiter for 16 years, and into its current Saturn period which lasts 20 years, and so on.

If beans had begun trading only a day later, then the cycle would have begun from the next constellation which is ruled by Rahu. The number of degrees the Moon has transited through a nakshatra will determine how much time is left in the initial cycle. Thus if the Moon were in the final degree of its constellation, the initial cycle will begin in the last section of the cycle. All of these calculations are now quickly performed by the many fine software packages currently on the market.

Within major cycles are sub-cycles that also unfold in a set sequential pattern. The sub-cycle begins with the planet ruling the major cycle and then continues in sequence. For example, the current Saturn period for soybeans started with a Saturn/Saturn period in September 1979, and it continued into a Saturn/Mercury period, followed by a Saturn/Ketu period, and so on. The major Saturn cycle will finish in 1996 and then soybeans will move into a major Mercury cycle starting with Mercury/Mercury, Mercury/Ketu, Mercury/Venus, etc.

In order to properly use the Indian time cycles and their smaller periods, one must have the *exact* time of the start of the first future's contract of a commodity. Each minute that one is off can lead to changing the prediction low or high by 4 days. O'Non and Remnick illustrate the importance of the exact time using a brilliant analogy from physics. To launch a rocket ship to the Moon, knowledge of the precise angle, time, and location of the launching on earth are necessary. If it is launched at just a slightly different time and angle, it will miss by 30,000 to 40,000 miles.

I have had to travel to the archives of the Chicago Board of Trade and other major exchanges to verify the first tick starting time, and I've collected an almost complete set of dates and times (which I make available to participants in my advanced seminars).

Predicting the effects of a period is based upon the natal chart placements at the time of birth. The positive or negative nature of these periods depends on the placement of the planet by house position, the houses he owns, the houses he aspects, the planets that aspect him, and the sign that he is in. For example, in a person's natal chart which has Jupiter in Cancer in the 9th with Scorpio rising, such a speculator or investor should expect astounding results during the 16-year Jupiter period since Jupiter owns the 5th and the 2nd (speculation and accumulated wealth), and it is exalted in the house of good luck and good fortune.

Indian astrology is thus especially fruitful for looking into one's own chart and seeing what periods will bring the most good luck and good fortune. W. D. Gann was noted for emphasizing the importance of trading off of one's personal chart, and my own experience supports this notion. Even when my market timing is objectively correct, if my own chart suggests a cycle of loss or obstacle, I inevitably get bad fills, miss a major entry by a tick, or get stopped out before the market goes my direction.

In Indian astrology, cycles are stronger than transits and aspects. This concept can explain why some Western astrologers are frustrated in their analyses. According to Indian astrology, if the underlying period is positive, then bad transits or aspects will only have a minor negative effect. But if the underlying period is negative, even good transits or aspects may not make a dent.

In market terms the cycle or Dasha often represents the underlying market sentiment. For example, in a bear market, when there is good news yet the market fails to rally, the underlying sentiment remains bearish, and no external event is going to alter it. More concretely, one can remember well the Saturn/Uranus conjunction of February 1988. It was commonly forecast that this would generate a sequel to "Black Monday." However, it failed to manifest, not only because of a special planetary combination (yoga) from Jupiter's trinal aspect on its own sign based on mundane astrology, but also because the underlying period in the 1792 natal chart, Jupiter/ Mercury/ Sun was neutral to slightly positive.

Application of Indian Cycles To Stocks

What is extraordinarily exciting about using Dasha systems for market prediction (and here I am emphasizing the most classically used Vimsottari Dasa system) is that it allows one to know the exact date that cycles change, to label them, and to quantify whether they are strong ups, minor ups, strong downs, minor downs, or sideways in direction. If one studies closely the 204-year history of the stock market, and if one is familiar with the rules for predicting and interpreting the Indian cycles, the previously mysterious factor(s) which seem to govern the behavior of stocks will no longer be a mystery.

For example, it is no accident that the bull stock market which began in 1982 coincided with the beginning of a 16-year Jupiter period which began in late August of that year. In general then, according to this system the market will continue to expand until 1998, since Jupiter is a "bullish" planet and is well placed in the stock market natal chart of May 17, 1792. Rises and falls within the current Jupiter cycle are explained by the sub-periods (Antardasas). These sub-periods can either amplify or diminish the strength of the major period.

Within this 16-year period, the transits of Jupiter, its directional changes, and aspects to it are especially influential since Jupiter assumes the second most important role in the NYSE chart next to the Moon, the chart lord. In 1998, when the Jupiter period ends and the 19-year Saturn period begins, Saturn will assume the second most important role.

A recent study I did of the NYSE explains how the Dasas can be used to spot short-term and intermediate rises or declines. Certain combinations lead to very predictable outcomes. To get daily timing on the stock market, one needs to examine four or five levels of Dasas to break the larger 20 and 2-3 year periods down into 20 and 3-4 day periods. Amazingly, the cyclical combinations that are negative on the larger scale will often prove equally negative on the smaller scale.

For example, a comparison of the October, 1987-February, 1988 fourth level cycles (Jupiter/ Mercury/ Venus/ Rahu, etc.) with the third level periods in 1901-1904 (Mercury/ Venus/ Rahu) reveals that the major lows coincide with a repetition of particular planetary combinations. This principle can also be extended to sections of other cycles in other years. For example, note the following:

Venus/ Rahu/ Saturn: (the Depression period of 8/28/1929 to 2/17/1930):

This covered a period of decline from a high of 372.06 on 9/03/1929 to a low of 230.07 on 10/29/1929. Jupiter/ Mercury/ Venus/ Rahu/ Saturn (12/04/1987) signaled another major low and decline to 1747 on the Dow after being as high as 2051 following the crash.

Jupiter/Mercury/Venus/Venus/Rahu (the 500+ point drop of 10/19/1987):

Here the third-level Venus period contributed to the direction of the decline as did a number of bearish oppositions, the return to an eclipsed constellation, and the sidereal transit of Uranus into Sagittarius. This one example indicates how the Venus/Rahu combination can be used to signal a sharp decline if it occurs within a particular combination.

This particular Venus/Rahu combination is only one of many historical combinations that one can label and study. Other combinations are bullish—such as when the sequence unfolds from a Sun period into a Moon period and on to a Mars period. For example, the stock market's last major Moon period went from August 1947-August 1957. During that time the Dow went virtually straight up from 179.74 to 492.32, a gain of well over 250%.

During smaller Moon cycles within larger periods, such as the Mars/Moon period (01/21/1964 to 08/21/1964), the market again rose (from 776-838). And in the Rahu/Moon period 01/31/1980 to 07/31/1981) the Dow climbed from 875-935. Even at the third level, we can usually count on a rally during a Moon period, such as the recent Jupiter/ Mercury/ Moon period (04/04/1988 to 06/13/1988). We saw a "surprise" rally that began in late May that took the Dow from 2000 at the beginning of the period to almost 2200 by the end of the period.

From the above examples, one can see the value of being able to label and quantify the cycles in order to predict the magnitude of the moves. As many cycle analysts know, one can often find major cycle lows and entry points; however, one may have no idea how large the move is going to be. The Indian time cycle analysis is a genuine solution to forecasting because it can predict the future—not just suggest it from the past.

Future of the Stock Market Based Upon Indian Cycles

[*Editor's Note: This article was received for publication in mid-1996.*] The Jupiter/Rahu period, set to begin in 1996, should lead to a major decline in the stock market into 1998 followed by a 19-year lackluster Saturn period from 1998-2017. We are likely to see basically sideways activity before we have a major global economic reorganization into 2017.

Conclusion

Anyone attempting to uncover the mysterious laws of nature that underlie the stock and commodity markets will be rewarded and intrigued by the depths of Indian astrology. The study of Indian astrology leads not only to knowl-edge of economic laws, but ultimately to knowledge of the self. Learning how to interpret one's own cycles and transits is as important for successful trading as any good timing system. A combination of the two is astounding-ly useful and leads to an awe-inspiring appreciation of the order of natural law.

While no astrological system should be used 100% to time market entries and exits, a combination of astrological and technical signals, and a knowledge of personal trading periods, can certainly stack the odds in one's favor and lead to the answer of one of man's greatest metaphysical questions—the relation-ship between his own consciousness and the universe.

Suggested Readings and References

James Braha, *Ancient Hindu Astrology for the Modern Western Astrologer.* Sarasota: Hermetician Press, 1986.

T. G. Butaney, *Forecasting Prices.* 5th Edition. Bombay, 1958.

Tom Hopke, *How to Read Your Horoscope.* Hawaii: Vedic Cultural Society, 1987.

Pandit Gopesh Kumar Ojha, *Predictive Astrology of the Hindus.* Bombay: Taraporevala, 1972.

Elizabeth O'Non and Allen Remnick, "The Art of Jyotish." Fairfield Source, Summer 1990, 22-25.

B. V. Raman, *Planetary Influences on Human Affairs.* Bangalore: Prakashana, 1982.

Barry Rosen, "Indian Fixed Stars and Time Cycles." *The NCGR Journal,* Winter 1989, 31-33.

Barry Rosen is a CTA and has been studying Indian philosophy (Vedic Science) for twenty years and Indian astrology for the past seven years. He began applying it to the financial markets in 1987. His newsletter, "Investor's Fortucast," began in August 1987 with a focus on stocks and is currently in its eighth year. He currently publishes a daily fax service on 22 commodities. For more information contact Fortucast Market Timing, PO Box 2066, Fairfield, Iowa 52556. For subscription information and a free copy of his newsletter, please call: 1-515-472-6866.

FIXED STARS AND THE LUNAR MANSIONS

Diana K. Rosenberg

According to Bepin Behari, *Nakshatra* (constellation or lunar mansion) means "that which never decays." The idea behind the use of this term for these ancient sets of asterisms may be the same as that which led western astrologers to refer to the stars as "fixed." Down through the long centuries sky patterns were the one unchanging element in the otherwise precarious chain of history, linking those who had gone before, and those who were yet to come.

No invading army, storm, earthquake or pestilence could touch or change the sky, nor (apparently) could Time itself. We know now that stars do have their own proper motion, and that due to a wobble in our planet's spin, precession of the equinoxes does, very gradually, shift the seasonal risings and settings of constellations. But to our remote ancestors, the sky was the one eternal, indestructible, unchangeable, and, ultimately, most sacred element in their otherwise uncertain experience of life on Earth.

To ancient sky-watchers, the mysterious and ever-restless Moon, like a queen on a tour of inspection, graciously attended each star-group in turn. Among the Arabs, these clusters became the 28 *Manzils* (stations, or houses); the Chinese also had 28, and called them *Sieu* (night-inns). The Nakshatras of India, however, numbered 27, slightly closer to the 27.3217 mean solar days of the sidereal month. [A 28th, Abhijit, associated with the brilliant 1st-magnitude star Vega, (alpha Lyrae, 21° 28 Sagittarius), was only used in horary astrology, although at least one source hints it was once a full member of an even earlier set of 28.].

It is only now, in the closing years of the 20th Century of the Common Era, that we have the tools to test Lunar Mansions, one of the most ancient of all known astrological usages. Do the traditional attributes of the Nakshatras really apply? Are they a reasonably accurate descriptions of the personalities and lives of the people born under them? These are the key questions I asked myself as I started what has turned into a lifelong query. Since my area of expertise is the fixed stars and constellations themselves, I have searched out the original star sets that determined each Nakshatra. Setting myself to studying these, some problems immediately become apparent.

For one thing, four of the Nakshatras definitely *do not* match the longitudes of their determinant stars! According to Dr. Valerie Roebuck, "it is still possible to look up at the Moon at night and know by its proximity to the star Betelgeuse (alpha Orionis, Orion's right shoulder) that it is in the mansion of Ardra." Yet Ardra does not start until 6° 40' Gemini, 1° 46' *past* Betelgeuse's position! Swati (6° 40' Libra to 20° 00' Libra) has as its traditional star Arcturus, alpha Bootes, but Arcturus is 0° 23' of Scorpio. And The Scorpion's red heart, great royal star Antares, (alpha Scorpii) the *lucida* of Jyeshta; glows at 15° 54' of Scorpio; yet Jyeshta *starts* at 16° 40' Scorpio.

Seven more of the mansions, as given, only encompass some of their "component" stars. The problem probably lies in the attempt to make each segment exactly equal, that is, 13° 20' of celestial longitude. The sky simply is not a neat and tidy place. Allowances should be made for the natural borders of the star clusters that the moon visits each month, as well as for the fact that her speed varies considerably. Another noteworthy fact is that some of the Nakshatras' star clusters lie above or below the zodiac: Andromeda, Aquila, Bootes, Corvus, Delphinus, Hydra, Orion and Pegasus—all having stars, comprising Nakshatras, which lie beyond the Moon's path. This indicates a strong probability that the borders of these regions were originally generalized, rather than specific.

Since, by tradition, the 6th Nakshatra has an undistinguished and somewhat malefic nature, I chose it first as my "guinea pig" to test these ancient waters. Ardra is, quite suitably, "The Moist One," sometimes symbolized by a teardrop. Ardra was originally ruled by the Vedic Storm God Rudra, who later became a fierce red form of Shiva, this mansion's ruler. Since much of early astrology was in the physical and mundane sphere, it is interesting that this definitely is an area of storms.

In 1989, the Moon and Jupiter joined in Ardra when Hurricane Hugo reached Charleston. The Moon was here when Hurricane Andrew struck Florida. The Moon and Mercury were here at the 1889 Great Johnstown Flood. Neptune was in Ardra at the 1900 Galveston hurricane that killed 6,000, Mercury in 1889 when a storm wave killed 100,000 in Bombay, Uranus at both a storm in 1530 that smashed Holland's dikes leaving 400,000 dead, and at the 1864 Bengal cyclone that killed 50,000. Saturn occupied Ardra at a Solar Eclipse in July of 1591 which produced four Atlantic hurricanes in one month: more than 100 ships went down! "Moist" indeed!

According to the *Vrddhayavanajataka* of Minaraja, the earliest surviving account of the significance of the Lunar Mansions dating from the late 4th century AD (there are earlier mentions of them, but in other contexts), a man born with the Moon in Ardra "will be of low character, without radiance or fame, devoted to his own kin and dominated by women, overcome by anger, ungrateful, and given to rashness." A woman born with the Moon here "will have her pride injured, have a wicked nature, be both phlegmatic and choleric, will have a character like that of the king of the gods (i.e., Indra), will know the weak points of enemy factions (rather unusual to attribute this skill to female!), will have great losses, and be shrewd and wise."

The *Brhajjataka* ("Great Natal Astrology") of Varahamihira said of those with the Moon here: "under Rudra's constellation (Ardra) "false and proud, ungrateful, violent and wicked." The only positive attributes to be gleaned from these are "devoted to kin" (interesting as the Gemini Twins were notably devoted to each other) and "shrewd and wise."

According to Dr. Valerie J Roebuck, though Ardra ("The Moist One") has as its symbol a teardrop, this does not necessarily mean only grief; it is, rather, passionate and full of feeling (one may weep with joy, for instance). There is also the moistness associated with sexual arousal, and passion of every kind. It the mansion of the Sun's rays and heat, and the oppressiveness of a hot climate.

These attributions are fascinating to me, because in the western constellations this segment encompasses the lower halves of the Gemini Twins. And directly below, *in the same longitudes*, are the stars of Canis Major, the Greater Dog, which in the Western tradition has always been associated with oppressively hot weather (this is the source of our expression "The Dog Days"). As for Ardra being "The Moist One," this is China's 22nd Sieu, "The Well," associated with cleaning, repairing, and purifying wells, as well as the cleansing of crime, expurgations, and concern for morals, law and order. It is always exciting to discover similarities and correspondences between and among the most ancient cultural sources. It indicates, I believe, the independent discovery, in remote times, of the energies of these figures.

Among those individuals born with the Moon in Ardra are the artists Rodin, Durer and Miro; composers Erik Satie, Sir Arthur Sullivan, and Stephen Foster; authors Emily Bronte, Guy de Maupassant, Thackeray, Thoreau and Thomas Hardy; scientist Sir Isaac Newton; and astrologers Paul G Clancy, Grant Lewi, Isabelle Pagan and Lois Rodden (where would modern astrologers be without Lois?).

Although some of these people are quiet, brooding loners, there is also an adventurous spirit manifested by Admiral Byrd, Anne Morrow Lindbergh, Empire builder Cecil Rhodes, explorer and oil entrepreneur Wendell Phillips, and Astronaut David Scott. Dr. Christiaan Barnard dared to perform the world's first heart transplant, and Walter Reuther defied the power of Henry Ford, forging the United Auto Workers union into a powerful political force (no doubt Ford thought him "false and proud, ungrateful, violent and wicked!")

It would seem that the Moon here at birth produces an edgy need to "test the borders." Examples are Janis Joplin, and at another level, heroic World War I nurse Edith Cavell who was finally executed by the Germans for helping allied soldiers escape from prison camps (perhaps she *did* "know the weak points of enemy factions"). Author Upton Sinclair wrote *The Jungle,* an expose of the horrors of the Chicago stockyards, a book that the enraged meat packing industry thought very "wicked" indeed!

As for violence, the murderers I've found with the Moon in Ardra were Herbert Deneau who, fearing his visitation rights would be curtailed, shot his ex-wife and child, then himself. Another is Richard Speck who, on June 13 1966, after drinking and taking drugs, entered a dormitory and knifed and strangled eight student nurses, one of whom he raped. He claimed to hate his ex-wife. Sepp Dietrich, Nazi SS officer and assassin, also had the Moon here. Ought we to consider these as corresponding to Vrddhayavanajataka of Minaraja's description: "low character ... dominated by women, overcome by anger, ungrateful, and given to rashness?" However, considering the high number of non-violent people with the Moon here, obviously we would need more evidence than this to verify the ancient, almost wholly malefic descriptions of the Moon in Ardra.

It is when we widen the range of usage, and include the other planets, as well as the angles, that Ardra's potential for producing some negative, harsh personalities becomes more apparent. Although even here, there are just as many positives to balance the equations. Nazi torture-doctor Josef Mengele (Ascendant), and serial killers Randy Kraft (Saturn), Peter Kurten, Myra Hindley (Jupiter) and Dennis Nilsen (Rahu) are all represented here.

Mass murderer Charles Whitman's Sun was here (an autopsy revealed a brain tumor) and cannibal/ necrophile/ serial killer Arthur Shawcross (Rahu) suffered brain lesions, pyroluria, and lead poisoning (apparently there are more than the average number of birth defects in this span of stars). As for "of low character," might not disgraced publisher Robert Maxwell (Mars), Nazis Adolph Eichmann and Heinrich Himmler (Neptune), gangsters Al Capone (Ketu) and John Dillinger (Sun), con artist Rita Faulkner (Mercury) and porn star John Holmes (Saturn) qualify?

Having thoroughly discredited this mansion, I must now make amends. For there are so many people born under Ardra that are honorable and eminent that they outweigh, in my view, the "low-lifes." Besides those already mentioned with the Moon here, there are, for instance, Mozart (Mars), Bach and Schubert (Rahu), Berlioz (Ascendant), Stravinsky and Schumann (Mercury), Arturo Toscanini (Uranus), Sir Georg Solti (Pluto), and Shakespeare (Ketu).

If it's character you're seeking, try Saint Augustine (Uranus), George Washington (Ketu), Winston Churchill, John Quincey Adams, Anwar Sadat (Pluto, Jupiter, MC), Justice Hugo Black, President Woodrow Wilson (Saturn), Joan of Arc (Neptune), Nelson Mandela and Saint Francis of Assisi (Pluto), Saint Frances Cabrini (Mercury), Red Cross founder Henri Dunant and Florence Nightingale (Venus), and hospice pioneer Elisabeth Kubler-Ross (Moon).

Some of the most powerful intellects the human race has produced have placements in Ardra: Blaise Pascal and G. Liebnitz, both philosopher-mathematicians, were born with the Sun here, as was Ignace Semmelweiss, discoverer of antisepsis. Jonas Salk and Sir Joseph Lister, medical pioneers, had Saturn here; and penicillin discoverer, Sir Alexander Fleming had Venus here. Albert Einstein and S. Ramanujan, the self-taught mathematical genius, had Ardra rising. It was also Sir Isaac Newton's Moon.

Indira Gandhi (Ketu, Pluto in Ardra) fit much of the Vrddhayavanajataka's description of the Moon-in-Ardra female: "...will have a character like that of the king of the gods (i.e., Indra; is it coincidence that her name was Indira?), will know the weak points of enemy factions, will have great losses, and be shrewd and wise."

Now that astrologers have computers and high quality data collections to work with, there is the opportunity to test, expand and perhaps "modernize" the ancient interpretations. Ardra is, as I have attempted to demonstrate, very much as the ancient texts have characterized it. But it is, I believe, much more as well. This perhaps reflects the fact that, in general, many of the ancient writings were necessarily quite cryptic and allusive.

When it comes right down to it, a list of nasties vs. good guys can get very boring. What fascinates me are the ordinary people who struggle with the energies within them, striving to find a way to use them as a ladder to the light. To me, these are the true heroes.

Wallace Hartley (Ardra Ascendant) came to his fate as the bandleader on the Titanic. He and his musicians found the courage to keep playing, calming the passengers, and none of them tried for places in the lifeboats. They all went down with the ship. Anwar Sadat (Pluto, Jupiter, MC Ardra) found within himself the courage to buck history and the ancient, deeply embedded prejudices of his countrymen, and traveled to Israel in the name of peace. He was later assassinated for his labors, but history will never forget what he attempted.

William Wilberforce (Rahu in Ardra) fought against the English slave trade. He did not live to see the Emancipation Act passed, but it was his groundwork that led to it. German Lutheran Minister Dietrich Bonhoeffer (Neptune in Ardra) went underground to oppose the Nazis. The Gestapo caught, impris-oned, and hanged him. His "Letters from Prison," published posthumously, are an inspiration to all those who oppose tyranny.

Truly, could anyone say these are "without radiance or fame?"

I have found that, rather than good/evil or right/wrong patterns, what the fixed stars offer are *issues,* i.e., certain classes of challenges and experiences that channel each soul to make choices that will (hopefully) advance its unique evolution. The Gemini Twins, Castor and Pollux, were rollicking, adventurous heroes who were devoted to each other, epitomizing true brotherhood. It seems apparent that the *real* challenges of Ardra are courage vs. cowardice, action vs. non-action, and the battle for self-control as well as devotion to others (the *brotherhood* of the Twins) that is the eternal task of the true hero.

For those interested in beginning further research in this area, I recommend these books:

Roebuck, Valerie J., *The Circle of Stars.* Shaftesbury, Dorset & Rockport, Maine: Element Books, Ltd. 1992. (Additional material, from the Vrddhayavanajataka of Minaraja, was graciously made available by Ms. Roebuck).

Behari, Bepin, *Myths and Symbols of Vedic Astrology.* Salt Lake City, Utah: Passage Press, 1990.

Walters, Derek, *Chinese Astrology.* Wellingborough, Westhamptonshire: The Aquarian Press, 1987.

Nash, Robert Jay, *Darkest Hours.* Chicago: Nelson-Hall, 1976.

Rodden, Lois M., *The American Book of Charts.* San Diego, California: Astro Computing Services, 1980. [*Editor's Note: I'm told this has now been updated, retitled Astrodata II and published by the AFA in 1988.*]

Rodden, Lois M., *Profiles of Women: Astro Data I.* Yucaipa, California: Data News Press, 1996.

Rodden, Lois M., *Astro-Data V: Profiles of Crime.* Hollywood, California: Data News Press, 1991.

Diana K Rosenberg, UAC and NCGR faculty, vice-president of The Uranian Society, has published articles in the NCGR Journal, Ingress, Memberletter, Urania, *and* Heliogram, *as well as* The Mountain Astrologer, Astrological Journal of London, The Traditional Astrologer, Dell Horoscope, *and* American Astrology. *Llewellyn's* Astrology *of the* Macrocosm *includes her chapter on Earthquake Prediction, and the NCGR's Essentials of Intermediate Astrology contains her essay on Fixed Stars. A fixed star scholar (according to Robert Hand, Diana is the expert on fixed stars), she has written a Workbook as well as a Correspondence Course on fixed stars and constellations. She can be contacted at: 100 La Salle St. (# 6A), New York, NY 10027. Phone: (212) 663-2243.*

A GOOD LORD/BAD LORD
APPROACH TO INTERPRETATION

Steve Stuckey

Vedic astrology offers many valuable techniques of chart interpretation and methods of prediction that find no equal in Western astrological systems. One of these is the assigning of benefic or malefic status to ruling planets for each rising sign irrespective of the sign a planet may, in fact, be tenanting. These rules are laid down in the *Brihat Parashara Hora* and are also mentioned in many Hindu books on astrology so will not be addressed here. Assuming the reader is basically familiar with the aforementioned rules, I would like to discuss a unique way of approaching natal chart analysis and synthesis using this technique.

The method is to first look at benefic or malefic lords for the Janma Lagna (rising sign) and Chandra Lagna (using Moon as the ascendant). Surya Lagna could also be used, but for simplicity it will be excluded from this discussion. This should be done prior to the usual assessment of the chart, i.e., planets in houses and signs, aspects, nakshatras, etc. All of these points are certainly to be included in the overall delineation, but at first glance, as a way of assessing the chart, determine the respective good and or bad lords. As an example, you will need to run the the well known chart of Marilyn Monroe with Cancer rising and Moon in Capricorn (June 1, 1926 at 9:30 AM PST in Los Angeles 34N04 & 118W15).

My first thought is directed at Mars (for the Cancer Ascendant) and Venus (for the Capricorn Moon) as these are yogakaraka planets for their respective Lagna, ruling both a trikona and a kendra house (5th and 10th for Mars and Venus). An immediate feeling for the combination of Mars and Venus comes to mind, i.e., beauty, passion, charisma, dancing and singing talents etc. The next step in the process is to look at the house placements of the planets. Venus is in the 10th from Lagna, and 4th from Moon aspecting the 10th. Certainly one might predict a strong predilection to a Venus occupation and the possession of many luxuries and comforts including properties.

Mars in the 8th from Lagna, and 2nd from Moon aspecting the 8th, gives a further emphasis on sex and the possibility of addictions. As Mars Bhukti was operating at the time of her death one might suspect that sex or excessive living (Mars conjunct Jupiter) contributed to her demise. This is the basic technique and when used as a "first glance" approach will give astounding results.

As an astrologer becomes more attuned to the Hindu method of chart interpretation, the mere mention of a particular sign sends impulses flashing along a galactic path to understanding. For Taurus and Libra, one asks: where is Saturn? For Cancer and Leo: where is Mars? For Aquarius and Capricorn, the question is: what's Venus doing? More examples will help to clarify this process.

Libra rising for Mahatma Gandhi made Saturn (lord of 4th and 5th) in the 2nd House of food significant for fasting, and along with his Cancer Moon, made Mars important by imparting vital physical energy and a warrior's spirit (Mars in 1st from Lagna). Libra rising, again for Adolf Hitler, almost gave him world dominion with Saturn in his 10th, and the Moon in Sagittarius conjunct Jupiter (as lord of the Lagna from Moon) gave him the basis for his belief of German race (and his own) superiority. Capricorn rising for Jeddu Krishnamurti made Venus (ruler of 5th and 10th) and the natural planet of love and beauty, especially powerful in the 6th House of service. Jack Nicholson and Christopher Reeves, both with Cancer rising and Mars in Scorpio in the 5th have shared a similar reputation as "super" men.

For Gemini and Virgo ascendants one naturally thinks of Mercury and Venus as benefics ruling respectively 1st and 5th, and 9th and 10th. However, Hindu astrologers also look for Mars as the worst malefic for Gemini (as lord of 6th and 11th) and Virgo (as lord of 3rd and 8th). In fact, Virgo rising is often associated with a harsh death (because of Mars ruling the 8th). Naturally all factors must be considered before rendering such a judgment

For Scorpio, the Moon, as ruler of the 9th, becomes a powerful benefic, just as Venus becomes a malefic and a powerful ruler of "lust" by ruling both the 7th (marriage partner and desires in general) and the 12th (pleasures of the bed). The Moon, also ruling the public, became a powerful planet for Elvis Presley, who had Scorpio rising with an Aquarius Moon in the 4th (aspecting the 10th House of career) and giving heightened emphasis to the relationship with his mother (4th House). Venus, as the yogakaraka planet for Aquarius (ruling 4th and 9th) is significant for pleasures in Capricorn (12th from the Moon) and for creativity (in the 3rd from Janma Lagna).

To take this technique of chart interpretation one step further, and always guarding against oversimplification, one might draw some generalizations from each Lagna. For instance, with Aries rising the Sun, Mars and Jupiter are generally benefic ruling the 1st, 5th and 9th. Therefore Aries natives may be thought of as bold (Sun/Mars), confident (Sun/Jupiter) and possessing knowledge (Jupiter as lord of 9th). In addition, they may have difficulty in communication, legal disputes, and troubles in concentrating (Mercury as a malefic ruling 3rd and 6th). Obviously if Mercury is well disposed by house, sign and aspect this would be offset.

For Sagittarius, positive qualities of confidence, religiosity and enterprise would be apparent with Jupiter, Mars, and Sun being good. But despite Sagittarius being the "good guy" he may be disappointed in affairs of the heart since Venus becomes the worst planet (ruling 6th and 11th). With Pisces Lagna, the Moon ,Jupiter and Mars are good, giving qualities of nurturing, sensitivity, compassion and positive action. However, with Saturn as a powerful malefic (ruling 11th and 12th), Pisceans may be undisciplined and unorganized. Many valuable insights into the original meaning of each sign can be gained by this technique and may also serve as a useful tool for memorizing benefic and malefic lords.

Steven Stuckey is a Hindu/Sidereal astrologer who first began studying Tropical astrology in 1968 at the age of nineteen. He later became connected to the Fagan/Bradley school of Sidereal astrology in 1971. After being initiated into the Vedic path, he began a study of Hindu astrology in 1979. He currently teaches at the Vedic School of Astrology in Los Angeles. He may be contacted for consultation and private instruction at: 3667 Dunn Drive (#4) Los Angeles, CA 90034, Phone: (310) 535-4969.

THE MANAGEMENT OF CONCEPTION
THROUGH ASTROLOGY

Kirsten Tingstad

During the past 21 years I have worked with the Western charts of over 3,000 clients to help them 1) conceive a child, or 2) prevent the conception of a child, and/or 3) select the sex of a child, and/or where possible, 4) prevent miscarriage. In more recent years I have become increasingly intrigued with Hindu astrology. In the Fall of 1994 I flew across the ocean to attend the four-day "First East Coast Hindu Astrology Conference" in metro Washington, DC This wonderful experience solidified my determination to reconsider my work from the Vedic perspective. I was pleased when the conference sponsor then asked me to contribute some of my initial conclusions to this anthology.

I was first inspired to this work in Bournemouth, England in 1974. At first the focus was totally upon improving the ability to conceive. I practiced with many people in Norway where I spent almost 18 years (one nodal cycle) from 1970 to the end of 1987. Many of you may know the book that inspired me. It was *Natural Birth Control* by Art Rosenblum.

During my years in Norway I also attempted two informal statistical studies among my clients. First I wrote to about 1,200 persons who had received special "conception calendars" from me since, even by that time, about 85% of my work was still in this one area. Later an additional 600 clients were contacted. Both of these investigations showed that 20-25% of the patients received the help they had been seeking. They conceived and bore the child they had been hoping for. The ages of these women were from 29 to 43 years.

Due to inadequate response data, no clear statistical picture emerged among those who had asked for a child of a specific sex. Oddly enough, almost everyone asked for a girl, and this is said to be the exact opposite of the preference in India. This is also in contradiction to Eugene Jonas, MD, discussed later in this article, who states that the ability to select the preferred sex is 100% possible.

Those who used "the system" for prevention were very pleased at not having to use pills and still being able to decide themselves when to get pregnant. Calendars controlling miscarriages were created using progressed aspects to determine when it was not advisable to conceive.

The system I had always used was developed by Eugene Jonas, a medical doctor from Czechoslovakia. His basic discovery is that a woman is most fertile when the degree angle in longitude between the Sun and the Moon is the same as the degree angle between these two heavenly bodies when she was born. As a student of the spiritual science of Rudolph Steiner this makes sense to me. Mr. Steiner has written that humans were split into the two sexes when the Moon parted from its connection with the Sun and the Earth, and from that time forward conception began to work as we now know it.

The main issue that evolved for me was how my accumulated experience could be integrated or supplemented with Hindu astrology. As I began investigating this matter, the books of V. K. Choudhry particularly appealed to me. Mr. Choudhry has subsequently been most generous with his time and help during our correspondence about his books as they relate to this matter. Let me now be clear that I am only presenting myself as a dedicated researcher; I am otherwise a humble student of Hindu astrology as it pertains to these matters. With this in mind, I have re-investigated about 35 charts of my Western clients after having converted their charts to the Vedic perspective, and I have some initial observations that I hope may hold some interest for you.

To evaluate the chances of conception, as well as when it is advisable to conceive, Eastern astrologers evaluate the 5th House in the main Rasi chart, plus the status of Jupiter (the karaka, or indicator, of children), as well as two divisional charts: the navamsha and the saptamsa. Please note that the mother's time of birth must be quite accurate in order for these two divisional charts to be accurate.

As far as I have been able to determine, Eastern astrologers are not at all interested in the Sun/Moon angle when considering the issue of conception. They examine the Dasa and Bhukti that is currently active, as well as the next period coming up, in deciding to give counsel about conception. If the Dasa and Bhukti planets are weak then the couple will be advised to wear gemstones and/or yantras to reinforce the strength of these planets. But mind you: your own thoughts every day are very important also. They must be positive and kind. The gems can't do it all.

It is interesting to see what happens when a woman has conceived a child when the Bhukti planet is a malefic, i.e., ruling the 6th, 8th or 12th, or placed there, either in her rasi or saptamsa. What I think I have observed is that the child to whom she gives birth seems to develop a type of systemic weakness which may not first be apparent until the child's adult years.

I am now thinking of a woman (see rasi chart 1, born 28 June 1935 at 21:44 GMT with a Lagna of 25-CP-44) who conceived a child in her Jupiter Dasa and Jupiter Bhukti around the beginning of August 1963. Jupiter was ruling the 12th in her saptamsa (not shown). The child was perfectly fine during her entire youth, and she is now a successful dentist. But when she (the dentist) herself became pregnant, she had a miscarriage of twins in the beginning of December 1994.

		Moon	Sun Mercury Ketu
Saturn			Venus
Lagna		CHART 1 Mother	
Rahu		Jupiter	Mars

When I reviewed the dentist's rasi and saptamsa, I noted that she was running a Rahu Dasa and Mercury Bhukti from the 17th of May 1993 to the 4th of December 1995 (see rasi chart 2 for the 3rd of May 1964 at 7:45 AM local time in Copenhagen. Lagna is 18-GE-47). Jupiter is combust in her rasi as well as Mercury (which rules her Ascendant). Her 5th House is ruled by Venus which is also weak.

	Sun Mars Mercury Jupiter		Lagna Venus Rahu
Saturn		**CHART 2** **Dentist** **(Child of Chart 1)**	
Moon			
Ketu			

In the saptamsa (not shown) her Ascendant is Libra with its ruler a weak Venus, and the 5th House is ruled by Saturn which rules the 8th in the rasi and is weakened by that link. Saturn is further debilitated in Aries in the saptamsa. In the 5th House in the saptamsa, we find Ketu in Aquarius aspected by Rahu, the Sun (strong both in rasi and saptamsa) and Jupiter (combust in the Rasi). So it could be said that there are a number of weak energies in this horoscope regarding the question of procreation.

If I had been asked to advise her about when to conceive, I would have suggested after the 22nd of December 1999, when the Sun Bhukti begins, because the Sun is very strong in her rasi. But she is currently expecting a child at the beginning of December 1995. As of September 1995 the pregnancy is running perfectly and medical scans show no problems. But I would suspect that there is the risk of some future weakness for the child.

However the mother is running a Rahu Dasa, and Rahu is strong in her horoscope which should help her (note: when I use the word "strong," this is a simplified observation and is not to be confused with information provided by formal systems of planetary strength such as Shad Bala).

But then again, in October 1995 her blood pressure became too high, so she had to stop her work as a dentist in order to protect herself and the child.

As we consider all this, we must remember that procreation is also an issue of occult philosophy. The imperfections with which mankind is born are often karmic, and these must be outgrown through our labors as social beings. It is not so simple as to just avoid these problems.

By the way, the dentist's brother was conceived about the middle of October when the mother was running her Rahu Dasa. Rahu is weak in the rasi for her because its position is in the last quarter of the last degree of Sagittarius, and her Mercury is also weak by position and combustion. Consequently the brother lives a good life in many ways, but he has developed a skin disease that runs through many generations of his family.

So this sample case just reinforces my impression, developed through studying many cases, that when the planets governing the ruling periods are weak during the fertile periods in a woman's life, then the risk increases of giving birth to children who will develop some subsequent noteworthy defect.

Let's now turn to the issue of prevention. In Western astrology, the Sun/Moon angle is also used to prevent conception. Women are advised not to have sexual intercourse during the three days before, and one day after, the day when the Sun/Moon angle repeats itself. And, of course, there should be no intercourse during the ovulation in the middle of the month between menstruations. Overall I have found this approach to be effective.

On the matter of the sex of the children, Dr. Jonas states that when the Moon goes through a masculine ("positive") sign during conception then the couple will have a son. When the Moon passes through a feminine ("negative") sign during conception then they will have a daughter. and more specifically: when the Sun/Moon angle repeats itself, and the Moon is in a feminine sign (but not the first or last five degrees) then a female should be conceived. However, all these sign-related statements are based upon the Tropical zodiac, and my limited investigation is not conclusive at this time.

Eastern astrology states that male planets in male signs bless the person with sons, and the reverse applies for females. But obviously it cannot be so simple as that considering that the charts of both parents must be considered as well as the status of many planetary factors (aspects, resident planets, divisional charts, and so forth). A stronger feeling is that if male planets are aspected by male planets during the run of its Dasa or Bhukti then a son will be born, and vice versa. In this regard Rahu and Ketu are both considered female according to Mr. Choudhry.

I suggest the reader study a little book by Mr. Choudhry titled *Divisional Charts* (published by Sagar Publications in New Delhi). But one thing I totally disagree with in his book is that conception can only take place during the Dasa or Bhukti of a planet that rules either the Ascendant, trinal or angular houses. My case studies have already shown this to be not true.

Here I can highlight some related ideas I have also seen mentioned in other sources but have not investigated. Note that there are also many specific yogas that pertain to fertility.

- Fertility is promoted if the ruler of the 5th is linked to benefics and there are no malefic aspects.

- Fertility is promoted if the ruler of the 5th is in an angle or trine and not otherwise under special stress.

- Fertility is promoted if the 5th house itself receives good aspects (especially in the absence of non-supportive aspects).

- Mercury, Saturn and a weak Moon are considered to support sterility if they link to the 5th house, or its ruler, with inadequate offsetting considerations.

- A weak or damaged Jupiter (by placement, sign, aspect, and so forth) will tend to deny children.

- Jupiter transiting the 5th, 7th or 9th will produce children if the Dasa or Bhukti is supportive.

- The total number of children a person is able to have is said to be related to the total number of planets occupying the 5th house from the Ascendant and from Jupiter (I also wonder about the Moon and the 5th position from the ruler of the 5th). But this is only said to be true for planets that are appropriate and with adequate strength.

- Alternatively, the number of children is said to be equal to the number of positive benefic dots (usually referred to as "bindus") in the 5th house from either the Ascendant or Jupiter (whichever is stronger) in the ashtakavarga of Jupiter. But this presumes an understanding of the concept of ashtakavarga that is itself beyond the scope of this article.

If you now ask me if I have yet compared Eastern vs. Western charts on the matter of miscarriage, the answer is "no." To this point I have only been interested in investigating the difficulties that seem to appear over and over for some people. But with regard to this issue, my initial impression is that it seems as though the planet ruling during conception was typically low in strength or ruling a difficult house. It is also said that there is often an interplay between the rulers of the 5th and 8th. But I have not yet fully investigated this.

People sometimes ask me if there is not a pattern for the man. In Western astrology there is not because we only work with the Sun/Moon angle for the woman. But now that I know some Eastern astrology, I would say "yes." You look at the related energies in the man's chart the same way that you would the woman's. Just the other day I found a woman's horoscope where the Moon was conjunct Saturn in her 7th House. The Moon rules procreation and Saturn delays events. This woman complained that her husband's seeds have very little energy, and I believe it!

In my work I also give advice to the married couple about herbal supplements that can reinforce the weak glands and organs related to the weak planets. They are also educated in eating in a healthy way with an emphasis upon organically grown vegetables, breads, eggs, and so on. I always strongly recommend giving up smoking due to its toxic effect upon the bloodstream.

In conclusion, let me reemphasize that the majority of my work has been with people who wished to conceive, or who wished to carry a pregnancy to term, but could not. The key point to be reinforced is that I have some statistical evidence that success in this matter can be enhanced through astrology. I have not found it very important to give "guarantees" concerning the choice of sex. since I am sure the incarnating soul chooses the sex which is right for its further development.

Kirsten Tingstad was born in Copenhagen, Denmark on 1 November 1930 at 2:18 local time. In her early years she pursued a career in fashion design. From 1960 she became very involved with the work of Rudolph Steiner. A mother of three, she moved to Norway in 1970 and began teaching astrology in 1974. There her mind was captured by the book Natural Birth Control *written by Art Rosenblum. This led to a strong career focus in this area. Her fertility work was featured extensively in the Norwegian media over the 18 years that she lived there. She has attended numerous seminars including in England, Germany and the US. Her rewrite of the Rosenblum book (retitled* Your Individual Day of Fertility*) is in the Norwegian library system and features an introduction by a local doctor who highlighted the astrological fertility work of Eugene Jonas MD. Write to: Attenbjerg 15, DK-3210 Vejby, Denmark. Phone: +45 4230 9071.*

FORECASTING WORLD EVENTS
Using Guru-Sani (Jupiter-Saturn) Conjunctions

Jan Willem van Doorn

Why are we using firearms today? Why do environmentalists receive so much attention and support these days? Why were discoveries overseas so successful in the 16th and 17th centuries? Why are the major traditional monumental buildings (like pyramids, temples and cathedrals) only being built in specific time slots? Why do nations migrate on a global scale every 850 to 900 years?

Every serious investigator of history will find that history repeats itself in an indefinite number of cycles. Every serious astrologer knows that these cycles must relate to the movements of "the stars." During all times, authorities have mentioned these cycles as a reference point for what has happened or was expected to happen. The major cycle generally emphasized in this respect is the Guru-Sani (Jupiter-Saturn) conjunction cycle of about twenty years. Nearly all material written on this subject is based upon the tropical position of these two Grahas (Planets). However a study of these conjunctions in relation to their *sidereal* positions reveals a number of special insights.

Let us first relate these conjunctions to the elements of the Râsis (Signs) in which they take place. These four elements are: Earth, Air, Water and Fire. If we follow historically the conjuncti-ons of Guru and Sani in the Râsis related to these elements, we find a rather consistent picture. Note that we are using the Ramân Ayanamsa, and the figures have been rounded:

Earth	2250 BC	-	2200BC
	1650 BC	-	1350 BC
	750 BC	-	500 BC
	100 AD	-	450 AD
	1000 AD	-	1300 AD
	1900 AD	-	
Air	2350 BC	-	1950 BC
	1500 BC	-	1100 BC
	600 BC	-	200 BC
	350 AD	-	650 AD
	1200 AD	-	1500 AD
	2100 AD	-	

Water	2100 BC	-	1700 BC
	1200 BC	-	850 BC
	350 BC	-	0 AD
	550 AD	-	850 AD
	1400 AD	-	1700 AD
Fire	1850 BC	-	1600 BC
	950 BC	-	700 BC
	100 BC	-	200 AD
	850 AD	-	1100 AD
	1700 AD	-	1950 AD

Generally the conjunctions remain in the same element for 250 to 300 years, and the total cycle through the four elements takes about 850 to 900 years.

The most interesting point is that during these "elementary" periods the quality of the very element itself shows quite clearly, not only on the gross level but also on the more subtle levels (examples to follow). Also we find an extraordinary refinement at the end of these periods just before the next element finally takes over.

The Binding Force Of Water

Let's take an example: the Water period from 1400 AD - 1700 AD. We recognise this period very well as a period in which voyages oversea were undertaken from the end of the 15th century (Columbus, etc.) and continuing during the next 200 years. Nearly every part on the globe, from the North Pole to the South Pole and from the East to the West, was searched for over sea. It was also the Golden Age of Holland, which in its strongest period was able to link the most distant places on earth over water by means of trade.

Many of the conjunctions during that period took place in Karkata (the Crab), the Râsi for both Amsterdam and Holland. Another interesting fact is that the Dutch master painters were able to bind their dye particles in such an unique way that even today's scientists, with all their modern techniques, still do not know how this was done, nor has anyone succeeded to this date in replicating the same.

The Life Of Fire

This recent period of Water was over-taken by our well-known period of Fire. Around the year 1700 (the over-lapping period), we experienced the application of fire unto water which led to the "invention" and development of the steam-engine, thus setting into motion the era of the Industrial Revolution. If we look back over the past 300 years we see a striking development of this element Fire penetrating gradually into all areas of human activity. We learned to move by fire (trains, boats, cars, planes, rockets), to make use of instruments by fire (all kinds of engines driven either by steam or electricity, or even now, laser energy), to speak and hear by fire (microphone, loud-speaker, telegraph, telephone, radio), write and read by fire (computers, telecommunications, laser printers), to see by fire (television), build by fire (in steel and glass) and last, but no least, fight by fire (fire! arms, atomic weapons, laser weapons).

The interesting, and at the same time alarming, point is that there seems to be a growing imbalance in the use and appreciation of the other elements at the end of an particular elementary period. Especially the United States is still a place where fire predominates, and this is nicely illustrated by the general custom to serve ice water at every occasion to cool down these burning influences.

We also see the application of Earth unto Fire which has led to the invention of the Silicon chip, now playing a very elementary role in the current period and the period to come. There also is the growing interest and influencial power of environmental movements with their plea to return to a more natural environment where the elements (with an emphasis on Earth) can play their natural role.

This simply means that the currently evolving period will necessarily turn the general attention more and more towards Earth, in all her gross and subtle qualities, and consequently more and more away from Fire. The United States should be very well aware of this fact because their current leading role in the world is based on their mastery over Fire, just as the Dutch at the end of the 17th century were masters over Water.

Why Not Use The Tropical Positions?

The reason for taking the sidereal rather than tropical positions and viewpoint is that the evidence shows the sidereal positions lead to a number of very useful forecasts, especially as it relates to the timing of major events for mankind. Take for instance the building of cathedrals, temples, Stonehenge and pyramids. Especially regarding the early constructions there is no consensus about the time when these were built because it is very difficult—if not impossible—to find a rather absolute reference for dating. However what is more unbiased than the factual positions of "the stars" at any point in time?

An in depth study of this might reveal some striking facts. A first impression shows that the cathedrals can be traced back to the previous Earth period (1000 AD - 1300 AD), e.g., Mexican pyramids to the Earth period of 100 AD - 450 AD, Greek temples to 600 BC - 200 BC, Stonehenge probably to 1650 BC - 1350 BC, and the Egyptian pyramids to 2550 BC - 2200 BC. In the same way major events of, for instance, migrations of the nations, the Commercial Revolution and epidemic diseases (like pestilence) can be related to Air periods.

Critical Period Ahead

All this leaves ample material for further study. Apart from referring these conjunctions to their element placements, it is also possible to relate these conjunctions to the Naksatras. This can contribute a futher level of refinement in observations and judgements. In the cycle of 850 to 900 years every Naksatra is hit once or twice giving a specific impetus for the time to come. What will happen at the time of the next conjunction (to take place in May 2000)? Depending on the Ayanamsa being used, this conjunction takes place in either Mesha (Aries) or Vrishabha (Taurus).

Generally speaking, there is no doubt that this conjunction will take place in the Naksatra Krttika which bears all the characteristics of fire, cutting and destruction. Just as the Sanskrit word "Krttika" implies, it should prove to be a rather "critical" period. It will lead either to a flaming out of the past Fire period (as is pictured so often in all the American movies, and which is easy to imagine because all the fuel is present), or to a restrained calming down of this fiery period along with a gradual building up of a (new) Earth period.

To aggravate the situation, a number of other factors are scheduled to be present like the (transiting) positions of Mangala and Râhu, and the lunar and solar eclipses from 1998 onward. These factors together put a very high strain on those in responsible positions. The previous times a conjunction took place in Krttika were in 1146 AD and 233 AD. These time periods were also of a rather unstable nature. However, if reason prevails, the coming period will be met as an evolution for mankind rather than a revolution of the elements.

Within the School of Philosophy the principles of Advaita Vedânta as well as Plato are practically applied. There are groups studying a wide variety of subjects including Vedic Astronomy, Astrology and Mathematics, which have been studied for the past ten to fifteen years. Also links are established with similar groups studing the same subjects in the United Kingdom and elsewhere. With specific regard to Vedic Astrology there is a special interest in Muhurta and Cycles and a number of lectures have been given on these subjects. A book is also planned on "Historical and Economical Cycles in the Light of the Stars". Contact: Jan Willem van Doorn, Velazquezstraat 4, 1077 NH, Amsterdam, Holland. Phone: 31 20 6798-004. Fax: 31 20 6798128.

PRACTICAL RULES FOR INTERPRETING THE LUNAR NODES

Bob Wendell

[This is Part II of a 3-Part unpublished series on the lunar nodes. Part I connects the abstract nature of these non-physical points of intersection in space to their transcendental nature as symbolic entities in Jyotish. A unifying spiritual role as the axis of evolutionary drive toward untimate fufillment, or Enlightenment, is developed in terms of their symbolic and geometrical relationships to the physical bodies from whose movements and positions their existence derives.

Part II now elaborates the mechanics for interpreting the innumerable specific ways in which these general, abstract evolutionary roles express themselves concretely in different lives. Part III considers the implications of the nodes for spiritual practice.]

The nodes' intrinsic natures are abstract. Yet they have specific, concrete effects in a native's life through the significations of the houses they occupy, the grahas they aspect, and most importantly, the grahas for which they each act as agent, and the houses these grahas own. It is necessary, therefore, to address some of the technical specifics for the nodes. Reminding the reader of the wide range of opinions on these issues, the author shares these specifics as he has resolved them for himself.

The Technical Specifics

A node acts as agent for the lord of the sign it occupies. The only exception is if the lord of the nakshatra occupied by the node is either conjunct or aspecting the node while its sign lord is not. Then the node acts as agent for its nakshatra lord. The nodes can have secondary agencies in addition to this rigorously defined primary agency. These secondary agencies include the nakshatra lord, but can also result from simply being conjunct a graha or aspected by it.

The nodes cast aspects in the same way as Jupiter, i.e., they cast a special fifth and ninth aspect. And they fully aspect each other in every chart because of their intrinsic 180-degree relationship. When one is active through Dasha lordship, the other is activated. It is only a matter of relative dominance.

Consequently, they appear to have many traits in common. Nevertheless, during interpretation one should bear in mind at all times the deep character of their polarity, and the differences their respective natures therefore represent. They work together to accomplish their evolutionary task, but perform fundamentally opposite roles.

Rahu and Ketu have their deep exaltation points at 16° Taurus and Scorpio respectively. These points are auspiciously approached from above because of the nodes' normal retrograde motion. The author has only seen one reference to these positions in a very concise and practical little book by Pundit Prashant Shah, *Essence of Hindu Astrology*. Despite being unaware of its origin, the author has adopted Pundit Shah's viewpoint for some very compelling reasons.

The author has developed an argument for these exact positions in a separate, as-yet-unpublished paper. It reveals the perfect symmetries existing in the relationships among the deep exaltation points of *all* the grahas. All the points are derived from the Sun, the Moon, and the 0 and 15 degree Aries points in the zodiac. (Fifteen degrees Aries represents the first house cusp of the natural chart as defined in Jyotish.) The whole symmetry breaks down, however, unless Rahu and Ketu are assigned the deep exaltation points given in Pundit Shah's book.

Rahu is considered by some to co-own, with Mercury, the sign Virgo; and Ketu, with Jupiter, the sign Pisces. This accords with Rahu's mundane, or earthy, exploring nature and fascination with new adventure, characteristics also associated with Virgo; and Ketu's status as Mokshakaraka, the significator of enlightenment, reflects the twelfth sign correspondence with the tail and final liberation. Rahu's Moola Trikona is held by some to be Gemini, and Ketu's, Sagittarius. Rahu is also said by some to co-own Wednesday with Mercury and Ketu, Thursday with Jupiter. Justifications for these views are developed by the author in the previously mentioned paper, using pattern analysis.

The true nodes are used to determine their exact positions, although for purposes of analysis, they are considered to be always retrograde in accord with classical usage. It is interesting that the rapid, slightly wobbling orbit of the Moon around the earth creates a very unique, sinuous, snake-like movement through the zodiac when the nodes' longitudes are visually graphed versus time.

This adds further specificity to their addictive/transformational release polarity as significators when considering the traditional symbolic association of snakes with healing and transformative power and the toxic nature of addictive substances and venom, as well as the systemic detoxification often associated with profound psychophysiological transformation. The nodes, and especially Rahu, have classically been associated with snakes and poisons, and by extension, venomous insect bites, rashes and infections, and morbid addictions to toxic substances.

The nodes require special consideration in the analysis of Dasas, transits, and of the interaction of transits with Dasas and their sub-periods. The author has evolved a systematized approach to interactive Dasha/transit analysis more general and lengthy in its application than an article specifically on the nodes justifies. This is developed in another unpublished paper, "Dasha/Transit Analysis for Precise Timing of Events."

The fundamental principle behind the method described in that paper is this: the transits of grahas ruling current Dasha periods, and the transit of any grahas through current Dasha rulers' signs or nakshatras, are heightened greatly in their significance. In the aforementioned paper, more detail is given on how the agencies of the nodes affect the rules for interpretation in this context of Dasha-transit analysis.

These rules apply to the physical grahas for which the nodes act as agents. The essential principle is that to judge the importance of a transit, these physical grahas must be treated as if they are the current rulers when the node acting as its agent is a period or sub-period ruler. The reverse is also true: when a transit occurs while a graha represented by that node is a current period or sub-period ruler, in judging the importance of the transit, that node must be considered as if it is a current period or sub-period ruler.

The Specifics Applied

The issues around which the nodes' primary symbolic characteristics express themselves—attachment for Rahu, release and transformation for Ketu—are understood in terms of the planet or planets for which each node acts as agent. For example, in a Leo Ascendant chart, the second and eleventh houses are owned by Mercury. If Mercury is in the eighth, it is in Pisces and therefore debilitated. If Rahu occupies the second house, then Ketu is in the eighth with Mercury.

The obsessive attachment of Rahu, since it acts in this chart as an agent of Mercury, involves second and eleventh house issues, and especially those in common with the natural significations of Mercury. The second house signifies nourishing values, such as mother's milk, food in general, family environment, early upbringing and education, speech, and liquid financial assets. The eleventh house signifies the realization of desires, especially social ones, and the social rewards for one's contributions to society, most especially income.

Among Mercury's significations are money and communication, so obsession with liquid assets, income, and social contact in the form of conversation are emphasized in this chart by Rahu's agency and Mercury's house ownerships. Rahu's obsessive/ addictive nature in this chart would have unfortunate consequences, since the planet he represents is debilitated in the eighth, powerless to deliver the success the native so intensely longs for.

Rahu's nature impels the native to persist, driving the very things he desires further from him. He likely stutters, or speaks nervously and impulsively, obsessively hovers over captive listeners, talks forever, and generally alienates everyone around him. He is likely stingy with money, selfish and thoughtless or worse in his methods of acquiring it, driving any potentially significant business from himself.

His spiritual evolution centers around letting go of these obsessions and expanding his sense of fulfillment to include others. He must eventually develop the ability to enjoy others' success in these very matters without feeling any pinch concerning his own lack. The intense karma in these areas exists for the very reason that it is necessary in this extreme to drive him toward the personal expansion he needs to find true fulfillment.

Ketu in Pisces, on the other hand, in this chart acts as an agent of Jupiter. Much depends, then, on the placement of Jupiter. A saving grace already exists in the location of Rahu and Ketu in their own signs. Despite Rahu's acting as agent for a debilitated Mercury in the eighth, Rahu at home in his own sign uplifts his nature and allows for rapid growth away from his early tendencies.

If Jupiter is in the fourth in Scorpio, a friendly sign, he fully casts his fifth aspect on Ketu in the eighth. This further improves the situation, and dramatically so. Jupiter spiritualizes and is a planet of principle. In kendra, he becomes powerfully activated in the native's life. So the underhanded side of Rahu mentioned initially, emphasized by his agency for a debilitated Mercury, is ameliorated.

Finally, Ketu's Mokshakaraka side is activated by Jupiter's full aspect. Among the hidden matters the eighth house signifies is the Transcendent. Jupiter's full aspect on Ketu here gives the chart owner very deep spiritual tendencies, and he likely experiences the Transcendent frequently, probably through meditation. Ketu is still conjunct a debilitated Mercury, and may indicate a chronic nervous disorder such as epilepsy, or some milder tendency toward it. However, the most important understanding is that the associated symptoms actually constitute the most manifest level of Ketu's long-term work in normalizing and integrating psycho-physiological functioning in the direction of full Enlightenment.

Robert Wendell works in the marketing department of Human Factors International, the world's largest and most experienced firm specializing in engineering psychology as applied to software user interface design. He worked in electronics for many years and has been a recording engineer. His degree is in music with a major in violin. He has performed professionally as a classical vocalist, is an accomplished choral director and is the founder and music director of Musica Sacra of Southeast Iowa, which specializes in the sacred choral works of the composers from the Renaissance, Baroque, and Classical eras. Bob has studied Jyotish steadily since 1986, and is fascinated with the prospect of discovering the relationships between musical structure and planetary significations, especially with respect to the potential use of music to heal the diseases associated with each planet. Contact: 2000 N. Court (7M) Fairfield, IA 52556. Internet: 102646.1023 @ compuserve.com.

The Astrology of Death
by Richard Houck

Are you transitioning from Western to Eastern astrology?   Consider the 400p. *Astrology of Death* from Groundswell Press ($21.95 + $3.95 shipping), a synthesis of Eastern and Western techniques that is already in reprint and translation. Here are brief extracts of what some critics have had to say:

Sergio de Del Castillo, writing in the main *Newsletter* of the world famous Johns Hopkins University and Medical Center, calls it: "very precise and scientific... strong evidence for the strange connection between nature and the timing of events... a powerful reference tool that marshals copious evidence to reveal the correlations between astrology and occurrences of death."

Margaret Millard, medical astrology author and MD, writing in *Considerations,* calls it: "a wonderful book... fascinating... clear... unique... a classic text that will not be equalled."

Lois Rodden, prolific author and editor of *Data News* (who rarely reviews books in her newsletter), wrote: "crisp wit, humor and common sense... probably the most stimulating astrology book I have read in a decade... exciting. We will do well to use his methods."

Chris Lorenz, reviewing in *Dell Horoscope*, calls it: "an eye opener... (that) will yield a profound respect for astrology's true capacity, and for Mr. Houck."

Joe Polansky, publisher of *Diamond Fire* magazine, writes: "wonderful, ground-breaking and seminal... the author will both thrill and enrage you... awesome... one of our first-rate astrological minds."

Edith Hathaway, reviewing in *The Mountain Astrologer*, says: "Houck writes with considerable verve, wit, passion, humor and dead seriousness, if you can imagine all these rolled into one... clear, concise and assiduous."

Mark Lerner, publisher of *Welcome To Planet Earth*, calls it a "comprehensive, fascinating, extraordinary masterwork... a brilliant text and reference work... an instant gold mine that will attract a lot of attention."

Gracie Astor Best, reviewing in the *Whole Life Times*, calls it: "phenomenal and entertaining... holds the attention of the reader... this is the book to revisit time after time... and pass down to your kids."

Michael O'Reilly, writing in *American Astrology*, says, "... Houck's book should be considered a landmark in what must inevitably become a standard diagnostic system... brash and to the point."

Dave Roell, in an *Astrology Center of America* advertisement, rated it "The #1 astrology book available in 1995."

James Braha, renowned astrology author, wrote in the Foreward: "Predicting death is neither the beauty nor the profundity of this work. [It is] a rich and subtle... treasure chest of penetrating astrological insights."

Groundswell Press is also the Exclusive Manufacturer of a

100 year (1920-2019)

SPECIAL SIDEREAL EPHEMERIS

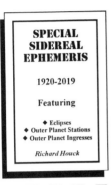

SPECIAL SIDEREAL EPHEMERIS

1920-2019

Featuring

♦ Eclipses
♦ Outer Planet Stations
♦ Outer Planet Ingresses

Richard Houck

**This Unique Booklet Flags
3 Important Phenomena:**

• **All Solar and Lunar Eclipses**
• **All Stations of Jupiter – Pluto**
• **All Sign Ingresses for these Planets**

With this efficient and focused resource, you can quickly spot these changes of condition that strongly impact your forecasting work.

ORDER FORM

Here is the information you need to directly order additional copies of this book, or other products and services, from Groundswell Press (or just to be put on our mailing list). Quoted shipping rates apply only within the United States. Call or write for out-of-U.S. shipping.

Hindu Astrology Lessons	$16.95	+$2.95 S&H
The Astrology of Death	$21.95	+$3.95 S&H
Special Sidereal Ephemeris	$10.00	S&H prepaid
Tapes of the 1994 D.C. Vedic Conference (call or write for list)	$12.00 (each)	S&H prepaid
Copy of Your Vedic Astrology **Chart** Materials (coded as in *The Astrology of Death*)	$10.00	S&H prepaid
Digital Astrology	Available in early 1998	

Make Checks out to: *Groundswell Press*. All checks must be expressed in U.S. dollars and must be drawn upon a U.S. Bank (or must reflect international postal agreements).

Classes, Consultations, Etc. contact: *Richard Houck*
                                              ARC Associates, Inc.
                                              P.O. Box 8925
                                              Gaithersburg, MD 20898
                                              Phone/Fax: 301-353-0212
                                              E-Mail:RichardHouck@worldnet.att.net

Coming in Early 1998...

Digital Astrology
by Richard Houck

Did you know there is a multi-thousand-year-old forecasting system from India that:

- Was specifically **reserved** for the current "Age of Metals"?
  (read that: machines, i.e., *computers*)

- Is based upon **bit switches** being turned "on" or "off"?
  (in other words, it's an ancient *binary* system;
  except, instead of binary, they called it *bindu*)

- And that these bits are clustered into groups of **eight**?
  (which, as you may know, is a classic *byte* of data)

The **spreadsheets** it generates are:

◊ uniquely powerful,
◊ easy to understand, and
◊ simple to apply.

Superficially, it's "just" transits. But using this book's clear "westernized" explanations and many examples, you will soon be able to see a whole new class of accurate natal and forecasting effects "pop out" from this automated pointing system that have long been hidden from you and your clients. But be advised: Once you really tune into this technique, you'll feel stuck with it for life!

WATCH FOR IT. FROM GROUNDSWELL PRESS.